Martha S. Bechtel
119 Messiah Village
P.O. Box 2015
Mechanicsburg, PA 17055

MESSENGER of GRACE

a biography of
C.N. Hostetter, Jr.

Christian Neff Hostetter

MESSENGER of GRACE

a biography of C.N. Hostetter, Jr.

E. Morris Sider

Evangel Press  301 N. Elm St.
Nappanee, Indiana 46550

Other books by E. Morris Sider

A Vision for Service: A History of Upland College

Fire in the Mountains

Nine Portraits: Brethren in Christ Biographical Sketches

Fruit from Woods and Sands: The Story of Houghton Mission (co-author)

Lantern in the Dawn: Selections from the Writings of John E. Zercher (co-editor and author of a chapter of biography)

Here Faith and Learning Meet: The Story of Niagara Christian College.

Portions of the material in this biography appeared in the chapter on C. N. Hostetter, Jr., in the book, *Something Meaningful for God,* Cornelius J. Dyck, editor, copyright 1981 by Herald Press, Scottdale, Pa. 15683 and are included here by permission.

Messenger of Grace © 1982 by E. Morris Sider. Printed in the United States of America. All rights reserved. No part of this book may be used or reproduced without written permission, except in the case of brief quotations in articles and reviews. For information, address Evangel Press, Nappanee, Indiana 46550.

Library of Congress Catalog Card Number: 82-71583

Cover design by Jeff Spencer

To

Ray and Ruth Zercher

valued models of the Christian Life

Foreword

*T*his book began more by indirection than direction. Several years ago I agreed to write a chapter on C. N. Hostetter, Jr., for a collection of short biographies C. J. Dyck was editing for the Mennonite Central Committee (recently published under the title *Something Meaningful for God*). I soon discovered sufficient materials to expand the chapter into this book-length study.

Even so, the biography is more a survey than an exhaustive treatment of its subject. C. N. Hostetter, Jr., was a churchman; his interests and sense of duty led him into many activities of the Brethren in Christ Church and related organizations. To write something about all meant that I could not dwell long on any.

Because of his long and varied service in the denomination, Hostetter's life is, in a sense, a history of the Brethren in Christ Church for a period of some fifty years, from about 1915 to 1970. I have, in fact, attempted to make the biography a sort of mini-history of the church in those years. Among other things, this meant that where there was need to be selective in sources and subject matter, I usually selected on the basis of how well the sources and subject helped to explain Brethren in Christ church life.

Biographers must beware not to make their subjects larger than their time and place, not to make them too central or too inevitable to the causes in which they were engaged. I have been conscious of this potential problem as I wrote the life of C. N. Hostetter, Jr. Ideally, in order to portray his exact place and role in the institutions and agencies to which he gave himself, I should have written a history of each. For this I had neither time nor space. Thus the problem, without doubt, remains.

This biography is obviously only one interpretation of the life and work of a man and his church. Some readers will find me too favorably disposed to C. N. Hostetter, Jr., while others will consider me too critically inclined. Some would choose other illustrations and details to paint the portrait of the man they knew. I write from the point of view of one who knew and admired him (indeed, he was a sort of model for me), but I write also as a historian who recognizes that historical writing requires that I put at least a little distance between my subject and me.

My use of his last name is no sign of disrespect for C. N. Hostetter, Jr. Again, I follow the accepted practice in historical writing: people no longer living are not referred to by their titles. Thus to use such terms as "President" Hostetter, or "Dr." Hostetter, or "Bishop" Hostetter would not be strictly in accord with the canons of historical writing. Similarly, to use the popular and affectionate "C.N." by which he was known to many seemed too intimate, too likely to become quickly dated, and not entirely appropriate for readers outside Brethren in Christ and Mennonite circles. Thus my general use of the last name only.

Since Hostetter's life and work is so recent and was in many cases of a confidential nature, I have taken perhaps undue liberty in withholding in the text and the footnotes some of the names involved in his work. I have not, however, attempted to hide the location of the sources to which names would otherwise be attached. Virtually all of these sources are in the Archives of the Brethren in Christ Church and Messiah College at Grantham, Pennsylvania. Thus all materials may be quickly found in the Archives, and used if clearance is obtained.

My greatest pleasure in the several years of working on this book is to thank the many people who have assisted me. First, I express appreciation to the members of the Hostetter family for their encouragement. Especially am I grateful that their encouragement came without restrictions on materials used or demands about what should or should not be included in the book. All biographers are not as fortunate in this respect as I have been. I owe thanks also to Messiah College for making time and money available for some of my research and writing. Dean David Brandt, as always, and in the tradition of good academic deans, stood behind me to make my work easier in a variety of ways. The assistance of Miriam Bowers in the Archives meant that I had more hours to devote to the book. Hers is the skilled hand that composed the index to this volume. On Ray Zercher I have here, as before, relied unduly in such matters as language and style.

Several of my students at Messiah College have contributed, in one way or another, to the writing of this biography. They include Claudia St. Onge, Sara Petrosky, Howard Kauffman, and Debra Hostetter. (Debra, who wrote a paper on Hostetter's early life and typed the manuscript, is a granddaughter of the subject.) Working with these students on this project had, for me, a special kind of satisfaction.

I am indebted to the readers of a third-draft manuscript. Nelson, Lane, and Ray Hostetter, William Snyder, Robert Kreider, Kenneth Hoover, Ray Zercher, Henry Hostetter, and John Hostetter gave creative suggestions and saved me from more embarrassing mistakes than I care to mention. They are, of course, in no way responsible for the errors that remain.

Leonard Gross, archivist for the Mennonite Church, once again proved to be a good friend and helpful adviser as I spent a week in the Mennonite Archives at Goshen, Indiana. I met with the same cooperative spirit when I worked for shorter periods of time at the Mennonite Central Committee headquarters in Akron, Pennsylvania, and at the Associated Mennonite Biblical Seminaries in Elkhart, Indiana. William Snyder, Executive Director of the Mennonite Central Committee, was a source of great encouragement in my work. I quickly discovered that I could impose myself without end on his good nature for advice and all sorts of information.

In collecting information for the biography I relied heavily on interviews. (I count as interviews two or three instances in which persons answered on cassette tapes a series of questions I sent them.) The names of some who assisted me in this way may be found in the footnotes. Here I name all the interviewees (in alphabetical order) and thereby say thanks to them: Atlee Beachey, Ernest Bennet, Allen Brubaker, Audrey Brubaker, Charlie and Ruth Byers, Laban Byers, Asa and Anna Climenhaga, Willis Detwiler, Amos Dick, Eber and Ruth Dourte, Peter Dyck, Esther Ebersole, Anna Engle, Ethel Engle, John Engle, Paul Engle, George Ford, Glenn and Beth Frey, June Byer Gibble, Edward Gilmore, Henry Ginder, Isaiah Harley, Clarence and Elizabeth Heise, Noah Heisey, Wilmer Heisey, Clara Hess, Kenneth Hoover, Paul and Lela Hostetler, Anna Hostetter, Henry and Beula Hostetter, John and Nellie Hostetter, Lane Hostetter, Nelson Hostetter, Ray Hostetter, Rachel Hubbard, Nelson Kaufman, Luke Keefer, Sr., Jacob Klassen, Virgie Kraybill, Carl Kreider, Mrs. John Lebo, Cyrus Lutz, Paul McBeth, Roy Mann, Harry Martens, John and Barbara Martin, Nellie Pattison Martin, Edgar Metzler, Earl Miller, John Moseman, Howard Musselman, Earl and Lois Musser, John and Barbara Musser, Charles Norman, Landis Ressler, John Rosenberry, Luke Showalter, Christian and Cora Sider, Earl and Elsie Sider, Mary Slaymaker, William Snyder, Clyde and Dorothy Jean Sollenberger, Aaron Stern, Jesse Steckley, Edgar Stoesz, E. J. Swalm, Erwin Thomas, Keith Ulery, Erland Waltner, Gerald and Lois Weaver, Roy Wenger, Samuel Wenger, Daniel Wolgemuth, Mark Wolgemuth, John Howard Yoder, Mary Wenger Yoder, Anna Zercher, Harold and Ruth Zercher, John and Alice Grace Zercher.

In addition to these interviews, a number of people at my request wrote letters providing helpful information. They include, George L. Classen, S. Iola Dixon, Elmer Ediger, Anna Engle, Paul Erb, Henry A. Fast, J. Winfield Fretz, Albert Gaeddert, Glenn Ginder, Waldo Hiebert, Mary Kreider, Robert Kreider, Herbert Mekeel, J. C. Penner, Dorothy M. Resconsin, Wendell Rockey, Donald Shafer, Andrew Shelly, John R. Sider, J. William Smith, Jr., J. B. Toews, Norman A. Wingert, and Thomas F. Zimmerman.

My debt is greatest to Leone—for her patience, moral support, and numerous assistances. There must be a special place reserved in heaven for wives like her.

E. Morris Sider
Messiah College, 1982

Contents

1

"On the Lord's Side"

*B*iographies traditionally begin with ancestry. That tradition is a logical one: persons are not only a part of all that they have met, but also a product of what has gone before. Thus ancestry is the point of departure for this account of Christian Neff Hostetter, Jr.

The line can be traced back to Jacob and Anna Hostetter who with their small children emigrated to the United States in 1712. They were among the many Mennonites who came from southern Germany and Switzerland in the years surrounding that date to settle in Lancaster County, Pennsylvania. Jacob and Anna obtained a farm along the Conestoga Creek. The land now lies within the southern city limits of Lancaster City.

A great grandson, also called Jacob, was probably the first Hostetter to become a Brethren in Christ (or River Brethren, as the group was then popularly known). The Brethren in Christ originated around 1780 in the northwest part of Lancaster County, near the Susquehanna River. The first members came from Anabaptist related groups, probably mainly Mennonites, and thus carried into the new body they founded such concepts as separation from the world, discipleship, and peace. But they also had been touched by the pietistic revival movements in Lancaster County in the eighteenth century, and thus they also brought to their new organization teachings on the crisis conversion experience and the heart-felt relationship with God.

Great grandson Jacob was born in 1799 and lived on a farm in West Hempfield Township, between Mt. Joy and Salunga. He became a River Brethren minister and around 1840 was elected bishop, a position which he held until his death in 1888 at the age of eighty-nine. His obituary in the local paper noted that his "honesty was proverbial," that he once served as a missionary to western states and as a "peacemaker to settle disputes in other counties," and that he "frequently acted in a satisfactory manner." The sign of the respect in which he was held by his church and neighbors is the attendance at his funeral of approximately 1,000 persons, driven in 400 "conveyances."[1]

Jacob's son Christian also held official position among the River Brethren—as a deacon. Christian had a reputation for counselling forgiveness: if the Lord forgives a person, he was fond of saying, then we should too. As a deacon, he opposed the beginning of a Sunday school in his church, but when one was started he insisted that all members should firmly support it.

Christian took over his father Jacob's farm and in turn passed it on to David, one of his four sons. Another son, Christian, obviously named after his father, was the father of the subject of this account.

This younger Christian was born in 1868, and grew to be a well-built, handsome man, just under six feet in height. That together with his pleasant personality made him a popular figure in the community, and one of the attractive persons at local parties, particularly, of course, to the young women. One of them, Ella Neff, a Mennonite girl from near Millersville, was his partner on a date arranged by her sister. This blind date led to romance and eventually to marriage in 1891. Christian and Ella bought a 130-acre farm near Washington Boro in Manor Township, about eight miles south of the home farm, and moved on to it a few months after their marriage. Typical of the Lancaster County farmers in those days (and some since) they set out to pay for the farm as soon as possible by growing tobacco.

Neither Christian nor Ella were members of the Brethren in Christ Church at the time of their marriage. That position changed, however, with the birth in 1892 of Harris, their first child, when Christian was thirty years of age. The sense of responsibility for giving proper moral and spiritual guidance to their child led them to attend a prayer meeting where they made a commitment to "take the way," as the Brethren in Christ then referred to the act of conversion.

Conversion to the Brethren, among other things, meant a

visible change in life style. Thus Christian and Ella put on the plain dress of the church. Unlike some other members, they also discontinued growing tobacco, since some church leaders had begun to preach against its use. This latter step was a bold one. Local opinion held that if a man did not grow tobacco he was either wealthy or lazy.[2] Hostetter's neighbors predicted that he would fail in farming, and thus would soon be growing the plant again.

But in this they were mistaken. Not only did he not grow tobacco again but his sons did not even help the neighbors with their crop. Instead, Hostetter turned to mixed farming. He planted fruit trees—mainly apples and pears—and sold the produce on the Lancaster market or peddled it locally to the residents of nearby Columbia or elsewhere. He also grew potatoes, which he sold to the townspeople, who put large quantities in their cellars for the winter. Milk and eggs, too, became part of his sales, which he announced by whistling through his fingers as he moved down the street.

From this mixed farming, Hostetter did financially well. He was a good businessman and was progressive in his farming, making use of the expertise then available, and buying the first hay loader and manure spreader in the community, as well as one of the first automobiles. His buildings were always neat and in good shape. He gave the air of prosperity.

And yet he was not a rich man, as some thought. That was in large measure owing to his attachment to the church and his giving of himself to it in time and money. Rather quickly, Hostetter became one of the leading Brethren in Christ churchmen. Converted in 1892, he was elected a deacon in 1906 and a minister in 1907. Five years later, in May, 1912, he was ordained bishop of his local Manor-Pequea District, a position he retained until his resignation in 1942. In several instances he served as non-resident bishop to districts having internal difficulties or which for a period were without a resident bishop (Grantham, Morrison Cove, and Cumberland Districts being cases in point).

Christian Hostetter, however, was probably most noted for his interest in foreign missions. It is no accident that a number of missionaries among the Brethren in Christ came from his district. In 1910 he became a member of his denomination's Foreign

Mission Board, which he served, first as secretary, and then, on the death of John R. Zook in 1919, as its chairman until 1944, when he was made an emeritus member. In 1921-1922, with David W. Heise of Canada, he made a deputation tour of Brethren in Christ missions in Africa and India, returning just in time to be elected moderator of General Conference, held that year in S. R. Smith's abandoned noodle factory in Grantham.

That office, too, was a sign of Hostetter's churchmanship. He was elected moderator of General Conference five times, and assistant moderator six. He became General Conference secretary in 1916 following the death of S. R. Smith and held that position until 1927. He also followed Smith in the presidency of Messiah Bible School and Missionary Training Home (now Messiah College), the denomination's school founded in 1909. He held that office for five years, largely because in its early years the school had need of a churchman whom the denomination could trust.

Thus Hostetter played a large and influential role in the life of the church. A popular saying around General Conference time, when the business of the church was conducted, was that if one wanted something done he should see Christ Hostetter (as he was often called).

All of this suggests a man greatly devoted to the program of the church. Some people thought he was too devoted, since he seemed sometimes to put the church ahead of his family. While some admired, others wondered about his going off on church business between the death and funeral of his three-year-old-daughter Mary. Perhaps those who wondered did not know that he had done so at the encouragement of his wife. The same devotion to church was shown when he spent the year abroad on deputation work, leaving care of the farm to his wife and teenage sons Henry and John.

Hostetter's effectiveness as churchman was, of course, in part owing to his devotion to his denomination, but it was also owing in part to a friendly, diplomatic manner. Like his bishop grandfather he was good at mending disputes and healing wounds. He listened well and encouraged people to speak; one man's opinion, he held, was usually as good as another's. And he approached his leadership roles as a servant. When he became bishop he remarked to his wife that now they could serve everyone—even ministers and those no one else wanted to serve. Such attitudes were enhanced by a friendly face and gracious manners. "He was easy to love," says one who remembers him. "People looked on him as a god," reports another.

Hostetter's style of leadership may be seen at close hand in his bishopric, eventually comprising the Pequea, Manor, Lancaster, Refton, and Newtown congregations. As in most cases in Lancaster County up to the 1930s, the congregations met together on Sunday, rotating from one church building in the district to another. Over his congregations Hostetter exercised a benevolent paternalism. He counselled rather than expelled offenders. Although he assumed that his members would dress in the plain way, he did not preach plain clothes. The same with tobacco; while personally persuaded against growing the plant, he did not speak against others growing it or working in the harvest. After his missionary deputation in 1922, because of the desperate needs and famine he saw abroad, he rigidly abstained from eating candy for years after his return; he did not, however, preach that others should not eat candy. If General Conference passed what he considered to be a too legalistic piece of legislation, he would soften its effect on his district by either remaining silent on the issue or trying to modify the way in which it was carried out. Thus the Manor-Pequea District had the reputation under Hostetter of being moderate, relaxed, and relatively progressive, at least for a Pennsylvania district.

Given his frame of mind, it is not surprising to learn that Hostetter associated rather easily with non-Brethren in Christ groups, an attitude that was not customary with many of his fellow members in the denomination. He felt most comfortable with Mennonites (he had, of course, married a Mennonite and he sometimes preached in their churches), but he also attended the services of other denominations in the area, particularly after his return from abroad, when he was asked to speak to non-Brethren in Christ audiences about his trip. On one occasion, he shared in conducting a funeral service with a Roman Catholic priest.

It is tempting to see Ella his wife as a model for a bishop's companion. On Sunday morning she took her place on the front seat in the "amen corner" at the head of the ministers' wives. She was usually the first to give a testimony when "testimony meeting" time came around. The women of the church, including the young girls, always received from her a greeting and an inquiry about their welfare.

Ella was small and invariably dressed in plain black clothes, always neat and dainty. A source of long-standing amusement in the Hostetter family was her answer when as a guest at dinner she was offered a piece of pie. "I think I will have just half a piece," she would say, but would somehow manage to obtain the other half as well. Although small and dainty, she was also determined and resourceful, as she needed to be to carry on the home and farm during her husband's many absences.

To be born to parents such as Christian and Ella Hostetter and to grow up in such a district as Manor-Pequea was to be of significant moment to the life and career of Christian Hostetter, Junior, Christian and Ella's second son.

The younger Christian was born on Jaunary 22, 1899. As his second name, his parents gave him Neff, his mother's maiden name. He was seven years younger than Harris, and was followed by two other brothers, Henry and John, and by two sisters, Mary (who died at age three) and Ella. Because Harris was considerably older than the other children, young Christ (as he was popularly called by an abbreviation of Christian) served as the elder brother to the rest of the children. It was not out of character for John to call out to his older brother one night in a thunderstorm: "Christ, are you there?" and to roll over and go back to sleep when Christ assured him that he was. As older brothers often do, however, Christ somtimes led his young brothers into situations where they got into trouble, but he himself was usually clever and diplomatic enough to avoid the blame.

The home life of Christ and his brothers is what one might expect, given the character of the parents. There were few rules in the home, and thus few confrontations. The father in his home as in his district preferred to lead by example and suggestion, by guidance, not restraint. After he was fourteen years of age, as Christian, Jr., sometimes remarked later in his life, his father seldom said no to him.

At age five, young Christ began to attend Prospect Hill School, a one-room schoolhouse located a mile south of his home. By all accounts he was a good student, and a caring one. One day the teacher fell while playing with her students in the yard, and everyone seemed either too embarrassed or afraid to help her. Christ, however, naturally and easily walked to where she had fallen and helped her to her feet.

Three of his interests in these early years were pigeons, baseball, and books. Early in his teen years he began to raise pigeons commercially. He spent considerable time building pens, buying and selling stock, and purchasing feed, all apparently without much financial success. But Christ was fond of his pigeons; sometimes they could be found in his room, sitting on his bed.

School was the place to indulge his love of baseball. His bishop father eventually ceased to play ball with his sons, explaining that it was proper to play ball with children but not with older people.

He early developed a fondness for books, and while still a boy began to build his own library collection in his bedroom. As a teenager, he encouraged other young people and children to borrow his books.

Christian Junior's bright and attractive personality earned him a growing popularity in the community. The young teenager found this development pleasing and responded with a growing interest in the more sporty, entertaining activities of the surrounding area, such as racing buggies down the local roads. That, of course, became a concern for his parents.

But his parents did not need to worry for long, because shortly before his fifteenth birthday, Christ made a commitment to become a Christian. The occasion was a revival service in his home church of Manor. A series of meetings had been scheduled to begin in the last part of December, 1913, and to run for several weeks, with the well-known T. Avery Long, then of Texas, as evangelist. When Long was detained because of floods in Texas, the bishop himself began the meetings. This was not Hostetter's most comfortable role (he was hardly emotional enough to fit the image of evangelist), but as bishop he seemed compelled to act. But by the time Long arrived on January 3, the revival effort had resulted in the conversion of young Christ and several other youths in the congregation.

On the first Friday of the meetings, Christ, now well under conviction, determined he would make his commitment that evening. He was unable to respond, however, when invited to do so at the end of the service. A great fear gripped him: surely he must be hopelessly lost. When he went home he knelt beside the stovepipe going through his bedroom and begged God to give him strength to take the necessary step. Should God not see fit to do so, he promised to do his best to help others find the Lord (a not uncommon fear and resolution in those days among the Brethren in Christ).

His fears, however, were unfounded. According to the practice then current, the invitation to become a Christian was not an altar call (not, at least, in the Manor-Pequea District), as it later became. Instead, the leader invited the congregation to sing a hymn while standing, and those who wanted to become Christians to remain on their feet after the audience had seated themselves at the end of the hymn. Young Hostetter's commitment was made in this fashion—without apparent emotion or physical manifestations. Others followed him in the act on succeeding nights, including his two brothers and a number of other young people in the congregation.

Hostetter always considered this conversion experience to be the major turning point in his life. Certainly this appears to be his thinking at the time of his conversion, for a few days later he began to keep a diary. His early diaries, which he wrote from 1914 to 1918 and for part of 1923, are an invaluable source of information about his early spiritual pilgrimage, as it is as for the other events in his life.

The diaries show that from the time of his conversion Hostetter was seriously, almost precociously, concerned about his spiritual growth. He wrote on January 11, 1914, that Avery Long had come home with his parents for dinner and had then gone visiting with them in the neighborhood in the afternoon; he, however, remained in his room reading the Bible and praying. He was rejoicing as he recorded that in the evening service eighteen persons "came out on the Lord's side" (then a common expression for conversion).

Two weeks later he wrote in his diary that he attended the Bible Conference at Messiah Bible School and Missionary Training Home, where his father had preceded him by two days to serve (as he frequently did) as a speaker. These Bible Conferences were the highlight of the year, for both the college and the denomination, at least for the Pennsylvania churches. The conferences were even a popular place for young people to spend their honeymoon, even for couples from as far away as Canada. Their popularity was owing at least in part to the school bringing to campus some of the best speakers in the denomination.

This was not the first trip that Christ Hostetter would have made to the Bible School, but it was obviously a significant one for him. For one thing, he travelled with several of his boyhood friends—Roy Mann, Henry Heisey, and Elmer Mellinger. It was a sort of boyhood outing for the three young teenagers. For another, they were able to hear some of the leading figures of the denomination; besides Hostetter, Sr., they included Christian C. Burkholder of California, J. N. Engle of Kansas, and H. K. Kreider, S. R. Smith, George Detwiler, and Eli Engle of Pennsylvania.

Above all, there was Lafayette Shoalts of Ontario, Canada, who was to have a signifcant influence on young Hostetter's thinking about the nature of the Christian life. Shoalts was one of the leading proponents in the denomination of second definite work holiness. Holiness was, in fact, Shoalts' trade mark, and for many years he carried the teaching with his strong voice and equally strong personality across the entire denomination, particularly in Pennsylvania.

On the first night of the Bible Conference and under Shoalts' powerful preaching, young Christ "came out for prayer and received a fuller realization of God's love," as he wrote in his diary. The excitement of the meeting must have been great, because he did not get to bed until midnight. The conference next day was a splendid one: "I received food for my soul," he noted.

The four teenagers combined some sight-seeing with the Bible Conference. They went through Smith's noodle factory and the orphanage (Treona) across stream, and before leaving on the train for Harrisburg, toured the state capitol buildings.[3]

Back at home, as the diary shows, Christ entered a busy round of church and prayer meeting attendance. With his father and brothers he went to revival services at Pequea where his father's boyhood friend, C. C. Burkholder (now bishop of the California church), was the evangelist. In the latter part of February he attended some of the revival meetings farther away at Cross Roads, undoubtedly attracted there by evangelist Lafayette Shoalts. A short time later he went to Lancaster to hear C. C. Burkholder again. In March he had the privilege of listening to Burkholder as evangelist in services at Manor and of talking with the great man in the privacy of the Hostetter home.

His diary reveals still other interesting activities of this spiritually sensitive fifteen-year-old. He recorded with great appreciation the prayer meetings he attended, usually in members' homes. He sometimes had "a good talk" with his father, as he usually put it. One morning before going to school he had a "long prayer . . . and put self to the cross. Praise the Lord."[4] He did some confessing as well, as on April 3 when he wrote: "I took a ride this eve to straighten up crooked things in my life." (Perhaps this included confessing his shooting of a pheasant on a neighbor's property despite the posted No Hunting signs.)

Then came his baptism, on Sunday, May 10. With other candidates for baptism and membership in the church, he attended several examination meetings prior to the event, as was customary in those days. On the day of the baptism, a large crowd gathered (2,000, he wrote in his diary, but this may be a somewhat exaggerated figure). Eleven of the fifteen baptized were young people—three Heiseys, two Manns, three Mellingers, and three Hostetters (Christ, Henry, and John).

This suggests that Christ Hostetter was not alone in his pursuit of the spiritual life. The past revival and baptismal service, with similar ones that followed, brought into the Manor church a group of spirited yet deeply religious young people. These youth found their social life, not in such "worldly" activities as fairs, dances, and the theatre but rather in the functions within the life of the church. Along with the Hostetter youths, they attended prayer meetings, Sunday school and Sunday services, harvest home (Thanksgiving) meetings, revival services, and General Conferences. Once each week they met in a singing school, rotating from home to home, where they learned how to read notes and to sing new songs.

The nature of the Manor-Pequea District was conducive to this youth movement, and the leadership worked wisely to promote it. The special young people's meetings begun at this time were a clear sign of the district's responsiveness to its youth. Very few other places in the denomination in those years would have permitted such a dangerous innovation to church life.

It is thus understandable why Christ Hostetter in his formative years should develop a positive attitude toward his church. The attitude was strengthened by the care his parents took not to discuss church problems in front of their children. The Hostetter children, one of them has observed, did not realize until later in life that there was anything wrong in the church.[5]

The sense of finding a satisfying, indeed happy, life within the circle of the church may be seen as one follows Christ Hostetter through some of the activities subsequent to baptism. Two weeks later, with some of his Manor young friends—John Heisey and his sister, and the three Mellinger boys—he was off to attend General Conference, held that year (1914) at the Fairland church in Lebanon County. A few days later, with three of the Heisey youth, he attended the love feast at the Elizabethtown church, where he listened to such church giants as J. R. Zook, Avery Long, H. K. Kreider, J. N. Engle, Moses Dohner, and D. R. Eyster (all of whom obviously had remained in the area following General Conference). Many of these same men and many other church leaders he talked to in his home, since his parents were widely known throughout the denomination. Young Christ spoke of such men in his diary with a tone of respect and appreciation.

Entries in young Hostetter's diary for November 28 and 29, 1914, are typical. After doing the "barn work" and sawing some wood, he, Henry Heisey, Forry Frey, and Elmer Mellinger (all young people near his own age) went to the Mt. Pleasant church where revival meetings were being held. They stayed overnight at the home of S. S. Wolgemuth. Next morning Graybill and Cecelia Wolgemuth "took us to Elizabethtown [church] in the auto. We went to Levi Musser's for dinner. Morris Stauffer's, Shelly's girls, Henry Hess and sisters were their *[sic]*. Went back to Wolgumuth's *[sic]* about 3 o'clock. Came home. Prayer meeting at D. Mell."

In the meantime, Christ had begun a program of memorizing Bible passages. Thus in the fall, while tramping corn as it was put into the silo, he memorized the entire Sermon on the Mount.

At the end of 1914, while still in his fifteenth year, he evaluated his spiritual growth. "I had a good year with my Lord," he wrote in the back of his diary, "the first spent in his service, although sometimes I am sorry to say I did not obey the Lord in everything, but the year is over and I am happy in the Lord. Determined to go through at any cost."

His diary for 1914 also shows another side of Christ Hostetter— the daily life of a Lancaster County farm boy. Of course, he is still in school, and sufficiently interested in his work to note new courses started and his success in others. But just as frequently he talks about noon and recess activities—fox chasing in the snow, "performing feats on the ladder," and playing ball.

By late March he left school to work on the farm, as most farm boys did in order to help with the spring activities. Although slight of build and still only five feet, two inches in height, he appears to have taken virtually a man's place—spraying fruit trees, spreading manure, plowing, planting (potatoes, corn, fruit trees); later cutting hay, picking fruit, cultivating corn, threshing (both at home and at the neighbors'), making cider, filling silo, husking corn; and in the winter sawing wood and butchering hogs. He assisted his mother at the Lancaster market in selling fruit and vegetables (perhaps helping her to place the poorest quality on top of the basket, a practice for which his mother was noted). And he suffered through a bad case of poison ivy, as he did every summer.

Christ took a great interest in the farm, as evidenced in his obvious delight in working and by his recording in the back of the diaries the amount of the year's harvest. His entries for 1914 are a guide to the nature and quality of the Hostetter farm: 480 bushels of potatoes, 1,000 baskets of peaches, 280 bushels of apples, several hundred gallons of cider, 1,000 bushels of wheat, 14,000 bushels of corn, and a "good yield" of alfalfa.

Early in 1914 and following the death of her husband, Ella Hostetter's mother came to live in the Hostetter home. As the oldest son at home, it became Christ's duty to take his Mennonite grandmother to visit her Mennonite friends and sometimes to attend worship in such surrounding Mennonite churches as Habecker's, Masonville, and Millersville. This obviously greatly strengthened the tie he already had with the Mennonite world.

II

"Over the Hills Around Grantham"

The year 1915 began in much the same way as the previous one, with Christ Hostetter attending revival meetings, love feasts, and in January the Bible Conference at Grantham. This time he traveled to the school with a larger group of Manor young people—his brother Henry, Fred Frey, George Frey, Henry Heisey, Elmer Mellinger, Fanny Heisey, and Roy and Leighton Mann. Here he witnessed the ordination to the ministry of S. R. Smith's son, Joseph, and again came under the influence of Lafayette Shoalts' preaching.

On March 24 he attended Prospect Hill School for the last time. To celebrate that occasion his father gave him a Hamilton pocket watch. Five days later, and accompanied by Howard Mann, he set off for Grantham again, to enter Messiah Bible School and Missionary Training Home as a student for the final, spring term of the school year.

Although founded only six years earlier, in 1909, the school had already established a reputation for being a serious and highly motivating place in which to study. Certainly the rules were strict, at least by today's standards: few courting privileges, virtually no organized athletic activities outside of gym classes, early rising (6 a.m.) and early retiring (10 p.m.). Students came to school to study, not to waste time, although a high school and an elementary school connected with the institution guaranteed that the campus would not be uniformly sober. That many were older students earlier denied opportunities for education beyond elementary school only enhanced the note of seriousness. Then, too, many of them were strongly convinced that they were preparing themselves for future activity in the church, some as missionaries, particularly foreign missionaries.

Grantham was an exciting place for these young people, virtually all of whom had come from the farm. At the school they received the best teaching the church could offer, heard the famous men of their denomination (as at the Bible Conferences), and met (and later often married) many of the brightest and most forward-looking young people in the denomination. Certainly C. N. Hostetter, Jr., always considered his student days at Messiah Bible School and Missionary Training Home among the most important in his early life.

He attended the school from 1915 to 1917 and then again from 1920 to his graduation in 1922. In the first year he took the General Preparatory Course, designed to give students without high school some academic subjects. Thereafter he followed what was called the Bible Course. Thus his work was largely taken in biblical studies, although his records show that he also took courses in such subjects as arithmetic, algebra, grammar, civics, music, orthography, rhetoric, expression, typewriting, and bookkeeping.

He spent many hours with his books. Several of his notebooks survive; they are obviously written with great care from notes taken in the classroom. Early morning study was his custom. He noted in his diary in the fall of 1915 that because he had returned a week late to school after working on the farm, he was beginning to study as early as 3:45 in the morning. Many diary entries state that after "sweeping up" (probably his room) on Saturday morning he spent the rest of the day on his studies.

Such industry paid off well for Hostetter. Many of his report cards survive; these reveal that with very few exceptions he made A's in all his subjects (in conduct and deportment it was always so). One faculty member who made a pedagogical practice of beginning his search for responses from students least likely to answer correctly, usually reserved Christ Hostetter for the end, according to stories that still persist. Years later another of his teachers, Alma Cassel, was to say that as a student, Hostetter was "an especially alert and capable student," and that she still remembered "with pleasure the excellence of his themes."[1]

Hostetter immediately entered into the extra-curricular activities of the school. He joined virtually all of the campus student organizations—the Miltonian Literary Society, the Missionary Circle, the Young People's Society, and the Purity Association. In fact, he quickly assumed leadership positions in these organizations (despite his relative youth), obviously a commentary on his ability, as well as on his warm, although sometimes reserved personality. In his first term he was elected vice president of the Missionary Circle and president in the following school year.[2] In the spring of 1916, when elections were held for officers for the fall term, he obtained three major posts: President of the Purity Society, and Vice President of both the Missionary Circle and the Miltonian Literary Society.[3] And in his final year at the school (1921-1922) he became class president. The popular opinion in the school was that if you wanted something done, and done well, Christ Hostetter should be put on the committee.[4] A fellow student later wrote that Hostetter surely would have been named "Student of the Year" if such honors were given in those years.[5]

These leadership roles were good practice for future work in the church. So too were other activities. In October, 1915, he and other students successfully petitioned the faculty to permit them to form a group to practice public speaking; they held their meetings on the top floor of Old Main, unfurnished at the time because of lack of funds. He took part in numerous debates. In March, 1916, with Paul Baum he successfully defended the proposition that military "preparedness is better for a nation as a future world power." As if to make up for that unseemly victory, with the help of future missionary Ella Gayman he won the negative side of the resolution that in the present crisis, conscription was the best policy for the United States. Next year he lost a debate in which he argued that intelligence was the greatest achievement of man (Roy Wenger won with an argument for physical achievement).[6]

Similarly, he frequently gave speeches in the student organizations to which he belonged, including one on Longfellow, another on peas and beans (an illustrated talk), and others on how to live the virtuous life and making one's education practical. The same with music: he was sometimes a member of a group specially formed for an occasion (in those early years of the school there were no permanent music groups)—a chorus (as choirs were called in those days) for the 1916 Christmas program, a duet with Ben Books for the Miltonian Literary Society, a mixed quartet for the Purity Association, and more. Hostetter's spiritual life and religious activities at the school more than kept pace with his academic and extra-curricular activities. On January 22, 1916, on his seventeenth birthday he received what he always referred to as his sanctification experience. It occurred during the annual Bible Conference, and, not surprisingly, under the preaching of Lafayette Shoalts, the evangelist during the conference and accompanying revival services. After what must have been a powerful sermon by Shoalts in the evening, a large number of people (probably mostly students) went to the altar, including Hostetter, for what he called in his diary "more definite things." Shoalts himself dealt with Hostetter at the altar (and was criticized by a faculty member for the way in which he did it).[7] The experience was obviously an emotional one for Hostetter. He wrote in his diary: "My glasses had to go tonight. Sanctified holy about 1 hr. after midnight. Glory!" Two days later he was still "praising the Lord for glory in my soul." What he felt for himself he wished for others, and thus in April of the same year he promised at the students' prayer meeting "to pray every day with someone for the spiritual uplift of the school."[8]

At the end of the year, Hostetter in his diary reflected on this experience and in a somewhat calmer though no less certain mood considered its meaning for him.

> I praise the Lord this evening for his nearness to me this past year. There had always been a doubt in my mind as to having been sanctified and baptized by the Holy Ghost [obviously a reference to his experience in January two years earlier]. This doubt was removed by the Lord baptizing me with the Holy Ghost on Jan. 22nd. From that time forward I have realized what it means to work for God under the influence of the Holy Ghost. I have been spending from 20-40 minutes in prayer in the past year daily. Over the summer it was not that much and I felt it in my spiritual life. I have also enjoyed victory as I never did before . . . .[9]

Messiah Bible School and Missionary Training Home offered

Hostetter a variety of religious activities in which he could become involved, and he made the most out of them. From the school he was able to attend revival meetings, love feasts, and other services in the surrounding churches.[10] As a member of the Missionary Circle he took seriously its call to practical missionary work in the community. His diary shows that although still only in his middle teenage years, he visited local people who were either in spiritual or physical need (including a blind woman). He frequently took with him on these visits other young people from the school, including future minister Ben Books and future missionary Amos Dick.[11]

Because of his own spiritual commitment and leadership qualities, Hostetter soon became something of a model and counsellor for other students. Some of them retained memories of Hostetter walking down the hallways singing a currently favorite song, "There's Something More Than Gold."[12] He recorded in his diary that one night he was called out of bed to pray for a fellow student, and did not get back to his room again until after midnight.[13] Elmer Steckley, one of the Canadian students, on his return home in the spring of 1916 reported that when he was about to leave, Hostetter came to his room to pray for him, even though the two had not been much together throughout the year.[14] Another student, Charles Eshelman, later wrote of the way in which Hostetter had given him good counsel from time to time when Eshelman was disturbed by unreasonable demands being made on him by the church. "You counselled, encouraged and prayed with me," Eshelman wrote, "to hold steady within the church of our choice. The walls of Lawn Annex if able to speak would reproduce your words of spiritual insight, understanding and strength. After your thoughtful counsel and ardent prayer you extended a sympathetic hand across the small study table. My decision for the church was reaffirmed."[15]

This same kind of counsel and encouragement Hostetter offered on other levels as well. A fellow woman student later thanked him for the way in which he "comforted me after an unkind joke was played on me. I've never forgotten your Balm in Gilead."[16] A classmate, future missionary George Paulus, had difficulty with the "dead languages," as he called them. "Greek was like a Chinese riddle," until he went to Hostetter for help. The same student was seriously ill during one summer between school sessions. Hostetter wrote him a letter, "a bit flattering perhaps," Paulus recalled, "but full of sincere expression of encouragement. This letter remained for long a select keepsake."[17]

If all of this seems very serious, it is helpful to know that there was another side to Hostetter that appeared during his Grantham days. He seems to have enjoyed what social and recreational activities were available. When he played, it was obviously with vigor. Thus he had to replace two windows that he broke while playing in the gym in October, 1915.[18] In winter he enjoyed a "good refreshing snowball fight," as he once put it.[19] He frequently swam near the dam upstream from the campus, as early in the year as possible (on April 9 in 1915). He took part in ball games created in ad hoc fashion. In the spring of 1916 he joined with others to organize a boat club, and spent considerable time in helping to build the boat house and to paint the boats, and afterwards in boating.[20] In 1917, when the school finally allowed tennis to be played, Hostetter helped to lay the courts and presumably played tennis.

In fact, in 1922 when the editors of the first student yearbook produced by the school wanted to include an article on the athletic program, they chose Hostetter to write it. It is tempting to see a design in this arrangement. Athletics were still as much frowned on as ever by large sections of the denomination, particularly in the more conservative areas of Pennsylvania. A recent flurry of disapproval had resulted from the beginning of a club-like organization called the Recreation Association, and the wind had not yet died down. Now, however, an article on athletics was to be published by the school. Who better to write it than Hostetter, whose reputation was solid, who, as we shall see, by this time was a minister, and whose father was the esteemed Bishop Hostetter, now on a missionary deputation abroad?

Hostetter's article, entitled "Brain and Brawn," although guarded at points, makes a good case for athletics, under the right conditions. He acknowledges that sports are secondary to training for Christian service, and that exercise is preferable to competitive games. "We believe," he writes, "the shovel, the ax, the hoe, etc., have some advantage over the baseball bat and the tennis racket." Nevertheless "recreative exercises" have a proper place in letting off the "excess steam" of youth and are necessary to "remedy physical defects and develop a strong, well-proportioned physique." He assures his readers that all exercises and athletics are carefully supervised by the faculty and the Students' Recreation Club. No one, he claims, was ever hurt at the school in any way by athletics, not even those fellows who swim the year round in the Minnemingo (Yellow Breeches) River.[21]

Hostetter's reference to manual labor may have been a personal one. He was sometimes employed by Enos Hess (his uncle and vice-president of the school) to prune and graft fruit trees on the Hess farm; Hostetter, of course, had acquired the skill to do so on his father's farm. On a spring day in 1917 he trimmed the shrubs and dressed the roses of teacher Edna Booser.

Of all his recreational activities it was the long walks he used to take (sometimes with others) that he seems most to have enjoyed. He took one on a day in May, 1916, with Daniel Wolgemuth, and on the way they stopped to read *Love Stories of Great Missionaries.* "It was quite inspiring," Hostetter noted in his diary, "and surely gave me a desire to let God direct our social affairs."[22] In one of the school years he formed a close friendship with three other young men, including Jacob Long, who later wrote of the four "tramping over the hills around Grantham, along the trails of the Yellow Breeches or assembling in one of our rooms, [attempting] to solve many of the world's problems in general and those relating to the Brethren in Christ church in particular."[23]

In the spring of his second year at Grantham, Hostetter travelled with Roy Wenger (another student who was a close friend) to the love feast at Air Hill, near Wenger's home. The May day was warm, so the two young men rolled back the top of Wenger's small Saxon convertible, put on goggles, and in this manner rolled on to the church grounds at Air Hill, perhaps somewhat to the dismay of the more conservative Brethren. According to his friend, Hostetter moved with considerable ease and delight among the young "sisters" on the grounds; Hostetter records in his diary only that he was at the love feast at Air Hill, that he stayed overnight at Roy's home, and that they had "a good feast. Well attended."[24]

For some unexplained reason, Hostetter did not return to Grantham for the fall term of 1916. He spent the rest of the year at home, working on the farm, and attending as many of the revival meetings as he could, particularly those conducted by Lafayette Shoalts. On December 28 he visited his old school—Prospect Hill—and the next day spoke to the teacher about teaching school.

At this time in his life, a teaching career appears to have been very much on his mind. When he returned to Grantham in January, 1917, he picked up where he had left off in his Bible Course, but he also took some pedagogical subjects and did some practice teaching in the campus model school, which gave instruction to the children in the orphanage across the stream. He enjoyed his teaching, especially on the last day when the children gave him a "bouquet of beautiful roses as a parting gift."[25]

On May 31, at Lancaster, he took the examinations for the Provisional Teacher's Certificate. Although he passed the tests and obtained his certificate, he discovered that when he went to the Public School Building five days later to obtain a school, all the teaching positions had been filled. In the late summer of the same year (1917) he attended a methods class for teachers at Millersville, and next year in November he again wrote an examination for teaching (his fourth), but still a teaching career did not open for him.[26] His main occupation thus remained farm work, although for a while he was hired as a substitute mail carrier for his local mail route. He did have a school of sorts, however, in a singing class that he organized and taught, and for which he used the popular Randall Singing Book of simple secular and religious songs.

During these years at home he began to move into active work in the church. He learned more about the denomination by driving for his father when the latter travelled about on church business. (The elder Hostetter, on buying his first car, a Franklin, took it to a field for driving practice, but almost immediately ran into a tree and never fully trusted himself with the Franklin again.) Young Hostetter, instead of sitting in the car, accompanied his father inside to the meeting or business session. He liked to say in later years that this was excellent training for work in the church.

In the Manor congregation he was one of the officers in the Young People's group and very often gave talks in its programs.

In the spring of 1918, he was elected Assistant Sunday school superintendent. His mail route provided a good opportunity to invite children to his Sunday school.[27] In the following year, he was appointed to two committees of the district—the Missionary and Ministerial Program Committee, and the Sunday School Advisory Board. In 1918 he became involved with the Sunday school at the Lancaster City mission, and in February, 1919, was elected its superintendent.

The Hostetters were strong supporters of the Lancaster mission. The pages of the *Evangelical Visitor* show that they (both parents and children) gave frequent gifts of food and money to the project. The father assumed a bishop's oversight of the mission and frequently attended and spoke at its services. It was thus natural that his sons would become part of the program.

Hostetter junior attacked his work with great enthusiasm. Two days after his election as superintendent, a revival campaign began at the mission under evangelist J. R. Zook. On the first day, a Sunday, Hostetter went out into the streets with George Haagen, a fellow worker, to distribute invitations to the meeting.[28] He returned to the city from the farm every evening to help in the revival, usually arriving home after midnight. "The Lord most graciously answered our prayers in respect to Lancaster meetings," he wrote in his diary for March 10, 1919. "Praise His dear name. Some ninety visited the altar for various things. Quite a number of town people saved and sanctified . . . some were healed. God did most graciously bless."

Hostetter had for his helpers in the Sunday school a largely young group of people (including his brothers Henry and John) who possessed considerable esprit de corps for their work. Since the Sunday school was held on Sunday afternoon, the young people from the Manor and Pequea churches could assist, and could work out their creative energies in a mission venture. Under the leadership of twenty-year-old Christ Hostetter, they filled the mission building with scholars and then took the overflow to an adjacent house. According to estimates, it was probably the largest Sunday school at the time in the denomination.

By now, he had become involved on another, wider level of service to his church—assisting his father in his work as General Conference secretary and as chairman of the Foreign Mission

Board. In fact, young Hostetter became so busy with his many farm and church activities that he wrote in his diary on April 15, 1919 (after a silence lasting from March 13) that he probably would be forced to abandon his diary. He must have already made the decision to do so, since, unfortunately, there is no entry again until the beginning of 1923.

From his earliest days, Hostetter had been fascinated by General Conference. His father had gone off each year to sit with that body, and he held executive office in it. As a boy, Hostetter spent hours reading through the published minutes of the conference, as well as the *Evangelical Visitor* (the denominational periodical) and the *Directory* (the list of members of the denomination, with their addresses).[29] As a teenager he attended all the General Conferences held in Pennsylvania.

By 1917 Hostetter was working as a sort of private secretary to his father on General Conference business. In April of that year he read and mailed the proofs of the General Conference program, and sent out notices of the event. After the conference he helped his father to arrange the minutes into publication form, proofread the galleys, and did most of the indexing for the volume.[30] Much the same is recorded in his diary for 1918 and 1919. In the latter years he was recording secretary for General Conference, held that year in the Antrim church in Franklin County, Pennsylvania. "A smart young fellow," reported Isaac Swalm of Hostetter to his son Ernest when he returned home from the conference to Ontario, Canada.[31]

In 1920 Hostetter again accompanied his father to General Conference, this time held at Stayner, Ontario. Here he assisted his father as a "private secretary," to use his own words. Here, too, he met for the first time Ernest J. Swalm who was to become his lifelong and intimate friend. The two discovered that they had much in common—a love for reading the *General Conference Minutes,* an excellent knowledge of the church and its leaders, and a strong interest in entering the ministry. Hostetter remained for several days after the conference ended, spending much of the time visiting in the Swalm home. On one of those days he joined a group of the area young people on a picnic to the nearby mountain, riding there in a buggy with Swalm's sister Pearl. On his return to Pennsylvania he crossed Lake Ontario on a boat, rode a trolley up the Royal Gorge, and caught his first sight of Niagara Falls.[32]

And then in 1921 he became General Conference secretary *pro tem,* owing to his father's absence abroad. This meant, among other things, that much of the preparation for General Conference of 1922 fell to him. His father sensed the burden and perhaps the temptation to self-pride that the position might bring such a young man, and thus wrote from the Saharsa Mission in India that he should not allow General Conference to pressure him into serving in an official capacity in that office.[33] If such a possibility threatened, the father was able to head it off by arriving home one day before General Conference began (held that year in Smith's noodle factory in Grantham). His son, however, conducted the election for moderator, which resulted in the choice of the senior Hostetter, who also at this conference was appointed to a five-year term as the conference secretary.

In the meantime, in 1920, Hostetter had become a minister. These were still the years when ministers were elected to their office (whether or not they professed a personal "call"). These were also the years of the multiple ministry when several men in the congregation, having been elected and serving without ministerial salary, shared together in the work of preaching and visitation.

Unfortunately, the lapse in his diary prevents us from knowing much about the reasons for and the details of Hostetter's election, or about his reaction to it. Perhaps most striking and obvious in the situation was the election to the ministry of one so young (twenty-one years of age) and unmarried at that. In those days, such situations rarely occurred among the Brethren in Christ.

Several factors help to explain this unusual development. It did not hurt his chances at election that he was a son of the well-liked bishop (such relationships were not unusual in the denomination), but that in itself would not have been sufficient for his election. Ability and character were more important. Young Hostetter had given considerable proof that he possessed both. One of the ministers in the district declared that at the age of twenty Hostetter had the maturity of a man of fifty.[34]

Hostetter was elected by the entire district, as was then generally the custom. His ordination was on Sunday, June 28. His father performed the service before a crowd that overflowed into the aisles and across the back of the room. It was an emotional occasion; some in the audience wept.

In the fall of that year he returned to Grantham to complete the Bible Course. Because of his studies he eventually had to give up his work at the Lancaster Mission to others. In its place he did some speaking both at Grantham and in the surrounding Brethren in Christ churches. Early in 1922 he gave an address at the denomination's Pennsylvania State Council on how to enhance cooperation between the young and the old in the church. "His sermons," declared the yearbook for 1922, "show the result of prayerful meditation upon the Word of God."[35]

In his last year he was elected president of his class, and he wrote the class song. His last act as a student was to give the graduation oration at commencement in May, 1922. In it he identified the enemies of the cross (the title of his oration): modern education, social betterment and moral reforms, religious education that taught that people were basically good. All of these could be combated by holding up to men the cross "in its sublime beauty and matchless power."[36]

His graduation marked the completion of an important phase of his life; he now stood on the threshold of a promising future. He had at an early age earned a growing reputation as an exceptional young man and had won considerable deference even from older churchmen. He was not unaware of his position, or of the dangers inherent in it. When asked by a friend while still in school how he managed to remain level-headed, he replied, "George, this is one of my greatest temptations. I pray much to stay humble."[37] Besides ability, he was obviously possessed of the quality of self-examination.

III

"To Establish My Own Home"

*I*n the spring of 1922 while still in school at Grantham, Hostetter and three fellow students—Albert Engle, Norman Wingert, and Jesse Steckley—discussed their common hope to do some evangelistic work during the summer months. They received permission to do so from the Home Mission Board (which insisted that their project be self-supporting), and in mid-summer set out in Norman Wingert's car in search of fields to conquer.

They quickly came to the view that it would be best to divide into teams of two. Jesse Steckley and Norman Wingert settled on Ickesburg in Perry County, some thirty-five miles northwest of Grantham, where they held meetings in the town's lodge hall. Hostetter and Engle settled in Iron Springs, about the same distance from Grantham, several miles from Gettysburg, near the town of Fairfield.

Iron Springs is about three miles into the mountains. In those days it was a rough community, many of the inhabitants of the area being moonshiners, bootleggers, and ex-convicts. The woman moonshiner who worried that a forty-five gallon barrel of home brew would not last the weekend is illustrative of the community's style. What the people of the area knew of the gospel was little enough: no religious service had been held in Iron Springs for a number of years, and the last revival ended with the two preachers getting into a fight over the offerings.

The two young preachers were not entirely unaware of the community's character. But they were very much in earnest, and prepared to take the risks. Besides, before beginning they had gone into the woods to pray about their venture and had there received assurance that they should proceed.

They obtained permission to use the local schoolhouse, which stood unoccupied during the summer months, and obtained room and breakfast in Fairfield. Having no car, they walked the several miles to Iron Springs and their visiting. Neither did they have much money for food. Fortunately, wild berries were in season, and these the young evangelists ate along the road until some of the people of the area took pity on them and invited them for meals.

Mornings were spent in studying, afternoons in visiting, and also in praying in an old stone quarry (many mountain people heard the prayers and were attracted to the services by them). Hostetter and Engle took turns in preaching, and singing solos and leading the singing. In spite of the community's reputation, the evangelists suffered no harm, although one evening they were taken by car to their room in Fairfield because, as they later discovered, some young men of the community had planned to throw eggs at them on their way home.

The revival, which began in August, ran for three weeks, spilling over into September. Over a dozen people were converted, including Iola Dixon, future long-term home mission worker. When the services were discontinued, Albert Engle, accompanied by other students from Grantham, returned each Sunday in the fall to conduct a Sunday school. The work begun at Iron Springs by Hostetter and Engle continues to this day.

At the end of the summer, the four young evangelists came together to divide their offerings. Engle and Hostetter had nothing to bring after expenses; Steckley and Wingert had just enough money for each of the four to receive one dollar. This was not much to show in a financial way for a month of hard work. But Hostetter always looked back with much fondness on this first revival that he conducted, and over the years he frequently returned to Iron Springs to preach and to attend anniversary services.[1]

A few months later, on November 9, 1922, he was married—to Anna Lane of Lititz. She was one of two children of Samuel and Mary Lane, operators of the Millway Hotel near Lititz. Anna grew up helping to wait on tables and serving alcoholic drinks. She attended high school at Lititz and in her senior year at the age of eighteen began to teach at the local schoolhouse. After two years she became a waitress for the United Zion Church home in Lititz. The United Zion Church was a small, conservative group that had broken from the parent Brethren in Christ body in the mid-nineteenth century. The church had remained conservative, including in its "plain dress." Anna's father was not at all pleased that she was among such religious-minded people. So she returned home, but was soon back again with the United Zion people, this time to work at nursing in the home. While there she became converted in one of their revival meetings.

Because she found nursing to be difficult, she returned again to her parents. But when she became a member of the United Zion Church and began to dress plainly, she met with opposition from her father, who threatened to make her leave home. She prayed about the problem and received the answer to "Follow me." So she packed her suitcase and went to the United Zion Mission in Lancaster city. Phares and Cora Sweigert, who attended the mission, took Anna to their home in Elizabethtown, where she lived for two years.

While with the Sweigerts she gave a talk one Sunday to the United Zion Sunday school at Annville. S. R. Smith, Messiah Bible School and Missionary Training Home president (whose background was United Zion) heard her speak and invited her to come to Grantham, insisting on helping her through school when she protested that she had no money. She came in the fall of 1916 as both student and teacher, instructing in the commercial and typing courses. Hostetter took at least one course from her. He noted in his diary for January 10, 1917 that "because Anna Lane had a very bad cold, he took charge of her typewriting class."

After her graduation, Anna returned to the United Zion mission in Lancaster. By this time Hostetter was becoming active in the Brethren in Christ mission in the same city. People from the two missions were frequently together in Sunday school, church services, and street meetings. Thus Christ and Anna continued to see each other, and he was increasingly attracted to her. This is not surprising. She was obviously intelligent, decidedly pretty, deeply spiritual, and being seven years older possessed greater maturity than most of the girls of Hostetter's own age. Much about her was a recommendation to pursue a courtship.

Thus one Sunday when she was at the Brethren in Christ mission, Hostetter met her as she came out of the restroom and asked if they could be friends. She professed to be puzzled, and reminded him of the difficulties: a difference in age and churches, and the likelihood of her being disinherited by her parents because of her religious stand. Hostetter declared that he did not care about any of these difficulties (perhaps he was challenged by them), and so she consented to be "special friends." His diary does not record this event (undoubtedly because at this point there are many blank pages), but the entry for January 22, 1919 (Hostetter's twentieth birthday) suggests that the special friendship had already started and that the two young people were even then planning for the future: "Spent some time talking with Anna Lane. Truly God is worthy our trust, and *will* deliver us."

In June of 1920, Anna attended Hostetter's ordination to the ministry at the Manor church. He was aware of her coming, since she had written to tell him she would be there. As Hostetter later told a friend, at the beginning of the service he looked over the audience to locate her, and having done so, for the rest of the program could see only her dark eyes looking at him.[2]

Both were back at Grantham in the fall of 1920, she to teach and he as a student. These were not the days in which a courtship could be too actively pursued at the school, but Hostetter did find opportunities to go to her classroom to talk, and to take walks with her (since she was a teacher, they did not need a chaperone). Sometimes they traveled together between Grantham and Lancaster. With another student couple, Earl Sider and Elsie Sheffer, they once attended an evening revival service at the Brethren in Christ church in Mechanicsburg five miles away, traveling there by train to Harrisburg and by trolley from Harrisburg to Mechanicsburg. There were, however, no trains available after the service. At Hostetter's suggestion, the two couples separated and walked back to Grantham—Christ and Anna by way of Bowmansdale, and Earl and Elsie by way of Shepherdstown, both couples arriving on campus at the same time. Did Hostetter have this planned before starting? At least it seems one of the most daring escapades of his young life.

As his graduation in 1922 approached, however, Hostetter seemed to have second thoughts about his friendship with Anna.

What these were it is difficult to determine. Perhaps they had something to do with Anna's father who, although by this time largely reconciled to his daughter's lifestyle, was not happy about her marrying a "plain" man and could not believe that Hostetter really cared for his daughter. In any case, Hostetter suggested that they discontinue their friendship, or at least stay apart to give themselves a chance to think about their relationship.

Thus Hostetter spent the next several months removed from Anna, on the farm and at Iron Springs. But at the end of the revival at Iron Springs in September he returned to Anna at Lititz, his mind made up. He told her that he had prayed much about their relationship; he now more than ever wanted to marry her. In good romantic fashion, he proposed to her on his knees, and she gave an immediate yes.

The wedding was held in Anna's home, the father of the bridegroom performing the ceremony. Both Anna and Christ had wanted to be married in the Hostetter home (no one in the denomination in those days married in the church), but Hostetter insisted that by marrying in Anna's according to her father's wishes she could help heal the estrangement that had earlier existed between father and daughter.

The wedding was a large family affair. Samuel Lane, who by now had become convinced that his daughter was after all doing very well in her marriage, provided a large wedding dinner of stuffed turkey, cake and ice cream, with all the trimmings of a typical Pennsylvania-Dutch meal.

There was no traditional honeymoon immediately after the wedding. Typical of many newly married couples of their social and religious circles, Anna and Christ remained in her parents' home for several days, after which he returned to his own house. For about a month the two got together for weekends and on other occasions. Only later in 1924 did they take a belated honeymoon, to Niagara Falls.[3]

A week following their marriage, Anna was consecrated as a minister's wife in a Manor prayer meeting. At the same time she changed her membership to the Brethren in Christ Church.

A few weeks later (in December) the Hostetters joined Albert Engle and several other workers in a winter revival at Iron Springs. The Hostetters had volunteered to serve for only room

and board, which they received on invitation from the Weltys, a
local family who had been converted in the summer revival. The
house was small and crowded with eight people, including the
Hostetters; they shared their bedroom with Iola Dixon, with only
a curtain separating them. But this was a successful revival.
Whereas the earlier one had reached virtually only women and
children, this one resulted in the conversion of about twelve men
and boys. "The day of revivals is not yet past," Hostetter wrote,
encouraged, in his diary on the last day of the year. That evening
they left for Lancaster, spending the night in a Gettysburg hotel,
listening to the bells sound out the old year as they prepared to go
to bed.[4]

When the Hostetters returned to Lancaster they continued to
live with their parents, only now together and on a rotating basis.
By this time, he had begun to sell stereoscopic sets and thus was
absent from home for days at a time. In the first two months of
1923, he worked the area around Gettysburg and Hagerstown,
Maryland, with several other salesmen.

But he did not enjoy his work. He soon discovered that people
everywhere were plagued by salesmen and did not want to listen
to another one. Hostetter was not accustomed to such indifference.[5] Also, times were economically bad for selling such items.
He had some success among the Mennonites and members of the
Church of the Brethren who recognized a kindred spirit when
they looked at his "plain" Brethren in Christ suit. But what money
he did earn appears largely to have disappeared into repairs for a
1917 touring car which he had bought about the time of his
marriage.[6] "Had a flat tire outside of Hagerstown," his diary
reads for one day. "Had the tire off the rim three times before it
was repaired."[7]

What he most disliked, however, was the style of salesmanship
his employers seemed bent on demanding of him. To make good
money he needed to win prizes in competition with his fellow
salesmen. This opened the way for practices which he thought
were not consistent with his position as a minister. He had a frank
talk with his supervisor abou the matter, and when no improvement seemed forthcoming he resigned his position early in
March. "Educationally," he admitted at the time, "I received
quite a training in meeting and dealing with people. There are

strong temptations in work of this kind for one to lose out spiritually as there is a constant touch with all classes and in efforts to make a sale one must guard not to use undue persuasion, etc."[8]

It is almost certain, however, that one of the major reasons for giving up this sales position was Hostetter's decision to accept placement as the pastor of the small Brethren in Christ congregation at Refton, a village about ten miles south of Lancaster city. The church there was, in a sense, an outreach of the Manor-Pequea District. Simon Graybill, one of the ministers of the district from 1878 to 1898, was a very able and relatively progressive minister. Under his leadership, the Brethren in the southeast part of the district began to meet for services in the town schoolhouse at Quarryville. Around 1903 and after Graybill's death, the group started to worship in the Strasburg Temperance Hall and then moved again in 1912 to Refton, where they rented the church building owned by the Church of the Brethren.

Up to Hostetter's coming in 1923, Refton had always been a small congregation and rather out of the way, as far as the rest of the district was concerned. For a number of years the closest minister in the district lived eight miles distant. There was clearly a need for a minister to reside in the area. Hostetter welcomed the chance to fill that need. And in so doing he helped to move the district away from the system in which services rotated from one church building to another to one in which each congregation had one or more resident ministers and each developed a separate and regular program of worship.

The Hostetters spent several weeks in fixing up a small house in the village—painting, papering, installing book cases—and on March 26 moved in. "This marked the day," Hostetter's diary reads, "when I left my parental home to establish my own home."[9]

Two years later he built his own house in town—an attractive, two-story house—for $7,600. Part of the money came as a gift from Anna's parents, and part as a loan from his uncle David. He did not hesitate to build well; he considered such a move a good investment. Neither was he afraid to borrow money (within reason). Some years later when advising his brother John along the same lines he indicated that the debt he held from his uncle made him work harder, and thus in time he earned more money.[10]

Although pastor, Hostetter had, of course, to find his own financial support. Throughout his years at Refton he did this principally by relying on his abilities as a salesman. His first job in this new community was selling peanut butter for John Moseman, a Mennonite minister of Lancaster city who operated a wholesale business in peanut butter as well as a vegetable produce market. Hostetter served as Moseman's area sales representative, working on commission and covering territory as far away as Allentown and Reading in the northeast of the state to Franklin County in the southwest. Area colleges and retirement homes became part of his contacts in addition to stores and similar establishments.

He appears to have enjoyed selling peanut butter. Undoubtedly this was owing in part to a congenial employer who gave Hostetter considerable flexibility to carry on his church work. Some years after he was no longer selling peanut butter, Hostetter wrote to his former employer: "I always remember with keen appreciation your personal assistance when a young self-supporting minister was struggling to solve the two-fold problem of this life—support his family and give the church his best."[11] Perhaps part of his enjoyment of the job may also have been that at the end of a sales trip he always brought home the peanut butter remaining in the sample containers. Not surprisingly, peanut butter became one of the main staples in the Hostetter family diet.

In 1928, however, he shifted from selling peanut butter to selling calendars. In this he worked for the Gerlach-Barklow Company of Joliet, Illinois. As a sideline, he sold scripture text calendars printed by a local Amishman. Hostetter made this shift because calendar sales were more seasonal in nature, the bulk of the sales coming largely at one time in the year. This left him freer for his pastoral work at Refton and especially for his growing ministries in the denomination.

He was very successful in this new work, making as much as $3,000 in a depression year. This despite the fact that he discarded all the "girlie" calendars sent to him by the company as a part of his display stock. Neither did his Brethren in Christ plain-cut black suit which he always wore seem to have hurt his sales; in fact, it may have helped, since he was certainly in appearance far different from the "city-slicker" image that many salesmen had in those days.

Hostetter believed that good salesmanship meant good treatment and servicing of customers, even though at times it did not seem economically practical to do so. This attitude complemented the warm and interested personality (in contrast to other salesman types) that he brought to his contact with clients. Altogether, it was difficult to say no to him.[12] Hostetter himself attributed part of his success to his devotional life, as he explained in 1939 to a young salesman, John Zercher: "I found in sales life it was necessary to keep my own devotional life warm and my spiritual perspective clear. I was then not only in a position to radiate testimony for our Savior, but I was even in a better position to do the best for which I was responsible [making sales]."[13]

The Hostetters supplemented their income by planting a large garden and keeping chickens; some of the produce, including chickens, Anna occasionally sold on the Lancaster market. And almost from the beginning of their married life, they invested in stocks and bonds. Thus on October 12, 1923, six months after starting to work with Moseman, Hostetter wrote in his diary that he bought that day at Lancaster four shares of Armstrong Cork Company's preferred stock—"7% payable quarterly at 112."

In his pastorate, Hostetter exercised many of the qualities that made him successful as a salesman. During his first year, he organized a Sunday school and served as superintendent until someone else could be trained to do it. His congregation in 1925 purchased the building which they had been renting from the Church of the Brethren. Around the same time, Hostetter began to conduct regular worship services rather than the occasional one that took place only when the rest of the district came in their turn to Refton.

He quickly established a reputation for friendliness. When he shook hands, his parishioners remember, he used both hands—as if to be doubly friendly. This attitude extended to people beyond his congregation, showing itself, among other ways, in giving needy people food supplies.[14] One day he came home to find one of the church's loudest critics moving to another location. Hostetter helped him move, milked his cows, and ate supper with the family. The man became a great admirer of Hostetter, later was converted, and joined the church.[15]

Visiting in homes, Hostetter believed, was highly important to a successful ministry. Speaking at the Bible Conference in Grantham in 1928, he insisted that the better a minister knows his people and their needs the better he can preach to them. Thus "if the preacher is invisible through the week he is apt to be incomprehensible on Sunday." The lack of such pastoral visiting he considered to be one of the greatest weaknesses of the Brethren in Christ Church.[16]

At the same conference, he spoke on preparing the sermon; from his words we have presumably some of the ideas he attempted to practice at this stage of his ministry. Preparation is crucial, he maintained, for an effective sermon and ministry.

> It is not fair to the congregation to have Saturday night or Sunday morning arrive and the minister still be asking himself these questions, "What do the people need? What will the Spirit give me?" Every minister has had experience where in special times of need truth was very graciously revealed to him. However, to regularly rely on the inspiration of the moment to provide a message is to pave the way to failure and will inevitably produce a barren ministry. It's like a housewife who can once in a while set on the table a quick lunch which the family appreciates, but not often— she will have to draw on her store of provisions and canned fruit and vegetables.

This was good preaching. Hostetter was probing a weakness in Brethren in Christ church life.

Beyond preparation, he insisted that the minister should not "hesitate to challenge unscriptural practices of his people," but he should do so in wisdom and love. To prevent twisting the Scriptures, the texts should be studied in context and with parallel passages. Illustrations should be used as windows (some Brethren in Christ preachers were opposed to that view). But there are, he warned, wrong ways of using illustrations: "It is a sad fact that ministers sometimes overdraw illustrations or ascribe them to their own experience or observations when such is not the case. No man can remain spiritual and continue such a practice." In all of this, a minister should preach for a verdict—for results.[17]

From time to time, however, Hostetter had doubts about the effectiveness of his own ministry. These moments usually occurred when he became too busy in his sales and church work beyond Refton, but also when he detected pride within himself. A poignant passage appears in his diary on November 18, 1923, eight months into his pastorate:

> My soul is under a crushing burden tonight. My ministry has fallen so short to what it should have been. I have allowed temporal duties to preoccupy my mind. Time for study has been curtailed and minimized. My messages have not been heaven born as they should be. Not enough of prayer and prayerful scripture searching. Not enough concern of the lost of earth. Not enough personal work. Not enough visiting. Several appointments forgotten. Occasional thoughts of self while preaching. Oh merciful Father, forgive thy servant for this temporary burying of talent— this failure to give it to the "exchangers."

He ends the passage by praying for help "to seek first the kingdom of God and His righteousness."

One of the significant marks of Hostetter's ministry at Refton was his organizaton in 1929 of a Vacation Bible School. It is not clear from where he obtained the idea for the school. His was the first to be conducted not only in the surrounding area but in the denomination, although later in the summer two other schools were conducted elsewhere in Brethren in Christ congregations.

Hostetter himself led the Vacation Bible Schools, which grew each year in size—from an enrollment of 71 in 1929 to 216 in 1933. Children came from miles around—in cars, farm wagons, even a truck. Part of the excitement of the school was to see the vehicles roll on to the grounds and to inquire how many each held. "The little church," one of his nieces has recalled, "was crowded—basement windows, upstairs, little corners—there were all kinds of places where we met. We had hand-work, scissors and paste—things you didn't have in church those days."[18] In fact, the school grew so large that it spilled out of the church and into the Hostetters' house, into the local grade school, and finally into the United Brethren church in the village. Partly because the students came from many different church backgrounds, Hostetter chose a teaching staff that was in large part interdenominational, including some who were Mennonite. This was obviously a fortunate venture. Writing in the fall of 1933, President Enos Hess of Messiah College evaluated the Refton Vacation Bible School as the most successful school that he knew.[19] It is not surprising that Hostetter came to be seen as an authority on Vacation Bible Schools, frequently being asked to speak and write on the subject—at General Conference, at Grantham, and in the *Evangelical Visitor*. An article in that paper in 1933 outlines what in Hostetter's views are the values of the Vacation Bible School: it gives greater prestige to the church in the community, increases Sunday school attendance, teaches regular attendance at Sunday school, and greatly blesses any community. (In another article, he made the timely point that the schools also help to increase the quality of Sunday school teaching.) These values can be translated into reality by a well-planned course of study, and by teachers who are willing to do nothing else for two weeks except give themselves to the school.[20]

As the Vacation Bible School suggests, Hostetter was in effect a pastor to a constituency wider than just his Refton congregation. He had, for example, an effective ministry to the Mennonites. This was partly because the Mennonites in the surrounding area had no regular services, and partly because many of them liked the more evangelical style of Hostetter and the Brethren in Christ. Many Mennonites visited the Refton congregation on special occasions and for house prayer meetings; some worshipped there regularly. Hostetter spoke in their churches. He refused, however, to capitalize on this situation; thus under his ministry few, if any, of the local Mennonites were taken into the congregation as members.[21]

Over the years, a strong attachment developed between Hostetter and his congregation. "Tomorrow morning," he wrote to a friend after an absence from Refton of seven weeks, "will be the first Sunday morning I have been with the Refton people since in May. If they are half as glad to have me as I am to be home, we will richly enjoy our renewed fellowship."[22]

Perhaps an even more telling illustration was Hostetter's refusal to accept other, more promising pastorates. He twice rejected an offer from the Abilene, Kansas, congregation (both offers followed revival meetings he held there). This was a considerable rejection. Abilene was an attractive, growing congregation, and was the only one of two in the denomination that provided a salary. On the second offer, Hostetter wrote to his elderly friend, M. G. Engle, the Kansas bishop, to ask what he would think if he accepted the position. Engle was hoping that Hostetter would come to Abilene, and so he replied in his characteristically brusque way:

> What do you expect me to say about Abilene's request? I expect you to say the decision on your heart and if you want encouragement from the Bishop it will be O.K. with him because I think he and C. N. Hostetter would get along alright. "Would it surprise you if I would accept?" More surprising things have happened and are happening right along.[23]

If Hostetter was, in fact, tempted by this second offer, he put the temptation aside to remain with his Refton people.

His parishioners reciprocated the affection. "We never dreamed he would leave us," one of them said when Hostetter eventually left for other work in 1934. His successor, Cyrus Lutz, discovered that his hardest task was to follow Hostetter in the position. "One sister in the congregation," he remembers, "came to me and said that if I would do things just as Brother Christ did them, everything would be all right. It was a very heartbroken congregation when Christ left."[24]

During the years of his pastorate, Hostetter's influence in the denomination rapidly grew, and young as he was he quickly moved into a leadership position. His evangelistic work serves as a good illustration. The demand for his services, particularly as a tent evangelist, were great almost from the beginning of his career, and Hostetter responded with enthusiasm.

In doing so, he played a leading part in one of the most significant and characteristic movements in Brethren in Christ life during the 1920s and following decades. By now, revival services had been accepted everywhere in the denomination, and were being used in many, if not all congregations as the main tool for outreach in the community.

Tent meetings were a form of revival meeting that, although beginning as early as the 1890s among the Kansas Brethren, had just become generally popular in the denomination at the time that Hostetter commenced his evangelistic work. Some districts, as well as the Canadian Mission Board, purchased their own tents, using them in their own areas and sometimes renting them to other districts or congregations. They were an attractive form of evangelism: the tents, of course, had greater flexibility for use than church buildings, and thus could, if it seemed the part of wisdom, be moved away from the church and set up in the best place to reach the unsaved. They were also something of a novelty, perhaps possessing for many non-church people an image (subconscious or otherwise) of the circus, and thus could attract outsiders in a way that a Brethren in Christ church building could not hope to do.

This evangelistic spirit and especially the use of tent evangelism owed much to J. R. Zook. For more than two decades before his death in 1917, Zook had moved across the denomination as one of the first and most successful evangelists in Brethren in Christ history. A few months before his death in 1919 he had urged General Conference to create and finance "flying squadrons" of evangelists that would be ready at virtually a moment's notice to answer a call to conduct a revival. He had especially recommended the use of tent evangelism for these flying squadrons.[25]

It is very tempting to read Zook's influence on Hostetter and the work in which he was becoming deeply involved. Hostetter had listened to Zook speak on a number of occasions—at Grantham, love feasts, and revival meetings. Most significantly, Hostetter attended the 1919 General Conference at Air Hill (as recording secretary to his father) and had there heard Zook plead for his flying squadrons (unsuccessfully, as it turned out). Years later Hostetter wrote that Zook had taken a personal interest in him as a young member at the Air Hill conference, and that Zook's "passionate interest in developing a witnessing church captivated me. I still remember some of the things he said on the floor of that conference 50 years ago." In the same passage, Hostetter credited the beginning of tent revivals to Zook's 1919 conference speech.[26] It is also tempting to see Hostetter as picking up the great man's mantle when Zook died a short time later.

Hostetter conducted his first tent meeting in the summer of 1923, a few months after moving to Refton and one year after his first revival at Iron Springs. The setting for the campaign was the Howick church near Fordwich, Ontario, about forty miles northwest of Kitchener.

Howick was one of the older congregations in the Canadian church. Its membership, however, had steadily declined until there was only a handful remaining (Hostetter in his diary writes of only eight or nine being present for communion). According to Hostetter's diary, part of the difficulty was the strong conservatism that the elderly, gentlemanly Bishop John Reichard and his fellow church officials promoted, including in dress. When some women did not consistently wear the prayer veiling outside of church, the leadership objected. The result was further withdrawal of memberships and some friction among those who remained.

Other problems faced the young, twenty-four-year-old evangelist. He arrived in the farming community in July, in the middle of the hay-making season. More than that, the Howick members were seen by the community as good, honest, but in some ways odd sort of people. There had consequently been little, if any religious interchange between the Brethren in Christ and even their churchgoing neighbors. "Different people tell us," Hostetter noted in his diary, "that this is a very hard place to work. Some, 'If you get anything accomplished here, you will do well.' "

But Hostetter set out to do well. First, the tents were staked in a field—a large one for an auditorium, another for a kitchen, and three small ones to serve as sleeping quarters for the evangelist and his assistants. These workers (as such assistants were called in tent meeting terminology) were Levi and Anna Schell from the Markham congregation; Mary Sentz from Harrisburg, Pennsylvania; and Alma Bollinger from the denomination's Mt. Carmel Orphanage at Morrison, Illinois. "A blessed group of helpers," Hostetter thought. "They are spirit-filled, and good team workers. Praise God for this blessed band!" That bringing together of workers from various parts of the denomination was also typical of Brethren in Christ tent meetings.

With these workers he held two prayer sessions a day. He began his own prayer and study early in the morning. For much of the rest of the day he visited, often borrowing a car and striking off on his own. He visited everyone—Brethren and non-Brethren alike, including one woman whose house, according to his diary, "was one of the most filthy homes in which I ever was. The odors were such that I minded it in my stomach when I went on the pulpit [in the evening to preach]." Sometimes he helped the farmers with their work.

Predictably, the tent meetings started slowly, with only a handful of people attending the first nights. But Hostetter's warmth and visiting and pulpit ministry soon began to draw the community to the tent. By the middle of the second week the tent was crowded each night, and by the end of the campaign sometimes as many as 100 people stood around on the outside.

The entire community seemed to attend—Mennonites, Presbyterians, Methodists, Evangelicals, and what Hostetter called "non-professors." The local Mennonite minister came to his church one Sunday evening to find that all of his congregation had gone to the tent. The Methodist minister had the same experience; he himself went to the services, declared this to be "the most spiritual meeting" he ever attended, took part in one of the services, and invited Hostetter to speak in his church (which, for some unstated reason, Hostetter declined to do).

Soon the word spread over the Canadian church of the phenomenal success of the meetings at the impossible Howick church. Lafayette Shoalts, who obviously looked on Hostetter as a sort of protegé, could not resist traveling all the way from his home near Wainfleet to confirm the good news for himself. After listening to Hostetter preach a sermon on "What Shall I do with Jesus Who is Called the Christ?" Shoalts declared that he had never heard a sermon like it.[27]

Hostetter's own feelings may be caught in his diary entries; they are a mixture of expressions of delight with the success of the meetings and of concern that such success should not go to his head. "The attention is almost perfect to a person," he wrote on a Wednesday night. "No whispering, no shuffling. God is speaking to souls." In another entry, he is thankful that "God has been

helping me most graciously. I never spoke with so much freedom
. . . . I am praying that he will give me a tender heart—much more
tender. So that I can weep over the erring." Toward the end of the
meetings, he wrote excitedly: "What a glorious privilege to be in
Christian service. Take all, yes every bit of glory, Father."

The elderly Bishop Reichard was understandably swept off his
feet. He admitted to Hostetter that the meeting "far exceeded our
fondest hopes." Writing an account of the campaign a short time
later for the *Evangelical Visitor,* Reichard reported that fifty-two
people had received help at the altar of prayer. "We praise God,"
he added in a tone of typical understatement, "for His wonderful
love manifested in sending to us this divinely arranged campaign.
It is acknowledged as a God-send to this community . . . ."[28]

It was hard for the Howick people to allow such success to
stop; they persuaded Hostetter to remain for an extra half week.
Before leaving for home the young evangelist had a frank talk
with the elderly bishop in which the two discussed Reichard's
responsibility for caring for the revived congregation. Hostetter
particularly encouraged some activity for the young people, a
number of whom had been converted in the meetings.

The diary does not reveal the honorarium that he received
($150 had been raised in offerings during the meetings), but he
took with him the profuse thanks of the Howick people, and a
gallon of good Canadian maple syrup, which he had no trouble in
getting across the border at the Buffalo because no one asked him
to open his baggage.[29]

The Howick revival was followed next year (1924) by five
revivals—at Refton in February (until Willie Myers arrived to
take charge), at Graterford (where one of the converts was the
future Bishop Jacob Bowers), and three tent meetings in the
summer in Canada.

The first of these tent meetings was held near White Pigeon,
about six miles north of the Bertie church. The tent was pitched in
an open field near a crossroad, in an area containing no Brethren
in Christ. Mary Sentz returned from Pennsylvania as a helper
and was joined by Eva Hoover of Ohio, and Earl and Elsie Sider
(schoolmates of Hostetter at Grantham) from Ontario. During
the campaign, a strong wind levelled the large tent; next day
Hostetter helped to repair it for use. The result of the meetings

was eight families in the area inviting the Brethren in Christ into
their homes for prayer meeting; in the following year, the Fred
Lichtenberger family joined the Bertie church.[30]

At the end of this campaign Hostetter and the workers piled
the tents on a wagon and hauled them some thirty miles west
where they restaked them in a wooded area south of Fenwick and
where they were joined by another worker, Helen Ready. Here
the campaign was jointly sponsored by the Boyle and Wainfleet
congregations. Again storms plagued the tent; almost every
night, it seemed, the men spent much of their time pounding the
tent stakes into the ground. Here, however, some of those converted later became members of the Boyle congregation.[31]

Hostetter held a third tent campaign that summer north of
Toronto, near where the Oak Ridges Brethren in Christ church
now stands. Little is known of this meeting, however, except for a
few passing references in the diary in later years.[32] He conducted
revivals in 1925, including three in Kansas (at Abilene, Belle
Springs, and Bethel). By this time he was well launched on an
impressive career which took him over the entire denomination in
Canada and the United States. Between 1923 and 1934, there was
no area where he did not hold at least one revival. Altogether, in
these eleven years he conducted forty-seven campaigns.[33]

He began to go to Virginia in the early 1930s, for summer
revival meetings. In 1933 he took two young men, Cyrus Lutz and
Harold Martin, with him as helpers. They preached in a schoolhouse near Sylvatus and pitched two small tents (one for sleeping
and the other for cooking) in a Primitive Baptist churchyard
across the road. Bathing and laundry were done in the nearby
river. During the day the three men conducted Vacation Bible
Schools at Sylvatus and Farris Mines, and visited in the
community.

Hostetter took a great interest in the people of this area,
perhaps because of their mountain character. One of them a
Primitive Baptist, could not understand the need for revivals,
since God saved only those who were elect. Hostetter asked him
to explain his own conversion experience. "Well," the Baptist
said, "I started to go to the meetings and I fit it and fit it [fought it]
until I couldn't fit it no longer, so I just gave up." Hostetter told
him that God had given him conviction and asked whether some

people could not have the same experience by coming to the meetings, to which the Baptist agreed that Hostetter was probably right. Another, a woman, informed Hostetter that she took snuff but would like to get rid of the habit. Hostetter told her that he knew a good way to do that—come to the meetings, tell the people about her problem, and ask for prayer. That, however, took more courage than she could muster. "What dear people they are," Hostetter wrote of the Virginians in later life as he recalled this summer's work among them.[34]

Reports in the *Evangelical Visitor* suggest several common features of Hostetter's evangelism. He deliberately structured parts of the revival for children ("children's meetings," as they were called in the denomination), in this following a practice earlier begun by J. R. Zook. In 1931, while holding a summer tent meeting in Michigan he took a day off from his labors to visit the Mt. Carmel Mission, one of Walter Taylor's projects, where he spent the time speaking to and singing with the children.[35]

A second feature commonly reported is the simplicity and clarity with which he spoke. (Perhaps this was noted because people thought a graduate of the Bible College would use high-sounding speech.) His messages were "simple and clear, yet forceful and appealing," the reporter for the Rosebank, Kansas, congregation wrote in 1933.[36] Brother Hostetter preached "in his usual interesting and straightforward manner," a Palmyra member had written a year earlier.[37] Such reporting is substantiated by Charlie Byers (himself to become a prominent evangelist in the denomination) who first heard Hostetter in a revival at Chambersburg: "I was just a youth. This young preacher preached like I never heard preaching before. He reasoned of righteousness and judgment . . . . I was so impressed by his logic."[38]

As a leading and very effective evangelist, it was inevitable that Hostetter should be asked to share his views on evangelism. This he did at General Conference, State Council, Bible conferences, and in late 1932 in a series of three articles in the *Evangelical Visitor.* The articles are particularly helpful in gaining an insight into Hostetter as evangelist. They present a young man with much enthusiasm for his work, with a strongly evangelical approach to the conversion experience and the Christian life, and with an awareness of the possible negative effect of success on the evangelist.

Revivals, Hostetter notes in the first article, are not man-made—they are directed by the Holy Spirit. "No church," he writes, "[even] by organization of the highest type of brotherly cooperation can of themselves produce a revival." Prayer is the focus of the second article (a timely topic because revivals usually featured "cottage prayer meetings" in the afternoons). Prayer is necessary to combat the "hosts of sin" pressing hard against Christ and his church—"worldliness and sensuality, indifference and carelessness, false teaching and blasphemy, carnality and hypocrisy, vice and uncleanness, . . ." Against these we can pray: "Pray earnestly, unceasingly, until God's messenger flashes on the scene."

The third article gives an insight into Hostetter's methodology and his concern that a successful evangelist maintain a proper spirit. He entitles this article "A Soul Winning Preacher" and takes John the Baptist as his model.

> His sermons were not spoiled by the conspicuous 'I' which so frequently hinders the effectiveness of truth . . . . He preached the weighty themes of sin, repentance, and the Lamb of God . . . . No cheap jokes, no clap-trap, no trifling, no pet standard of right and wrong, the product of the preacher himself . . . . He did not aim only at convincing men of sin, nor would he have been satisfied only to see emotions stirred and see tears flowing or hear voices shouting. This fearless preacher trained his gospel hot shots straight at that seat of life and destiny—the human will.

Don't be too quick, Hostetter continued, to accept compliments from people, such as "I learned some new things today." That means nothing until you get such people "to yield—to act—to obey."[39]

Still another sign of Hostetter's growing influence in the denomination was his placement by General Conference on committees, and most notably on the Home Mission Board. General Conference placed him on this board in 1924. The following year the board named him its secretary, a position which he retained until 1946 when he became chairman. Hostetter also served in the companion position of field secretary for the Church Extension Board during its short existence (1926-1928). The only record, however, of his work in this position is a trip that he made back to Howick in 1926 to explore with Bishop John Reichard a change in the congregation's leadership.

The office of secretary was a significant post, especially for one so young. As secretary, Hostetter not only took minutes of board meetings but also carried on much of the correspondence with workers at the mission locations. In Hostetter's hands the position became the key one on the board.

Thus in 1926, within a year of his selection as secretary, Board Chairman M. G. Engle was writing to Hostetter to tell him to proceed as he thought best on a case.[40] In the same month, Hostetter's handling of a delicate problem at Howard, Pennsylvania, brought board approval: Levi Sheetz wanted to sell his horse and buggy and apply the money from the sale to run a car for church work, but Hostetter persuaded him to give the money to the board treasury, which would make a periodic payment toward travel expenses.[41] In 1927, Engle passed on to Hostetter the handling of a difficult case in Canada, because, Engle wrote, "you excel me in words."[42]

In fact, Hostetter eventually gained something of a reputation for running the Home Mission Board, a reputation not entirely justified. On a delicate issue in 1938, a bishop of the church accused Hostetter of answering letters and making decisions without consulting others—in fact, of acting like the board itself. Chairman Engle in his customary bantering way once wrote to Hostetter to say it had come to his ears that there was "a question as to whether or not the Home Mission Board is a one-man [Hostetter] show."[43]

Since most of Hostetter's career on the Home Mission Board falls after the time of his pastorate, fuller consideration of his activities and contributions to that board appears later. It is significant to note here, however, that he was active in helping to begin a new work at Arcadia, Florida, in selecting Paul McBeth to be its pastor, and in making several trips to the mission when the congregation developed severe internal dissension. In his position as board member he went periodically to Kentucky and

Virginia, and beginning in 1930, following the revival movements
that broke out in Saxton and the surrounding area, he made
frequent trips to central Pennsylvania.[44]

There were still other church appointments in these years of his
pastorate. He was a member of the committee appointed in 1929
to draw up a *Manual of Church Doctrine.* In 1930 he became a
contributing editor to the *Evangelical Visitor,* and in 1932 an
Associate Editor to the paper.

What did this busy life as a salesman and churchman mean for
his family life? During their years at Refton, all of Christ and
Anna's four sons were born—in order, Nelson, Lane, Ray, and
Glenn. Hostetter's frequent absences from home meant that his
wife was usually left with the care of rearing four lively boys.

Hostetter regretted the absences from his family, but seemed
constitutionally unable to slow the pace of his work to give
himself more time at home. Returning from his tent meeting in
Howick in 1923, he wrote in his diary: "Oh how good to be home!
How I do love to be with the one who is dearest of earth to me!"[45]
A few days later he somehow managed not to go to work so he
could remain home and help his wife dig potatoes and pick
plums.

Sometimes there were family holidays together. In the summer
of 1924, the Hostetters with Anna's parents and Nelson (then a
baby) traveled through the Shenandoah Valley in the Lanes'
seven-passenger Buick.[46] They repeated the trip in 1928, this time
to the Shenandoah Caves and with three sons—Nelson, Lane,
and Ray.[47] And in the summer of 1930 the family accompanied
Hostetter to Michigan, New York, and Canada for seven weeks
of revival meetings.

There are other parts to the family picture. There is the
mischievous Lane who will not behave in church so his father
brings him to the pulpit while he preaches, only to have the cute
little fellow make faces at the audience behind his father's back.
There are the wonderful occasions when the boys go with their
father to the store and he buys them ice cream cones—a great
delicacy for children in those days. And there is the playful
interchange between husband and wife, as when Hostetter disci-
plined one of his sons. He told Nelson that he did not want to
spank him but since somebody had to take the punishment,

Nelson must spank his father. When Nelson understandably refused, his father said, "Well, then Mother will have to do it." So mother gave father a good, hard spanking. "But Anna, I did not think," Hostetter joked later, "that you would hit so hard!"[48]

IV

"Enjoyed Soliciting the District"

*I*n May, 1934, while conducting a revival campaign in the Nottawa District of Canada, C. N. Hostetter, Jr. (as he was now being called) received a telephone call from John Martin, secretary of the Messiah Bible College trustee board, informing Hostetter of his election to the presidency of the college. He consulted several friends, including E. J. Swalm in whose home he was staying, and then telephoned back his acceptance of the trustees' decision.

The situation at the college appeared to the trustees and others to call for a change in the presidency. The school was in financial difficulty. It had always been so, but the economic depression, at its height by 1934, made the situation desperate. The school's debt had grown until by 1934 it stood at $20,000, an enormous sum in those days for economically conservative Brethren in Christ. In addition, cash gifts were falling off and student income was decreasing because of a declining enrollment.[1]

Morale, both in the college and in the constituency, was low. Students perceived a need for more aggressive leadership. The editor of the student paper, the *Clarion,* in the January and February issues plainly declared that new people and new methods were needed to deal with the college's problems.[2] Although in the March issue the leadership replied that readers should shed the statements like a filthy rag, the criticism could hardly be undone. Many in the constituency saw the president, Enos Hess, as an extremely dedicated man, but more the educator than businessman or churchman. (Charlie Byers' was a typical constituency reaction: when as a youth he heard Hess use the big word "psychology" he had no idea whether Hess was talking about the Blue Ridge Mountains or some other unrelated matter.) Under these kinds of pressure, Hess submitted his resignation. Although understandably disappointed by these developments, he remained with considerable grace at the college to teach until his death in 1941.

This helps to explain why a change in the presidency occurred; it is necessary to examine further why the new president should be Hostetter. Clearly a leading recommendation was Hostetter's reputation as a churchman. By this time, he was known over the denomination for his work in evangelism and on the Home Mission Board. His pastorate had been successful, his Vacation Bible School widely copied. Here was a capable and trustworthy servant of the church into whose hands the presidency of the college could with confidence be delivered.

As a churchman, on the other hand, Hostetter had been a valuable friend of his alma mater. In virtually every year following his graduation in 1922, he had returned to Grantham in January to be one of the speakers at the Bible conferences. (He was a favorite of the students, partly because they were required to take notes and found his sermons easy to follow.)[3] And beginning in 1930, he was for each year the guest teacher in the six-weeks winter term course beginning in January.[4]

Hostetter had also been among the first to bring the college to the constituency. His Refton congregation issued the first invitation to the men's chorus of any congregation in the denomination. That was in the early part of 1927. Following the invitation, the chorus, under Earl Miller, rented a hall in Paradise and another at the YMCA building in Lancaster, intending to give programs to which admission would be charged. A winter storm, however, kept people away. A financially disastrous weekend was rescued by a generous offering at Refton.[5] Two months later, while conducting a revival at Manor, Hostetter invited the men's chorus to give a program before he spoke on a Sunday morning.[6] Over the next several years, music groups returned to Refton on a periodic basis.

In addition, Hostetter had spoken out for education in public places, knowing that such was not the popular thing to do. At General Conference in 1927 he gave a major address showing how education can be of service in the evangelistic and pastoral work of the church. He made similar presentations again at General Conference three years later, as well as in the safer territory of the school itself.[7]

Hostetter thus stood as a bridge between the church and the college in the days before his call to the presidency. This bridge may be further illustrated by two addresses he gave at the fall homecoming in 1933 and reported in the *Clarion*. In the first, he urges students to be loyal to the church. The school came into existence to help the church, although, in fact, the two "would never be able to get along without each other." For this reason students should be thankful, not critical, of the church, not least because of the opportunities for Christian service it offers young people. In the second address, he reverses the emphasis. He points out, obviously for the benefit of the denomination, the degree to which the college is a good influence on the church and the extent to which the graduates have engaged themselves in Christian service. For its own good, the church needed to perpetuate that kind of influence.[8]

In measurable terms, Hostetter had probably made his greatest contribution to the college as an officer of the Alumni Association. Beginning in 1923 when he was elected vice president, he gave continuous service in the Association. He was the main force behind the Association establishing an Alumni Memorial Fund in 1925.[9] Under his presidency (he was elected in 1928), the Association decided to use the Fund to construct an alumni auditorium. Hostetter headed a team of workers who, by 1930, had expanded the fund to $11,000. Then the campaign slowed because of the economic depression, and Hostetter wanted to resign. He was, however, too valuable to the Alumni Association to allow that to happen, so he was given two vice presidents to help him with his work.

Hostetter remained, and in 1933 the Association decided to proceed with construction, even though the total amount had not been fully raised. This was an important moment for the alumni, and Hostetter was credited for bringing it about. His "enthusiasm was contagious," wrote one of his fellow alumni officers. "We came to believe that we could get enough money to build . . . in spite of the depression."[10] His work on the project supported the image of Hostetter as a successful manager and promoter, and as one much interested in the progress of the college.

Altogether, then, Hostetter was a logical choice for the presidency. He was so obviously a good choice that his name was being mentioned several months in advance of his appointment, and he had, in fact, been sounded out. He had turned the probings aside, mainly, it appears, because he did not hold an academic degree. But the pressure had been maintained, not least from the alumni, several of whom made a special trip from Grantham one day to plead with him to accept the presidency.

Thus when the call came to Hostetter at Nottawa, he was not caught unawares. His taking counsel with a few friends was a last, characteristically cautious act before making a decision of such magnitude for himself and his family.

The situation at Messiah Bible College that occasioned this change of leadership had its parallel in many church colleges across the country; certainly it was so in every Mennonite-related institution. Crises in finances as well as church and identity problems in such institutions resulted in shoe-string financing (sometimes insufficient in itself), denominational criticism of the college, and frequent change in leadership. The institution at Grantham was simply part of a more general picture.

In the early summer of 1934 the Hostetter family moved on to campus, into the cement block house built by Enos Hess which stood where the Climenhaga Fine Arts center is now located. The college bought the house from Hess in 1935, and it remained the Hostetter residence during the years of his presidency.

Hostetter set to work at once on the problems that plagued the college. Student discipline and morale were among them. He placed himself as faculty advisor on several key student organizations, including the Missionary Circle and Hapantes, the latter, in effect, the student government and publisher of the *Clarion*. Whereas attendance at the required Tuesday evening student prayer service had been lax, faculty now decided to check attendance as a means of enforcing the rule.[11] And in the spring term, Hostetter had the faculty at work bringing up to date all the rules that should be considered active, obviously with a mind to their better enforcement.[12] Out of the background of this work, he and the women's preceptress, Pearl Swalm, wrote a new students' guide.

Results followed. Two years after coming to Grantham, Hostetter wrote to Ben Thuma, whom he was attempting to bring to the campus as preceptor (dean of men), saying that "we have 'tightened up' a great deal the last two years in college discipline," and maintaining that "the student body has responded most splendidly and I believe you will find our group disposed to respect authority and cooperate with the college."[13] This was not reading too much into student opinion. Many students liked the aggressive leadership of this new president, not least because he made them think more seriously about their school experience. *Clarion* Associate Editor Carlton Wittlinger, writing in the October issue of 1934, reminded his readers of the problems of the past, but expressed optimism for the future under the new president's leadership.

> There was a time in those days gone by when we feared for the future of our beloved alma mater. The storms beat hard on her foundations until the very supporting timbers rocked. And we were sad as we looked on for every blow our institution received rebounded unto the very heart of each one of us who loved her . . . . But after a short time on the campus [after the beginning of the new school year] I knew that the crisis had past . . . . Gone was pessimism and in its place reposed glorious expressive optimism . . . A new day [has] dawned for MBC.[14]

Students, of course, were essential to the college, and thus Hostetter set out to reverse the trend of decreasing enrollments. That there had not been a systematic approach to student recruitment is suggested by a faculty minute of January 30, 1933, which shows that the faculty spent some time on that day discussing the need for some plan to obtain more students. By January, 1935, Hostetter had developed a proposal, undoubtedly with the help of his faculty, and had obtained trustee board approval for it.[15] The details of this plan are not spelled out in the minutes of the board, but from other sources it is not difficult to deduce it: continuing use of faculty as they travelled to contact prospective students; sending out music groups to indirectly and attractively advertise the school; and developing systematic lists of students to be contacted and followed up.

Thus in the spring of 1935 he wrote to alumnus Adam Byers, then principal of Ontario Bible School, for a list of students who might be interested in continuing their studies at Grantham.[16] On the same day he sent letters to the pastors in the denomination asking for the names of all students in their congregation attending high school.[17] When Business Manager Jesse Brechbill was about to leave for Kansas in early summer, Hostetter was able to turn over to him fifty-one names of Kansas high school students he should contact while in the state.[18] Beyond this, his correspondence shows many personal letters and contacts made with students in these early years of his presidency. Here, obviously, was an attempt at a more efficient approach to student recruitment.

Much of the college's difficulty was financial in nature. Hostetter attacked the problem directly and at once. He accepted for himself a salary of only $800 a year, which stood in marked contrast to the approximately $3,000 he had earned as a salesman in the previous year. Until at least 1940 (perhaps even beyond that date), he returned to the college all income he made from speaking engagements, including revival meetings.[19] He not only continued to keep staff salaries low, but could even suggest to a prospective preceptress that she work for nothing in exchange for room and board and free tuition for whatever school work she might wish to take on the side. Not surprisingly, his offer was declined.[20]

There are other examples of Hostetter's carefully husbanding of the college's funds. The first *Bulletins* (the school's periodical for public distribution) under his administration were printed in mimeograph form rather than in the regular type of the previous issues. Dissatisfied with the rates for electricity being charged the college, Hostetter protested to the Pennsylvania Power and Light Company and warned, apparently without effect, that the college might be forced to return to being serviced by the local power plant if the rates were not reduced.[21] When attendance at the annual Bible conference in January, 1936, was low because of bad weather, he did not hesitate to send the speakers from Pennsylvania only $2.00 for both speaking and expenses, although this was less than usually paid.[22] A few months after sending these $2.00 checks, Hostetter was asking the Musser

Brothers, poultry farmers, for a quotation on *cracked* eggs for the college.[23]

Over the years the amount of unpaid student bills had been steadily growing. The principle of students not paying their bills was an entirely unacceptable one to Hostetter, careful business man that he was; besides, the money, if collected, could help ease the school's financial bind. Thus he set out vigorously to collect the debts.

His correspondence on the subject in his first years as president is large and usually diplomatic. During his second year, he wrote to one student, congratulating her on her recent marriage, and adding that in such a situation she should pay her school bill so it did not become a millstone around her neck. He had, he went on to say, "personally guaranteed this account to our Finance Committee. I was exceedingly anxious to have you come to MBC and I told the Finance Committee that I was particularly sure you would take care of the obligation."[24]

He sent a similar letter to one of his favorite students saying that he was shocked to find that the student had a continuing debt. "Now let me be very frank with you," Hostetter wrote, "even if it is painful. Are you going to fool around with this account and neglect payments until you finally will criticize and hate MBC because we took you at your promise? . . . We need the money and need it badly but for your own good you will need to pay this bill more than what we will need to receive the money."[25] He consistently refused to send out student transcripts in cases where a school bill remained unpaid, even in an instance in which the president of Taylor University pressured him to do so in order that the transferring student could sing on the university's quartet.[26]

A sensitive area in this problem of school debts was collecting money from students who had been given free tuition on condition that they become home or foreign missionaries but who had gone into other areas of church work instead. Technically speaking, they still owed the money. But the subject was so sensitive that nothing had been done about the situation.

Hostetter, however, picked up the problem. In a typical letter he explained that he himself had not been able to qualify for the tuition credits even though he had been a pastor and evangelist since leaving school. The perceptive reply to Hostetter's letter by the former student turned pastor was that the school obviously "feels inclined toward a rather strict interpretation of the text of these notes, which, of course, leaves me with many others ineligible even though, needless to say, service has been at considerable sacrifice from the material standpoint."[27] Hostetter's letters usually indicate, however, that, while still insisting on the notes being paid, he was flexible about the timing of the payment, particularly with persons in direct Christian service.[28]

Of course, for college financing more was necessary than merely husbanding funds and collecting debts. Messiah College presidents, then and now, have provided the leadership in obtaining money for the college in the church and community publics, and Hostetter was no exception to that pattern.

One of his first moves was to educate his constituency on how to give to the college. The *Bulletin* was a good medium in which to do this. The first issues under his presidency explain the various ways in which money could be given, including bequests and annuities (with a description of the latter).

Sunday schools, Hostetter recognized, were likely contributors. A few months after taking office, he wrote a letter to his superintendents in the denomination asking them to take an offering for the college by April 1.[29] He continued to appeal to the Sunday schools in this fashion well into the 1940s, and used the method to raise the money to repair extensive damages caused by fire in the science labs in 1937. Always in those letters he linked requests for money with requests for prayer for the spiritual life of the campus, thereby seeming, however indirectly, to couple the efficacy of the Sunday schools' prayers with their giving to the college.[30]

Contributions in food had long been a source of income for the college, and Hostetter encouraged his farming constituency to continue the tradition. Up into the 1950s he wrote annually to Brethren in Christ congregations in Pennsylvania to remind them that their canning of fruit and vegetables had significance for the college. The Grantham congregation had an annual canning bee at the college. Hostetter himself assisted in some of these bees, as on Labor Day, 1949, when he observed in his diary with obvious pleasure that he spent the day at the college helping twenty-five volunteers to can peaches for the school.

Such food donations were considerable. As late as 1950, a total of 4,602 quarts of fruits and vegetables were canned and donated in that year to the college by twelve congregations and three districts, including Grantham.[31] Other donations given consistently over the years were apples from Henry Hostetter, peanut butter from Henry Landis, and chickens from H. L. Eckhert. Hostetter acknowledged by letter all such gifts, and even the small ones, including on one occasion a basket of tomatoes.

Early in his presidency, Hostetter began to cultivate individuals as well as congregations for contributions. Virtually all of these were within the church constituency. The few occasions on which he contacted area people with financial resources were singularly unsuccessful. Obviously such people were not about to put their money into what may probably have appeared to them to be a small, sectarian school. Thus Hostetter turned to individuals in the denomination.

His uncle David was one of these. David Hostetter and his wife (an Old Order River Brethren) had no children but they had acquired some money, in part because of frugal living. David had lent his nephew $500 without interest to build his house in Refton. Now under his nephew's prompting he gave frequently to the college. He used to tell his friends, mainly in jest, that whenever he saw Christ's car coming down his lane he knew he would be asked for another $1,000 for the college. "You have been a liberal giver to the cause of the Lord," Hostetter wrote to his uncle in 1940 after the latter had made another gift. "Some members of the family have been called to the ministry and have served much more in public than has been your field of service but I feel certain that your reward for stewardship is just as valuable in the sight of God . . . ."[32]

Henry Trump was an elderly, retired bishop of the Brethren in Christ Church in Illinois, also with some money. Hostetter made a point of visiting Trump and his wife when he passed through Illinois, and arranged for the men's quartet to do the same. In the summer of 1939 he insisted that the quartet drive thirty miles out of its way to "give them a good visit and sing as many songs as they desire."[33] He humored the elderly bishop by assuring him that Trump's hard earned money would go only to students who work hard at manual labor and anything else required of them.[34] After the Trumps made another gift in early 1938, Hostetter wrote that he would read their letter at the next faculty meeting and then "have a special season of prayer unitedly asking God's blessing upon yourself and Sister Trump."[35]

Christian and Amanda Musser of Kansas were still another couple whom Hostetter financially courted. His acquaintance with them went back to 1925 when Hostetter held revival meetings in their church. The Mussers were attracted to the bright young evangelist, and over the years the three maintained an occasional correspondence on both money and spiritual matters. The Mussers gave nearly $50,000 over the years until their deaths in the early 1950s, at which time another $7,000 came to the college from their estate.[36]

Hostetter's touch with this elderly couple was a diplomatic one. At Christmas in 1947 he had the student body and faculty send thanks and greetings to the Mussers. "The spirit of the letters," Musser replied, "and the multitude of the signatures has *[sic]* taken us entirely by surprise and we are all broken up by our emotions. We really wept like a child and we want to pray for a few days so that I may know the mind of the master [about how much more to give]. And as I attempt to write, I feel a burden coming over me for the student body of the college . . . ."[37] Two years later, Musser counselled with Hostetter about a proposal made by the Abilene congregation that he buy the parsonage for the church and endow the salary of the minister. Hostetter encouraged him to accept the suggestion about the parsonage, but wrote against an endowed salary because it was an invitation for the congregation to become lazy.[38]

Much of Hostetter's soliciting for funds, not surprisingly, was for special projects and developmental needs. The first of these was the completion of the Alumni Auditorium, begun nearly a year before he took office, but far from being finished in mid-1934. Hostetter with the trustees gave some thought to borrowing enough money to quickly complete the project, but they decided that this was too risky and not practising good stewardship. Instead, they continued to follow the plan of "pay as we build and build as we pay."[39] A cartoon in the *Clarion* for May, 1935, shows two men working on the building—a bricklayer and Hostetter. In the first panel the bricklayer is saying that he needs more bricks (meaning money); in the last, Hostetter is replying: "O.K. I'll get them for you." In this pay-as-one-goes fashion the auditorium was completed in 1937, with a balcony added in 1939.

The next project was an industrial arts building, completed in 1940. For this, Hostetter carried on a large personal solicitation by mail.[40] Here his cultivation of Christian and Amanda Musser bore fruit. Much of the money for the project came from this Kansas couple, after whom the building was named.

By 1938, Hostetter had become concerned about the virtual nonexistence of any endowment or endowment policy. He wrote to one of the trustees in September of that year to say that the school's endowment was well below that of any other Pennsylvania college, and that the endowment had to serve both college and academy.[41] By 1941 there was need for action. Hostetter maintained that the college's membership in the American Association of Junior Colleges was being jeopardized (and thus its reputation with the State Department of Instruction) by not attaining the Association's standard of a minimum annual income of $12,500 from non-student sources. For the first five years, the college had received not much more than one-half that amount from such sources.

But to raise $200,000 in cash to provide an annual interest that would substantively meet the needed level of non-student income seemed impossible. The college thus took another route: it launched a Living Endowment campaign in which subscribers purchased $5 endowment units, paid on an annual basis. A total of 1500 units would assure the college of $7,500 each year in non-student income, which when added to other non-student sources would bring the school up to the $12,500 standard minimum.

Over this endowment campaign, Hostetter was made field representative (that is, director). He appears to have pursued his work more systematically than in previous similar campaigns by compiling a list of prospective subscribers (including some outside the church constituency), following up letters by personal contacts, promoting subscriptions when out in the churches, and, again, appealing to Sunday schools (the Elizabethtown Sunday school, for example, bought 20 units). By October, 1943, a total of 910 units had been subscribed, but remained short of the goal when a year and a half later the campaign was temporarily suspended. The campaign was reopened in 1949, but appears not to have quite obtained the projected 1500 units.[42]

In the mid-1940s, Hostetter led the college and constituency in what may be called the first long-range development plan in the school's history. The institution to this point had been a tiny one, and thus more or less able to survive on a year-to-year basis. Times and people, however, were changing. Hostetter had now had ten years of experience in his position and opportunities to think about possibilities for the future. The war in Europe was drawing to a close by mid-1945; soon Messiah Bible College could expect an influx of men who had either been in the army, or, more likely, in Civilian Public Service Camps as conscientious objectors. Already Old Main, which served as a dormitory and provided classrooms and administrative offices, was filled with both women and men students; obviously new housing had to be provided soon. With the ending of the war, building supplies would become available again, and funds to purchase the supplies would be more forthcoming from a constituency that, as everyone else, had prospered in the last several years.

Already in 1944 Hostetter was thinking of changes, at least in the existing buildings. He brought to campus three college administrators, including Goshen College President Ernest Miller, to recommend modifications in the structures and to suggest directions for future campus planning. Their principal recommendation was to leave Old Main standing (there had been talk of tearing it down), but to move its entrance to the opposite side, thus giving an inward orientation to the campus, which future buildings would also follow.[43]

While none of the committee's proposals were adopted, they appear to have served as a catalyst for Hostetter's thinking. In late February of the next year, Hostetter called a special meeting of the trustees to consider a recommendation he had drawn up for a building program to meet an anticipated rapid enrollment increase and which would cover the next fifteen years.[44] The trustees encouraged Hostetter to proceed with working out the details of the program, and then gathered again several months later to approve specific plans drawn up by Hostetter with the assistance of Harrisburg architect William Lynch Murray.

As finally approved, the new development called for a women's dormitory (the central element in the plan), a central heating plant, the transfer of the dining room from Old Main to the Alumni Auditorium, and a new administration building, library, and chapel when the funds became available. When a fire occurred in Hill View in the following year, the cost of remodelling the building from apartments to a music hall was added to the program. According to the Principles of Procedure for the plan, the need for new buildings had to be established and the money raised before construction could begin. "Bearing in mind," the Principles read, "the size of our constituency and remembering that we believe in the simple life, our buildings and renovations shall be planned frugally and economically, aiming to secure attractive, substantial, well-planned, well constructed buildings, avoiding elaborate ornamentation . . . ."[45] To accommodate these and future buildings, the college purchased forty-six acres of land from John Hess (Enos Hess's son) at a cost of $3,300.

The development plan, finally, provided for a fund drive, known as the Extension Fund Campaign, with a goal of $175,000. Hostetter was named Executive Director of the campaign, and over the next four years granted two semesters of relief from his teaching.

Hostetter characteristically threw himself into this campaign, doing much of the soliciting singlehandedly. By the first part of 1948, most of the $175,000 goal had been reached, and the trustees decided to proceed with the construction of the dormitory.

At this stage the campaign seemed to slow down. Hostetter tried some new approaches. With the local district officials he worked out quotas for the various church districts (the amount of the quotas, however, were not to be made public) and made some use of solicitors appointed in consultation with local church leaders. These new tactics helped to raise sufficient money to cover the cost of the dormitory, but other items, such as the changes in Hill View, furnishings for the dormitory, renovation of the heating plant and construction of a vault in Old Main, had added considerably to the estimated $175,000, and now around

$10,000 remained to be raised. The solution for the trustees was simple: in their meeting in October, 1949, they "decided to put this matter into the hands of the campaign director [Hostetter] and trust the Lord."[46]

Hostetter's later diaries begin in the latter stages of the Extension Fund campaign; they give us some insights into his work, as well as the response of the constituency. In early January, 1949, he went to Greencastle to canvas the Montgomery District with J. Lester Myers, the area's bishop. The quota for the district had been set at $1,000, which, with uncharacteristic pessimism, Hostetter thought was "a little too high." But after two days of soliciting, he obtained $1,047, and was obviously pleased. "I met many friends," he wrote after returning to Grantham, "and enjoyed soliciting the district."[47]

Next month on his way home from California he stopped in Kansas, where he obtained a $500 annuity from one person and a $50 cash donation from another. In May he traveled to Everett, Pennsylvania, to canvass the Clear Creek congregation, one of the mission churches he frequently visited as a member of the Home Mission Board. The members there gave him the very large (for them) sum of $485, which was probably as much an expression of appreciation for Hostetter as it was a personal interest in the college. Hostetter noted in his diary that he had "a lovely time with these people."[48] By this time, he was repeating visits to former donors: "Many folks have given 2, 3, or 4 times to the Extension Fund," he observed in his diary with an air of appreciation and some surprise.[49]

When the campaign ended, the Extension Fund was oversubscribed by about $10,000. Over one-half of that amount was given at the dedication of the new dormitory in November, 1949. Little wonder that Hostetter "choked with emotion" several times during the ceremony, as his diary records.[50] Virtually by himself he had raised nearly $200,000 (an enormous sum in those days, especially for a tiny constituency), and had done it at a cost of only 2% of the amount raised.

Including the new dormitory, the renovation of Old Main and Hill View, and a four-unit married students apartment constructed in 1952 from annuities, Hostetter claimed that the assets of the college now stood at more than $600,000. These assets he considered to be even more valuable because of their source. "These investments," he told students at a leadership retreat, "represent the gifts of thousands of devoted Christian men and women who believe in you young people who have come here to study. Many times these gifts represent great sacrifice . . . . The money comes to us because Christian men and women have denied themselves in order that they can help the Kingdom of God."[51]

Beginning in 1953, Hostetter led the college in another development program and fundraising campaign. He came home on April 23 from the spring meeting of the trustee board to write in his diary that this had been "a day that made history at Messiah College" because the trustees had decided to "go forward" with a new building program and to launch a campaign to raise the money. The heart of the building program was a library, a church (to be constructed jointly with the local congregation), and an increase of $50,000 to the endowment of the college. Other components of the development plan were a basement for a new administration building (to house dining room facilities), and a brick covering for Hill View. For various reasons these last two projects were abandoned, in part because some of the funds raised were spent instead on enlarging the science labs and adding to their equipment. The trustees set no figure for a campaign goal, except to rule that construction and renovations must be done on a pay-as-you-go basis, and nothing could be begun until $200,000 had been raised. The campaign to raise the money for these projects was called the Greater Messiah Development Program, and Hostetter was made its Executive Director.[52]

This program was more ambitious than previous ones, and thus although Hostetter was as fully involved as before, he had from the beginning more assistance. Jacob Kuhns was given a semester leave of absence from his teaching to help solicit, and Paul McBeth was appointed an advisor for publicity. Hostetter also had the assistance of a large Advisory Committee composed of twenty-seven persons from Pennsylvania, four from Ohio, and one each from the other states and provinces where the Brethren in Christ Church was then located.[53]

At first, Hostetter concentrated largely on the church constituency, as he had done in earlier campaigns. His diary reveals that for periods of time he solicited virtually daily, not only in Pennsylvania but also as far west as Oklahoma and on up into Canada. In fact, the only area in the denomination where he appears not to have campaigned in person for money was California, and that undoubtedly was because Upland College was located in that state. Early in the campaign, however, he had moments of doubt concerning the college's ability to conduct a successful fundraising effort, mainly because he discovered the denomination everywhere engaged in church building programs or interested in other projects to which they had committed money. Thus he returned one day from soliciting in Franklin County and recorded in his diary: "It seems everyone in the Brethren in Christ Church has already made committments [sic] in the matter of giving—building churches, etc., etc., etc. The Lord must graciously bless if we are to get our money for new buildings."[54]

But Hostetter had learned from earlier experience to be persistent. If he considered that a congregation had not given up to its potential, he simply returned to do some more knocking on doors. In some cases he did not expect too much and thus was not disappointed. After spending a day soliciting a Pennsylvania congregation from whose members he received little, he noted that, after all, the congregation was building a new church, and besides they had not criticized the college.[55] But Franklin County was a place where he did expect to obtain some money. When he received only $775 for a day's soliciting in the New Guilford District, he returned a few days later and collected another $850. And he was back again for more, for a total of $2,200.[56] In the same fashion, he spent three days in the Chambersburg area. He was finally satisfied when he had obtained $2,000; through his diary he thanked "the Lord for . . . blessing . . . this effort."[57]

Hostetter was candid enough with himself to realize that he was able to impose himself on his fellow churchmen because of his stature among them and the confidence they placed in him. Thus after his repeated and successful canvassing of the New Guilford District, he noted that there was probably a connection between his success in raising money there and his preaching that summer at the Roxbury camp (located a few miles away). "The campmeeting at Roxbury," his diary reads, "helped the solicitation I am sure. God blessed my ministry in the Word there and it greatly helped in the solicitation."[58]

By this time Hostetter had also learned that one of the most effective ways of raising money was to have a local church leader accompany him in his contacts. In soliciting the Mechanicsburg congregation, for example, he took with him Simon Lehman, one of the ministers. "I find it an excellent plan," he observed in his diary for that day, "to take their [the congregations'] men with me. It develops their interest in the program. And I usually get a larger subscription from them."[59]

In spite of his great efforts at soliciting money, Hostetter came to the conclusion that some new approaches would need to be taken to achieve the goal the campaign had set for itself. With this in mind, he spent about a week and a half in July, 1955, at a workshop on fundraising conducted by Syracuse University at Chautauqua, New York. (He rather proudly recorded in his diary that he took his meals in the Snack Bar and managed all three meals for about $1.90 a day.) The workshop made a case study of Northwestern University's program; Hostetter marvelled at how that university had built up their friends until they "get millions by bequests." As part of the workshop's exercises he wrote a brochure on promoting bequests.[60] From this point on in the campaign, Hostetter appears to have emphasized bequests, adding those that he received to the Greater Messiah Development totals.

Subsequent to this workshop, Hostetter also contacted at least two fundraising agencies and obtained from them what he called "good suggestions."[61] It appears that one of the suggestions they offered was to divide the constituency into districts, each to have a division chairman and solicitors. The campaigning in each of these districts was to have a "kick-off" rally in the form of a dinner.

Less than two months after the contact with the agencies, the college gave the first of these at the Fireside Restaurant for the Dauphin and Lebanon County districts. Present were forty-five persons, including thirty-two solicitors under Division Chairman John O. Hershey, who according to Hostetter did a "superb job" in presiding at the meeting. Hostetter was delighted with this new approach, as his diary suggests: "John Hershey and his wife thought my money solicitation challenge was 'terrific.' We had $2100 subscribed toward the $8000 goal [for that district]."[62] Other dinners followed in Ohio, Michigan, and elsewhere.

The fundraising agencies also seem to have encouraged the college to reach beyond its church and alumni constituencies, into the wider local community. At least around this time in the campaign, Hostetter began to make sustained efforts to contact the non-Brethren in Christ people of the area.

Already he had begun in the community closest at home— Grantham—where he visited every person or household, whether Brethren in Christ or not, whether known friends of the college or otherwise. He was pleasantly surprised at the reception he received, especially since some tension had developed in recent years between the college and the village. "These calls," he wrote in his diary, "are improving our community relations."[63]

Included in these contacts were members of the local Slate Hill Mennonite Church. Hostetter had long been friends with them, and sometimes attended their services. After spending a day soliciting among them accompanied by one of their leaders, Marlin Seitz, he observed that he had received a donation from everyone on whom they had called: "We had an excellent reception . . . . Our Mennonite friends have been most friendly toward the college."[64]

The campaign dinner as a soliciting device within the denomination was now extended to include the wider, mainly business community. The college gave one of the largest of these at the nearby Holiday Motel Restaurant. Hotel owner Eugene Zimmerman underwrote the $450 cost of the meal, which was attended by many of the leading business people of the local area. Several faculty members gave speeches in support of the college, the school's choral society sang superbly (according to Hostetter); Hostetter himself presided and spoke frankly about the needs of the college. "Those present," his diary claims, "agreed it was one of the best presentations on the work of Messiah College to the community ever carried thru. It made friends for us."[65]

By this time, Hostetter had begun to make personal contacts with the area business men. His first move was to discover who they were. Roy Shaull, a Mechanicsburg banker, helped him to compile a list of potential donors, as did Pennsylvania Senator

George Wade, Harrisburg architect William Lynch Murray, and area businessman John Blessing.

John Blessing was one of the discoveries of the campaign. In late December, 1958, he gave Hostetter, according to the diary, "a splendid interview. I found that he does not smoke or drink and appreciates the clean standard of life for which Messiah College stands."[66] Blessing introduced Hostetter to his brother William. Both on occasion accompanied Hostetter to introduce him to their business acquaintances and to help break down initial resistance to solicitation.[67]

In this fashion, Hostetter contacted much of the Harrisburg and surrounding business community, from Samuel Wilson (milk products broker) to the Hempt Brothers (construction firm) to Leon Kocher (whose coal mine Hostetter visited at Valley View). Included in these contacts were Josiah and Bessie Kline whose names had been suggested to Hostetter by the college architect, William Lynch Murray.[68]

The Klines had made their money principally in real estate, including rentals, were without children, and interested in philanthropy. After several unsuccessful attempts, Hostetter had his first visit with Kline on March 30, 1957. He found the visit and the man fascinating. He noted that Kline was practical and "strongly opinionated," and that he liked the economical way in which the college ran its affairs. Kline also informed Hostetter that he resented a college of the area offering him an honorary degree in return for a donation. The interview ended with Kline inviting Hostetter to visit him and his wife in their home.[69]

Kline's opinion of the college was substantiated shortly afterward when he visited the campus. Since the day he chose to come happened to be the annual spring clean-up (campus) day, he found students and faculty spread over the grounds, working in the yards and on the buildings. Kline was suitably impressed with the practical, work-oriented nature of the college.

These visits between Hostetter and Kline were followed by many more over the next several years. Hostetter, in fact, became something of a counsellor to Kline. Thus on going to Kline's office one day, he discovered that Kline had fractured his arm and nose in a fall, so he rushed to the Polyclinic Hospital in Harrisburg (one of the recipients of Kline's philanthropy) and had a "good visit" with his friend.[70] In July, 1959, Kline called Hostetter to his office to sound out with him some proposals for setting up another foundation to which he would give property valued up to $4,000,000. Possibly included in this arrangement would be a generous provision for Messiah College and two other area colleges.[71] Hostetter returned to the college to have one of the committees with which he was meeting spend time in prayer for Kline's decision. A few days later he wrote in his diary:

> Dear Lord, please (1) include Messiah College in this provision, (2) put into my own mind and heart what further I shall say to Mr. Kline, (3) forbid that receiving of money should burden our divine mission as a college, but make it stronger, richer, wider in its ministry for Christ and His Kingdom.[72]

In early 1960, Kline was in poor health. Hostetter repeatedly visited him, read the Bible to him and prayed, and once in his diary asked God to "please allow the dear man to live long enough to make clear provisions in his will for these institutions [Messiah and the two other colleges]."[73] When Kline had somewhat recovered, Hostetter persuaded him to become a member of the Board of Associates, which Hostetter had recently formed.

By the time Hostetter left the presidency in 1960, Kline was in the hospital. Hostetter took his successor, Arthur Climenhaga, and the new Director of Development, Ray Hostetter, to visit Kline and continued himself to make visits. Kline died in 1961, leaving a significant portion of his estate to Messiah College.

By the latter part of 1958, Hostetter was feeling pleased about his contacts with the wider Harrisburg area community. So much so that he and the Executive Committee of the Board of Trustees interviewed a representative of the Marts and Lundy fundraising firm and later hired the firm to make a survey of the feasibility of conducting a major, professional campaign among people and businesses outside the college's church and alumni constituencies.[74]

The results of the survey, however, were disappointing. Most of the thirty-eight area people surveyed said they would make a token donation to the college, but only two would help in any fundraising campaign. All who knew Hostetter spoke very highly of him as a person and as an administrator, but few knew the college in any significant way, and fewer still considered it part of their community responsibility to support the institution.[75]

During this fundraising campaign, Hostetter took the college's first steps in approaching large, nationally known companies for financial assistance. Through an introduction by George Wade, he had at least two interviews with officials of the Pew Memorial Trust in Philadelphia.[76] In late 1958, prior to attending a meeting of the denomination's Peace, Relief and Service Committee in Chicago, he met an officer of the Kresge Foundation in Detroit, who seemed interested in Hostetter's tiny college, but who did not react very well to his request for a $25,000 contribution on condition that it be matched with one of $75,000 from Kresge's Harrisburg store.[77] But Hostetter was back in early 1960 when he had a much better reception (though still no money), this time from Stanley Kresge, son of the founder of the Kresge stores. On the same day he interviewed an executive of the Kellog Foundation at Battle Creek, Michigan, but he came away convinced that there would not be much money coming to the college from that source.[78] And in May, 1960, he and Arthur Climenhaga met with officers of the Ford Foundation in New York city, unsuccessfully to propose a $50,000 grant for an African studies program.[79]

By this time the goal of $200,000 needed to begin the construction of the library had been reached—in a chapel service in May, 1957. Hostetter informed the students that $198,000 had already been raised. "I laid the matter before them," his diary reads, "and passed cards to the students. They subscribed $2200 and pushed the sum over the top .... Thank you, Father, for your blessing on this solicitation."[80] Construction began at once and was completed in late 1958, with the dedication of the building on November 1 (a "red letter" day on our campus, Hostetter declared). The new library had a capacity for 120 people in the reading room and for 48,000 volumes on the shelves. The reading room was named as a memorial for Russell Firestone, whose father Calvin, a Carlisle businessman, had given the college $21,000 in the early 1950s.

Before his retirement in 1960 the college and the church began work on a new church building—the next phase of the Greater Messiah College Development Program. Hostetter was chairman of the planning committee, which had done a major part of its work by the time Hostetter left the presidency.

This account suggests much growth on Hostetter's part as a fund raiser. He moved a considerable distance from the earlier years of his presidency when he sought money from only church and alumni constituencies for the most pressing, immediate needs, to the later years when he led the college in planning major development programs and campaigned for funds among a continually widening non-church community. In thus expanding the range of donors, actual and potential, he laid the groundwork for many of the contacts that the college presently relies on for financial contributions.

He was, as this also suggests, a good salesman for the college, as might be expected, given his sales career before he became president. He thought increasingly big, was positive in his approach, was obviously a man to be trusted. He disavowed high pressure tactics, but he was persistent and so convinced in what he was doing that it was difficult for people to refuse him. "I am not a high pressure solicitor for money," he once wrote to a prospective donor. "However I do have deep conviction about the importance of the place that the church school holds in the spreading of the work of the Kingdom of God . . . . We do not want anybody to give money unless the Lord leads and directs to that end."[81] That seemed to put Hostetter on the side of God, and thus who could easily resist?

These traits were widely known and sometimes commented on. John Zercher, his nephew by marriage, once wrote in a lighthearted fashion to Hostetter to say that after having received three letters in one week in which there was either a direct or implied request for money, he was suggesting that a fitting text to use at Hostetter's memorial service would be: "And last of all the beggar died."[82] Another churchman and longtime friend, Cyrus Lutz, wrote on the occasion of Hostetter's retiring from the presidency that his car was "seen too frequently in our communities in the interest of the college for us not to know whose heart and soul was in it. Sometimes when we felt we had done our share for Messiah College . . . a letter with a well known signature would arrive in the mail and spoil our smugness."[83]

Over this money that he raised, and over the college's funds in general, Hostetter kept a watchful eye. It helped that he was good at figures, that he read and wrote financial statements well (an accountant from another school remarked after auditing Messiah College's books that Hostetter knew more about college financing than most college presidents).[84]

Certainly he bent everything to balance the budget. "Our budget is always so difficult," Hostetter complained while working on the budget for a new year as he traveled by train to some meetings in Kansas. "May we know the correct point to set between teacher sacrifice and church gifts! How much should the church give Messiah College and not rob the other needs of the home church, missions and institutions?"[85]

The budget problems of 1955 were typical. In March, Hostetter and controller LeRoy Mann spent a day on the budget and still "the situation looked very difficult indeed." A few days later, Hostetter and the finance committee worked "hard and long," but affairs were still "very much out of 'kelter' with income shrinking and expenses up." Three days later they were so tied up with budget problems that Charles Eshelman had to substitute for the president at a speaking engagement in Hummelstown.[86] "The task of running Messiah College becomes more difficult financially every year," he wrote as he continued to wrestle with the budget for several days in December.[87] But the budget for that year was balanced, as it was for every year during his presidency except 1949-50.

But it was balanced only by demanding considerable sacrifice on the part of everyone. No frills were permitted, not even for Hostetter himself. To a faculty member who seemed to be implying that because the president had a new desk set others would want one too, Hostetter wrote that his old one had to be discarded after ten years of use and that the new one had been purchased at his own expense. "There are many, many convenient things," he pointed out, "that we have had to deny ourselves and our staff of in order to live within our budget .... I do not feel that we should supply these [sets] for all the desks of our people with other needs that are very pressing."[88]

The same concern to pinch pennies may also be illustrated in the inexpensive rooms he took in hotels when on college or church business. Very often it was in a YMCA building. Where he could, he took a room without a bath, since sharing a common bathroom with other guests of the hotel was invariably cheaper.[89] For much the same reason, he traveled by train rather than by airplane, although in this case he also enjoyed the opportunity to relax and do some homework that the slower travel permitted.

Perhaps the greatest difficulty Hostetter had in giving up the presidency was his concern that finances might not be carefully enough managed. Several months after his retirement, he walked through Old Main and noted with interest the renovations the building was undergoing. The changes greatly improved the place, he admitted in his diary, but he was afraid that they would cause great difficulty in balancing the budget. "The group is rather blindly counting on a new development director to automatically increase these funds. They will face some real financial problems before the year is through in my judgment."[90]

V

"A Good Advertising for Our College"

*H*ostetter's conduct of fund raising and his careful scrutiny of expenditures were part of a general style of administration—active, very much in charge, often taking on more work and responsibilities than he could manage.

His administrative duties were carried on at the same time that he taught two or three courses a semester (in only a few semesters during his entire presidency did he not teach at least one course), held revival meetings, and accepted an increasing number of church and church-related assignments. In 1951, in a moment of almost desperation, he listed his current activities. In addition to all the work connected with the presidency and the teaching of five classes, he was serving on thirteen organizations, boards, or committees outside the college, often as chairman. "I hardly have time," he added, "to do anything but what I must do."[1]

A more detailed examination of his activities more than confirms this general impression of a busy administrative life. Throughout his presidency, Hostetter located, interviewed, and hired the new teachers, and for most of these years consulted with faculty and staff about returning next year. As late as 1949, he sometimes helped to make out class schedules and to assign teachers to classrooms.[2] He assumed responsibility throughout most of his presidential years for the college publications. Repeatedly his diary records that he delivered copy for the *Bulletin* to printers in Harrisburg, later picked up and read the galley proofs, and even sometimes helped in the mailing.[3] He did the same for the college catalogues and the commencement programs, even on occasion carrying the latter to the auditorium and helping to distribute them before the ceremonies. And evidence suggests that as late as the 1950s he was writing some of the college's news releases.

Other similar detailed administrative activities he accepted as also part of his load. He assisted foreign students with their immigration papers.[4] A diary entry in August, 1953, reveals him helping a committee to make out work assignments for students for the coming year.[5] He planned the tours for the music groups at least into the mid-1950s; in late 1954 he asked a committee to take over this function because he was too infrequently on campus, but his next year's diary indicates that he worked all of one evening making out the itinerary for the octette on its trip to General Conference.[6] He helped to buy equipment and furnishings for the college buildings.[7] To the man who had installed a shower, he wrote to ask that he return to fix a drip that had developed in the plumbing.[8] And according to one source, he was not above cleaning lavatories that had been neglected by the student janitor.[9]

On several occasions, Hostetter temporarily took over an administrative office when it became vacant. This occurred at least twice in the 1940s. During the war years when men were virtually unavailable, he served the major part of a year as the dean of men. And in 1947, he was appointed business manager to do special purchasing and to direct the college store until a permanent appointment could be made.[10]

On top of all this Hostetter counselled students, acknowledged even small gifts by letters, sometimes gave visitors tours of the campus, took his turn at speaking in the chapel and the local church, and worked hard to obtain students. For most of his years at the college he was for practical purposes the admissions officer of the institution. In addition to his work on this level with the congregations and church schools noted earlier, he aggressively contacted high schools and arranged for Messiah College students to give programs in their assemblies, until some schools began to see such activity as undue religious promotion.

We have some good pictures in his diary of his work in soliciting students. Canada was a favorite place for such activity. Thus in the summer of 1951 he spent several days there, first at Niagara Christian College, then at Cheapside where he spoke with two young people attending Upland College. To arrange for transfer credits from Messiah College he went on to see officials at the Hamilton Normal School and the University of Western Ontario in London (where, he adds in his diary, registrar Helen Allison received him well). He ended his trip by talking with Niagara Christian College Principal Dorothy Sherk, who went over with him the problems of the Canadian educational system and a program of integration between NCC and Messiah.[11] Other pictures are of him soliciting for students among the Mennonites in the Morgantown and Ephrata area of Pennsylvania in June, 1955, among the Old Order River Brethren (Yorkers, he calls them), some of whom were his relatives, in July, 1958, and among the Brethren in Christ in Lebanon County in June, 1959, where he meets a growing problem—some potential Messiah College students plan to go to Upland College.

As the years went by, Hostetter found greater difficulty in handling all of this great activity. This, he recognized, was not only the result of his being engaged in many affairs outside the college but also because of the growing complexity of the college's life that came with the institution's development. "It is amazing," he wrote a year before his retirement, "how the duties of the President's office are multiplied since I took over here 25 years ago—more complex administration, money raising, student solicitation. These concerns have all increased in tremendous importance."[12]

Repeatedly in the diary he expressed weariness, although more often regret, that there was not more time in the day in which to do more work. "I'm so far behind in my work," he complained on December 26, 1953, "that I hardly know where to turn. Dear Lord, do help thy unworthy servant." The problem was more acute when he returned to his office after being away for some time. After several days in the Midwest on Mennonite Central Committee solicitation work, he came to his office where, as the diary notes, "I met lots of pressure—in fact I was really pressed with strong pressure. Many, many things waiting on me for decisions. Oh God help me!"[13] Returning from another trip to the Midwest in the same year he found "many conferences waiting on me. Many people to see. Not much more done today than to talk to people."[14] His frustration with correspondence in such circumstances is illustrated by an entry for February 1, 1958: he manages to make some progress on a large stack of mail, but admits, "I find the mails to be one of my greatest hindrances to effective long view executive action. These routine items would keep one busy if you would stop at that."

To keep up with his work, he was frequently up early in the morning to make his own breakfast and to be in the office by 6:00 a.m. Often his office lights were burning until midnight or after.[15] In 1951 he bought a Soundscriber dictating machine, which he found so helpful that he carried it with him almost constantly, using it on the train, in his hotel room, and on at least two occasions in the railroad station master's office.[16] By the mid-1950s he was so desperate for help that he repeatedly proposed to the trustees the hiring of assistants in public relations and student solicitations, proposals that were at first resisted because of the expense involved, but eventually granted.[17] But even then Hostetter seems to have been incapable of not taking an active interest in the work that he found himself too busy actually to do.

Naturally his faculty worried about his strenuous pace. Early in 1950 they sent him a letter insisting that "the demands made upon your time and energy long ago passed all reasonable bounds." As a result, the letter continued, the faculty stood in great danger of losing him as their leader, and that would be disastrous. A less rapid realization of the goals of the college, they urged on him, would be much preferable to a change of leadership. "We must admit," the letter concluded, "that we are laboring under an increasing sense of uneasiness and insecurity. No solution of the problem can be thought of apart from vigorous determined action on your part. We entreat you to take such action and to take it immediately."[18] One turns to the diary for Hostetter's response, only to find that he merely recognizes the receipt of the letter.

Why did he drive himself as he did, at the college and in his other work? The answers will become more apparent as this biography proceeds, but several observations of a general nature may be made at this point. Hostetter obviously had a great interest in all that he did, and thus found great difficulty in refusing to accept one more interesting activity. He also maintained that he found relaxation and relief by shifting from one assignment to a variety of others. He recognized also that he had

a good mind and excellent administrative ability, and that for
these gifts he needed to practice stewardship as much and as well
as he could.

A significant element of Hostetter's administration was his
development of the Board of Trustees and his relations with its
members. The size and nature of the trustee board shifted over
the course of Hostetter's presidency; it must be assumed that he
had a considerable share in bringing about the changes. When he
came to his office in 1934, the trustees met frequently and irregu-
larly, often according to demand. They concerned themselves
with many items of business, including annually interviewing
members of the faculty "in regard to their attitude to school
work," as a minute of 1941 records, which "occupied the greater
part of the day."[19]

Among the changes that occurred was the discontinuing of
these interviews in 1941. The minutes of the board suggest recur-
ring friction between board members and some faculty during the
interviews; perhaps dropping the sessions was Hostetter's way of
improving relations between faculty and trustees, as was his
introducing in the 1950s an annual dinner which brought
together faculty and trustees in a more relaxed atmosphere.
Instead of the interview, a questionnaire was used, but soon this
too was discontinued and the hiring and rehiring of teachers
became the president's sole responsibility, except for the annual
approval of names.

By the mid-1940s the board began to meet on a regular quarterly basis and in 1945 commenced to operate on stated guidelines
that more nearly resembled those of traditional institutions—
formulating and modifying policy, accepting financial responsibility, electing the president, and approving teachers.[20] Ten years
later the board was expanded to seventeen members. Shortly
afterward it began to operate with an Executive Committee.[21]

One of Hostetter's proudest creations was the Board of Associates, which first met in 1959. This Board was primarily composed of men and women from the local business community
(including Josiah Kline and Roy Shaull), and had the responsibility of advising the Board of Trustees on educational, financial,
and campus-plant matters.

Hostetter's relationship with the trustees appears always to have been on a high level. He took obvious delight in recording in his diary on January 20, 1955, a statement that was undoubtedly shared by all trustees: "Roy Wenger surprised me today in emphatically telling the Board of Trustees 'we have a better president than Wheaton.' He said 'God is with him when he speaks,' He said 'I told the Committee last night we have the best president of any college I know.' " In fact, as one of them has observed, the trustees revered him, hanging on to his words, and accepting his ideas virtually without question.[22]

Until the later years of his presidency, Hostetter seems not to have been greatly concerned about what is now called public relations, except as it affected the Brethren in Christ Church. Among his first efforts was a program of college music (Messiah Bible College Youth Hour) over WKBO, begun in 1935; two years later he became a regular speaker on the program, which continued into the early 1940s. The most effective public relations element of the college, however, became the music groups, whose use in the community Hostetter very actively promoted. In fact, for many years the college was undoubtedly known outside the denomination mainly for its music program under Earl Miller. "Your student body are outstanding in their musical ability," wrote a member of the Boiling Springs Lutheran Church in asking Hostetter for a music group, "and their reputation as musicians is known over the country."[23]

The Grantham Oratorio Society, organized in 1947 and singing annually in the Forum in Harrisburg, was clearly an important means of attracting favorable attention to the college. Hostetter freely passed out complimentary tickets, spending as he once noted in his diary, "the good part of one day visiting friends in Mechanicsburg and Harrisburg inviting them to the Hymn Festival Sunday afternoon (we must have our friends to whom we look for support learn to know us better)."[24] The performance of the Oratorio Society's "Israel in Egypt" in 1958 he called a "great one," and had words of praise for the director: "Earl Miller has done much for us as a music conductor. He towers above anyone else in the East as a group director of music."[25]

By the end of his presidency he was promoting the college in additional ways, including special conferences. Responding to the findings of Marts and Lundy that the college was not well-known in the area, he brought Clyde Narramore, a Christian psychologist, to campus in March, 1960, and invited ministers, guidance counsellors and others to attend. Over 550 persons accepted, leading Hostetter to see the event as a positive and significant way in which to end his career at the college.[26]

Public relations with the local Grantham community was of necessity a continuing concern for Hostetter and the college. Traditional "town and gown" tensions existed for even a Brethren in Christ school. Hostetter tried to lessen the tension in several ways. Beginning in 1942, the college usually made annual contributions to the Grantham Fire Company (by the end of the 1940s this was as high as $100) and in 1950 contributed $200 toward the purchase of a new fire truck.[27] For the sake of public relations, he was cautious about the college buying property in the village. "I will frankly state my own opinion," he wrote in discouraging the purchase of some apartments offered for sale to the college. "I do not think the college should own too much down town property. It gives us the appearance of a moneyed institution. We have enough property . . . now down town for good community relations in my judgment."[28] Two years later he recommended paying for some land that had originally been offered as a gift to the college: "I do not think," he advised the trustees, "we should cheapen ourselves nor our good will relations by trying to dicker [to force the donor] to stand by his original proposal."[29]

Some interesting correspondence with state officials shows that at times he acted as the village's unofficial spokesman. In one case he tried to get the village's name placed on state maps, and in another to get some stone delivered on Grantham Road when Highway 15 was being constructed. "The muddy condition of the last few days is a disgrace to any respectable community," he wrote in one letter. "We ought not be asked to drive our cars through a 'hog yard slop.' "[30]

The Grantham Water Company was a potential source of tension between the college and the village. Purchased by the college in 1939 from Ben Brubaker, a member of the Grantham Brethren in Christ Church, the company had difficulty in balancing expenses with income, despite Hostetter himself doing some of the work, including helping to sign up new customers, straightening out accounts with customers, and writing letters of good will.[31] The main problem was the relatively sparse population of the area (making extensions of the system expensive) and the correspondingly low rates charged by the company. Thus in 1951 the college filed with the Public Utilities Commission a rate increase estimated to bring in an additional yearly sum of $1,100.

Some people in the community strongly opposed this action, and called a public meeting at the fire hall on September 12. Hostetter encouraged town attendance and was there himself to answer questions. (This bothered one townsperson who claimed that it would be futile for him to go since everyone would be persuaded by Hostetter to the college's point of view.) The meeting was open and frank, and Hostetter, in fact, was able to get most of the attendants to agree that a rate increase was justified. He readily agreed to a suggestion that a citizen's committee of five should discuss the matter with the trustee board, and that until this happened the appeal to the PUC would not be activated.[32]

The trustees, however, decided to proceed with the request for a rate increase. Hostetter thus wrote a conciliatory letter to the company's patrons, pointing out, in answer to specific criticisms, that college residents paid for their water like anyone else, and that for practically all water companies, water is free at its source. He ended by offering to sell the company to the community—obviously, a diplomatic, tactical move.[33]

The hearing on the rates took place at the Carlisle courthouse in February, 1952. The citizen's committee appeared at the hearing to continue its protest, but after Hostetter had taken the stand for two hours, according to the diary "the opposition melted away and a general good feeling resulted."[34] The college had won its case, but had not destroyed its relationship with the community in doing so.

As all of this suggests, Hostetter became increasingly interested in developing good relations between the college and the community, but even so, he was far more interested in promoting them with the denomination. The church-college connection had brought him to the presidency in the first place. He never lost the conviction that the two bodies implicitly depended on each other for their mutual growth and strength.

We may thus expect to find Hostetter working in various ways to foster good church-college relationships. As with the community, he found the school's music groups to be one of his best instruments. From his first years as president, he wrote numerous letters to pastors and Sunday school superintendents suggesting the use of the groups, and advertised their availability in the college publications.[35] A letter in early 1937 to the pastor of the Des Moines, Iowa, congregation brought a typical, if somewhat warmer than usual, response: "Yes thank God we will be glad to have you come and give us a real *hot hot hot* Holy Ghost sermon and some Holy Ghost hymns, Glory to God."[36]

The result was that the male and ladies choruses (later mixed), male quartets, ladies quartets, gospel team quartets, and more, seemed always to be leaving campus during the school year for some appointment, or touring during holidays. Hostetter frequently took a quartet with him on his speaking engagements, and in the earlier years often used one during tent meetings in the summer. And almost everywhere they were well received. In many of the churches in the denomination, particularly those in more rural areas, the college's program was the highlight of the year, as apparently it was at Stayner, Ontario, in 1937. Ignoring E. J. Swalm's fears that the men's chorus might get stuck in the area's mud roads, Hostetter included that congregation in the itinerary. "It makes us wonder," the Stayner correspondent to the *Evangelical Visitor* reported of the singing, "if God could let mortal lips send forth His praises with such beauty; what must it be like to hear the angels sing. A large crowd attended each service."[37] This music ministry to the denomination continued, and in fact grew over the years of Hostetter's presidency.

There were, of course, some risks in sending young people out into the constituency, especially to congregations which contained critics of the college. Dress was often the problem. One person who had displayed in his store window a poster advertising the coming of a music group to the local congregation wrote after the program to say that the clothes the young people sang in were more modern than those shown in the picture—"a real deception of advertisement," he called it. He would display no more posters for the college. "I hope and pray that the plain people will soon see their mistake and fall in line regardless of college teaching."[38] In making arrangements in 1940 for a music group to sing in the Air Hill church, an official wrote to emphasize that the dress the young wear should be in order: "Last year the quartet came to our pulpit in white shoes, which was not appreciated by our group in general and we feel this has a tendency to weaken our efforts to keep our young folks conservative in dress and that is the reason we feel to offer a suggestion that the group be instructed to appear in moderately conservative attire."[39]

And up in Canada, Earl Sider wrote to impress on his former schoolmate and fellow tent worker that the Grantham young people would be acceptable at Wainfleet only if they dressed conservatively. Among other things, neckties and white shoes were prohibited on the platform. "Now understand me Christ," he explained, "I'm casting no reflections on either the Wainfleet Brethren or the young people . . . . But I'm desirous of breaking this prejudice [of the congregation against Messiah College] and believe by tact and cooperation it can eventually be done."[40]

Another criticism of the music groups was their apparent preference for "fancy music," rather than the good old gospel songs and hymns. One of the more moderate criticisms came from a strong supporter of the college, an Ohio pastor who wrote in mid-1935 to suggest that the music department "should not sacrifice too much of Christ for culture . . . . There is grave danger that much of the good will usurp that which is best."[41]

On such issues as dress and music, the views of the faculty as well as Hostetter himself were more fexible than many of their fellow church members. Hostetter had on one hand to give support to the faculty and their work and on the other to hold the reins sufficiently tight so that the church would stay with the college. He thus constantly appealed to students and colleagues to keep the church in mind in their more public roles. Students who did not maintain a "high standard of conduct," as Hostetter once put it, did not accompany the music groups when they went off campus. Enforcing this point of view led, for example, to cancelling the programs of one male quartet in the 1940s because of what was considered improper conduct.[42] A few years later when the male chorus returned from a tour, he met with the members to discuss the "irregular conduct" of some who played pool on the trip. In the evening he interviewed the culprits alone, and was satisfied that they "seemed very penitent and docile."[43]

Similarly with dress. For most of the years in office, the men did not wear neckties or the women light stockings when singing in public. In 1950, before the chorus left for a tour of Ohio in April, Hostetter wrote to director Earl Miller, suggesting to Miller that "it would be of advantage to our public relations" if he did not wear a tie. "I am sure you understand the general situation well enough to appreciate the basis for the suggestion."[44] A few months earlier he had several meetings with the women of the ensemble "about dressing their hair more modestly." He added with a mental sigh: "It is indeed a problem how to guide our young people right in this changing world."[45]

With the same concern in mind he wrote to the ladies quartet in January, 1948, because he had heard that they had been "too girlish and adolescent." He concluded at the end of a straightforward letter: "It does not do to sing sacred songs at one time and then speak or act in a way at another time that onlookers think we are silly or shallow."[46]

And over the years he urged the music department and its groups to try to accommodate themselves more to the music their audience appreciated. "I believe it would be very good," he wrote to Frances Smith in 1949 in a typical communication, "if our Male Chorus and Ladies Chorus would keep pretty much to the gospel song and hymn type of program and leave the heavier music for choral and oratorio."[47]

But good church relations involved not only activities off the campus; there was much on the campus about which critics thought they could find fault—guest lecturers and musicians included. A Lyceum program in April, 1937, by Percy Crawford brought a number of critical letters to Hostetter's desk, charging that the program was too "light and chaffy." One writer maintained that deeper spirituality should be expected at the school of a church which believes in holiness; a lecture like the one given previously on the Canadian Rockies "is better than a religious program that tickles the ears of the young people." The letter ended diplomatically by suggesting that Hostetter probably did not have much to do with the programming of this event; thus he might wish to pass on the correspondence to those who did.[48] To this and other letters Hostetter responded by indicating that he himself felt distressed over the undesirable features, and in one that the letter would be good support in "positively insisting on the elimination of this sort of thing from our programs."[49]

Such criticisms continued throughout his years of office, particularly in the later years when the college began to broaden the range of its guest lecturers and entertainers. In the fall of 1954 the women members of the Gage Singers appeared on stage in sleeveless and backless gowns with low necklines. Hostetter received the spate of letters he had expected. He reminded Earl Miller that "usually a frank, courteous statement of well-chosen words [to the entertainers] can clear such a matter satisfactorily without giving offense. We do not wish to offend our friends who back a Christian school which expresses itself on modesty of attire."[50] That letter was followed by an apology to the constituency, which appeared in the next (November) issue of the *Bulletin.*

At least in part for similar church relations reasons, Hostetter followed a very conservative policy on dramatic productions for most of his years at Grantham. In the spring of 1937, he wrote to the presidents of the graduating classes (academy and junior colleges), urging them to think more of quality than variety. "I am looking for many folks throughout the church to visit us enroute to General Conference," he explained, "and we believe your programs can present a good advertising for our College. As you know, dramatics and costuming are not considered advisable for these programs and the use of musical instruments should be somewhat limited."[51]

It was to be expected that when dramatic productions were finally permitted, some members in the church constituency would be critical. As late as 1957, one mother wrote to object to her daughter wearing a hat instead of a covering and having her face painted. "I certainly would not call that Christian. Would you want Jesus to come then?" she asked rhetorically.[52] Two other women who attended the same play were likewise critical. Hostetter sent the mothers' letters to the two faculty members who served as advisers to the production (a frequent technique in counselling colleagues on such matters), and to the letter appended a note that suggests a concern for both the constituency and the young people at the college: "As previously stated to both of you, I believe that in order to justify our course [of allowing dramatic productions] with fairness to our patrons, I believe we must use caution and discrimination in the use of make-up. Unless youth are guided by wise counsel at this point, they will tumble over themselves in reaction against the past conservative position of the group. This becomes the responsibility of wise teachers."[53]

The kind of faculty he chose, Hostetter realized, had significant church relations implications. He attempted to fill vacancies with Brethren in Christ and Mennonite faculty (both "plain people"), but if not with them, at least with persons who were clearly theologically compatible with the Brethren in Christ. And as with the students, the dress of faculty was an important issue.

This may be illustrated in the case of Jesse and Lucille Lady. In the mid-1930s they were both promising young people, she a nurse and he completing a post-graduate degree at Princeton Theological Seminary (in later years he was to become president of Beulah, later Upland, College). They would make good appointments to the faculty; thus Hostetter sent them an invitation in the summer of 1935 to return to their alma mater as teachers.

But it soon became apparent (in Jesse's letter of acceptance) that Lucille was wearing a hat rather than a prayer veiling, the result of the Ladys having been removed from Brethren in Christ circles for several years. Hostetter responded with a frank, strongly worded letter. The Ladys would need to give a definite commitment to Lucille's wearing a prayer veiling before there would be any hope of the trustees considering employing them for the next school year. He concluded by pointing out that "as an institution supported by the church in finances and students and expected to produce workers for the church, our program must be in harmony with the church, or we had better close the doors or sever our affiliation with the church."[54]

In the face of this strong letter, the Ladys withdrew their acceptance of the invitation. They are sorry, Jesse wrote to Hostetter: their strong wish is to come to Messiah, but they feel too strongly about the prayer veiling.[55] But less than two weeks later, Hostetter received another letter from the Ladys stating that they had reconsidered the matter: they now think the best move is to come to Grantham, and are now ready to comply with the college's position on the prayer veiling.[56] When they arrived on campus shortly afterward, Hostetter began to arrange for Jesse a busy round of speaking engagements in Sunday services, Bible conferences, and Sunday school meetings throughout the Pennsylvania area.[57]

A similar story may be told about J. Boyd Cressman, a member of the Old Mennonite Church (now Mennonite Church) in Ontario, who at the time was teaching at Ontario Bible School. In early 1940, Hostetter offered him a contract to teach at Grantham, providing he would set aside his necktie and wear instead a plain vest while on the faculty.[58]

Cressman was puzzled. He replied that he had been wearing a necktie at Ontario Bible School without "the slightest hint . . . that I should change my attire."[59] To this Hostetter sent a detailed response. He pointed out that Mennonites dress more conservatively in Pennsylvania than they do in Ontario. To have a person from a plain church dress in non-plain attire would not be understood by either the college's Mennonite or Brethren in Christ patrons, and would likely create an embarrassing situation for Cressman himself.[60]

But in this case, Hostetter was prepared to be somewhat flexible. Two weeks later he wrote to Cressman to suggest that it would be acceptable if Cressman wore a suit without a necktie, although the plain vest would be preferable.[61] Cressman, however, decided not to join the faculty, and shortly went on to become librarian at Goshen College.

At the same time, Hostetter was carrying on a correspondence with Howard Book about joining the faculty. Book, from Kansas, had been reared a Brethren in Christ, and was now teaching at McPherson College. Book replied to Hostetter's query by saying that such an appointment interested him, except that both he and his wife (from a Free Methodist background) were above the dress question and thus could not conform to the standards of the church on this issue.

Hostetter's reply to this letter is informative, for it gives us an insight into his own views in relation to those of the denomination. The strong suggestion of the letter is that his views on dress are somewhat more advanced than most of his fellow Brethren in Christ. How then, he asks in effect, can he (and, by implication,

Howard Book) remain within the church and be intellectually honest? Hostetter replied to his own question by saying that in being an acceptable and loyal member of the Brethren in Christ church he "has not resigned his privilege and ability to weigh truth individually." Any wide-awake person with a passion for God and righteousness will see much to improve in any good organization; what is needed is "a courageous stand for truth combined with the proper respect for properly constituted authority." He with others believes that some things need to be changed in the denomination, but he also is convinced that the Brethren in Christ hold a body of truth to which he can more fully subscribe than that held by any other group. Thus honesty means remaining with the church. Given the decision to remain, one's work at the college means taking a responsible position to the denomination that fosters the institution.[62]

As in other areas of his leadership at the college, Hostetter's insistence on a close conformity to church practices gradually relaxed. To judge by the school yearbook, some men faculty in 1953 were beginning to wear neckties, by 1960 the exceptions to the practice were few. Undoubtedly this in part was owing to a general change in direction on dress that the denomination as a whole was beginning to take. In any event, most faculty from those years agree that when neckties began to appear, Hostetter offered little, if any, criticism of the change.

In all of these ways, Hostetter attempted to bring the college and the church together. There were other ways as well. He inaugurated ministers' conferences at the college in 1940. He brought churchmen to speak at the college, in part for what they could do in promoting good relations with the denomination. Thus he once wrote to his academic dean, Charles Eshelman, to say that he had heard Harry Hock speak recently at Mechanicsburg, and since Hock "is quite influential and active in the church . . . it seems to me it might be well if we would have Harry over for a chapel service."[63] Similarly, early in 1951 he brought Henry Ginder to campus to speak to the faculty on what he would like the college to send back to the districts.[64] And he helped arrange for the five bishops (created after a reorganization of the bishoprics in 1957) to become voting members of the college's trustee board. "This I consider a desirable step," he woote to Carl Ulery, one of the bishops, "to keep the relationship between the college and the church in the years ahead."[65]

And over the years he encouraged young men to hold revivals and tent meetings during the summer and other holidays. Sometimes the response from the church was almost too good: in the spring of 1936, Hostetter wrote to John Hoke, father of student William Hoke, to obtain permission for William to remain after the close of school to help another student in a three-week revival at Canoe Creek, arguing that "we have more calls for capable young men to engage in Christian service this summer than we are able to supply."[66] At least one area Brethren in Christ congregation—Mt. Holly Springs—was begun in this fashion, when student George Kibler held a tent meeting in the town in 1954.

All of these efforts on Hostetter's part did not take care of all his critics. Church leader Charlie Byers has observed that in the earlier years of Hostetter's administration everyone worth his salt as a preacher or evangelist criticized the college for the problems in the church, and especially for the growing worldliness in the denomination. Thus, for example, if a woman student returned home from Grantham without covering strings, the college was obviously to blame. The criticism came from himself, he has admitted, as when in a presentation at the state council meeting in 1940 he blamed the college for much of the worldly drift in the church. Hostetter spoke to him after the meeting in a brotherly yet firm manner, pointing out that Byers as a church leader had done the college real harm, since what he said was not true.[67]

Hostetter's answer to a sharp letter in 1939 is again illustrative of his response to strong criticism from church members. The letter was written by the father of a young woman whom he had been trying to persuade unsuccessfully for three years to attend the college. "O how my soul is pained that we have a college at Grantham," the father complained. "Is it not drawing our members away from the simplicity that is the Gospel? . . . The doctrines that our old Brethren brought when I was young satisfied my soul when I yielded my soul to God. But today it is too much in the head and not a beautiful doctrine."[68] Hostetter responded by recognizing his correspondent's sincerity, but suggested that he would think better of the college if he knew more

about it. Thus most students, in fact, were more conservative
after they left the school than when they came, and the college
had an enviable record for preserving young people for the
church.[69]

Hostetter's patient, diplomatic espousal of good church-
college relations paid off well over the years, including with
Charlie Byers himself, who later said that it was mainly Hostetter's "careful guidance of the college and . . . understanding and
fatherly attitude and admonition to me that helped me to a wiser
position."[70] By the 1950s Hostetter felt generally pleased with the
support of the constituency, although he noted in some correspondence in 1953 that "there is a small margin of the group who
stoutly resist any change, who continue to voice their criticism on
the one hand, and a small group of folk with passion and interest
who seem to think that Moody Bible Institute and other similar
schools have a much better program than has Messiah."[71]

His mood is just as well caught in a diary entry following
homecoming weekend in October, 1956. Sunday was a beautiful
day, he recorded, and "as we travelled through the buildings on
'open house' it seemed as though many of our friends are really
backing Messiah College."[72]

VI

"And Eventually a Senior College"

*I*n his leadership of the more academic phase of the college's life, C. N. Hostetter, Jr., carried over many of the characteristics that served him well in the other areas of his presidency. And in doing so he helped to develop the institution from an academy and Bible school into a senior college and liberal arts institution.

He early looked to his own educational development. The lack of a degree had given Hostetter in 1934 some hesitation about accepting the presidency; thus at the first opportunity he began to remedy that deficiency. In the summer of 1935 he attended the Winona Lake School of Theology, returning for successive summers until he had completed the Th.B. (in 1937) and the M.A. in theology (in 1941). (The year following his graduation from the M.A. program he was elected president of the school's alumni association, a position from which he resigned the following year.) From there, he attended summer school at the University of Chicago from 1943 to 1945, graduating with the M.A. in Education. For his thesis at Chicago he visited and studied all the junior colleges in Pennsylvania, thus fitting himself for a later leadership role in the junior college movement in the state.

He also received two honorary degrees: a D.D. from Houghton College in 1945, and a Doctor of Laws in 1949 from Greenville College in Illinois, where his son Ray was a student at the time. (Messiah junior college graduates attended both institutions.) "Dr. [Leslie] Marston gave my citation," he notes of the degree from Greenville. "If I could have him speak for me at the day of judgment I would be fortunate."[1]

Education for the Christian, Hostetter claimed, was first and always training for a life of service and ministry, whether in the home as a wife and mother, in the school as a teacher, or in foreign lands as a missionary. He established this view in his inaugural address in 1934 when he pledged to make Christ central in all the life of the college and to challenge students for Christ and the church; that, he insisted, was why the school existed.[2] Twelve years later he made much the same point in an article in the *Evangelical Visitor.* Education for the sake of education, he wrote, degenerates into an instrument of harm. But our church schools are different; they do not exist for themselves. "They are service centers through which the Master wishes to work in carrying on His world wide program."[3]

How much freedom in the pursuit of liberal education Hostetter never deviated from that position, but over the years he also came gradually to an understanding of and appreciation for the role of the liberal arts in the Christian college. By 1945 he was conceding that the liberal arts had a place in leading people to a better understanding of themselves and their world, and thus to a wholesome integration of life.[4] Such sentiments increased until in one of his last pronouncements as president on the subject he could speak (and in the church paper at that) of a liberal arts education liberating men and women "from the earthworm society dedicated to leisure, wealth and recreation," and through imagination, feeling, and a knowledge of man's cultural heritage making them better fitted for service in the church and the world.[5]

Part of his growing appreciation for the liberal arts was owing to his reading of the ancient philosophers. He liked Plato for his teaching on the subordination of lower desires to the higher, and Aristotle for his insistence on moderation; these and other truths from the classical philosophers, he claimed, came to an "adequate and satisfying conclusion" in Jesus Christ.[6]

How much freedom in the pursuit of liberal education Hostetter considered tolerable depends in part on one's perspective. From that of the church constituency it was broad. He insisted, for example, that Roman Catholics could study at Messiah College without interference with their religious duties and with respect from faculty.[7] Strong pacifist though he was, he brought to campus as commencement speakers such vocal non-pacifists as Harold Ockenga and Bob Jones. In explaining his action in engaging as evangelist a speaker who seemed to have emphasized "continued confession" rather than the holiness position of the denomination, he wrote to John Martin, president of Upland College: "Personally I feel there is value for students to be exposed to some variation in teaching in order that their own beliefs and ideas and concepts can be formed, not in ignorance of other views, but taking in a satisfactory scope of religious thought."[8]

From other perspectives, he would have appeared too ready to defend the position of the church, even in the later years of his presidency. Thus, for example, on one occasion he called to his office for discussion a faculty member who, it was reported (without foundation), was advocating a divided chancel, and on another had strong words for a new teacher who he thought was too much influenced by non-Brethren in Christ theology.[9]

Hostetter's own rural, practical roots conditioned him to understand that education, as good as it was for most people, was not suitable, or even necessary, for all. When one of the academy students wanted to stay home to work on the farm in the second semester of the 1938-39 school year, Hostetter wrote to his father to encourage him to grant his son's wish: "If a boy wants farm work and farm life and insists on not going to school, I think, sometimes it is best not to force him to it and, if you see best to keep Edgar out, we will respect your judgment on the matter."[10] Neither did he encourage young people coming to the academy at a too early age, although the school had almost desperate need of money. "There are some things," he wrote to the mother of a prospective student, "in which the parent's guidance and help is strongly needed."[11]

On the other hand, he took a strong line with young people in the denomination who he thought should be in college but who were making excuses to avoid an education. One promising young man argued with Hostetter that it would be useless for him to come to Grantham because he was going to spend the rest of his life in farming. Hostetter replied that education prepares young people for "better and richer living whether you will spend your time on the farm, in a dairy or anywhere else . . . . The money that young people invest in developing their personalities and training their faculties is one of the investments that can never be lost and most things are very, very uncertain these days."[12]

He had more pointed words in a letter to a young man who wanted to enter the ministry without further education. "Success in the ministry," he wrote, "depends in no small way on what one puts into it in study and preparation, and these activities are virtually always better done in directed study [as at Grantham] than on one's own initiative."[13] When students spoke to him about staying out of school for a year or two, he cautioned them about the temptations of earning money and buying cars, and then not having the discipline to give up such things and return to school.[14] When a student yields to such temptation, he once wrote, he "sells his opportunity for college education for a pottage of money, personal pleasure, and individual freedom."[15]

From 1934 to 1960 Hostetter led the college in advancing from an institution offering a high school program, a two-year Bible course, and a junior college, to a four-year college offering degree programs in Bible and the liberal arts. In this academic progress, Hostetter and his colleagues worked within confining circumstances to improve the professional quality of administration and instruction. The goal for much of the improvement was accreditation.

One of Hostetter's earliest concerns was to improve the quality of teaching. He tried to do this by obtaining new teachers (such as Jesse Lady and Ben Thuma), and by sending older faculty back to school. He insisted that Enos Hess, former president and now sixty-six years of age, return to university for refresher science courses in the summer of 1938 (Hess wrote back from Pennsylvania State University to say that he was taking biology and chemistry, each eighty minutes a day, and was hunting up old acquaintances).[16] He required the same for Mary Hoffman, another venerable Messiah teacher,[17] and encouraged younger faculty, such as Ben Thuma, Clarence Musser, and Albert Brechbill to take graduate studies.[18]

At his and Academic Dean Asa Climenhaga's prompting, faculty in 1940 began to attend the educational meetings of the county.[19] Three years later, the Administrative Committee (of which Hostetter was chairman) made arrangements for faculty to be represented at such major educational associations as the American Association of Junior Colleges, the Association of School Administrators, and the Middle States Association of

Colleges and Secondary Schools.[20] Hostetter himself, beginning around 1940, consistently attended the annual meetings of several professional organizations, including those of the American Association of Colleges and Universities. Usually he was stimulated by these conventions. "One meets many educators at these meetings," he remarked in his diary following the American Association of Colleges convention in 1949. "One of the compensations of the job of College President is the wide association one is privileged to have with select men."[21] But occasionally he was disappointed, as at a meeting of the Association of Junior Colleges at Boston in 1952, where, he claimed, he "never listened to so many off color sex jokes."[22]

An early concern for Hostetter was to make easier the transfer of students from the junior college to other, mainly four-year, institutions. The academy had long ago solved such problems: it had been accredited by the Pennsylvania Department of Public Instruction as early as 1924. Since 1928 the Pennsylvania State University had accepted Messiah Bible College students without question, as had Elizabethtown College, providing their grades had been adequate. Students transferring to other institutions, however, often ran into difficulties, since the college was not listed in any source which the other institution could check. As a result, most of Messiah's junior college graduates transferred to other Christian colleges, such as Goshen College, Wheaton College, and Taylor University. Hostetter worked to expand the number of such institutions that would readily accept students from Grantham, including Houghton College, because, as he wrote to Claude Rees and President Stephen Paine, Houghton was the "only holiness school in full accredited standing east of the Mississippi."[23]

More than that, however, was needed, as Hostetter knew. Accreditation of some sort was crucial to the college's academic standing and the ability of its graduates to transfer courses. He had, in fact, accreditation in mind from the beginning of his presidency. In his inaugural address in 1934, he claimed accreditation as one of the goals of the college, and he kept that goal before himself and others, as when in writing to a prospective teacher in 1936 he said he was "looking forward to the time when we can become an accredited junior college and eventually a senior college."[24] One way in which to follow the academic progress of the college is to note the activities undertaken and the changes made in the program in order to obtain accreditation.

One of the steps was the college's role in the formation of the Pennsylvania Association of Junior Colleges. Both Hostetter and Asa Climenhaga attended the Association's organizing meeting in Harrisburg in February, 1944, at which Climenhaga was elected vice-president.[25] Beginning in 1947, Hostetter served five years on the executive committee, including one (1950-1951) as president. From this vantage point, in 1946 the college applied for and received junior college accreditation with the Pennsylvania State Council of Education.

Following this advance, and with an eye toward further accreditation, the trustees of the college in 1947 accepted a recommendation from the administration to upgrade the quality of teaching on the college level by hiring no one who did not possess at least an M.A. degree. At the same time, the trustees provided financial assistance for faculty members already on the staff to pursue graduate studies (the first Ph.D.s on the faculty were obtained through this plan).[26] In the same year trustees also agreed to provide some hospital insurance coverage and the beginning of a retirement plan.[27] For the students, a guidance program began in the latter 1940s, at the same time that scholarships became available in any meaningful amounts, owing much to Hostetter's initiative in raising and setting aside the needed money.

The next application for accreditation was to the newly-formed Accrediting Association of Bible Institutes and Bible Colleges. To be accredited by this group would assure being listed in the United States government blue book on Accredited Higher Institutions, a reference source used by colleges and universities in evaluating the credits of transferring students.

The college did gain accreditation by this group, but not as easily as might have been assumed. The team that visited the college was critical of several areas: low salaries (far too low for even a church school), too few volumes in the library (even a junior college must have 15,000 to 25,000 volumes), teaching loads (twelve to fourteen hours should be the rule rather than Messiah's standard eighteen).[28] Later in the year, the Association began to insist that future accreditation would be dependent upon institutions providing five years of training for the Bachelor of Theology degree (Th.B.) and, for those giving four years of work, a limited A.B. degree.

It was in part this new requirement, as well as the natural direction of the institution, that led the college in 1949 to apply to the Pennsylvania State Council of Education for the right to grant degrees in religious education and theology. The application was denied on the ground that the college did not have sufficient income from non-student sources.

At this point, Hostetter reactivated the Living Endowment League that had largely been quiescent since 1945 because of the Extension Fund campaign. A year later (in 1950) when Hostetter resubmitted the request and provided evidence of greater financial support, the college obtained the right to grant the Th.B. and B.R.E. (Bachelor of Religious Education) degrees.[29]

This, however, required a change in the charter, since the existing one did not provide for degrees. The new charter not only gave the college the right to confer degrees but also provided for a change of name from Messiah Bible College to Messiah College.

Action by the trustees to change the name had come several years earlier—in 1947.[30] That action, however, had caused some protest, including a letter to Hostetter from some former students now serving as missionaries in Africa. Hostetter responded by saying that the name presently being used no longer reflected the nature of the school, which included more than a Bible college. To name it after the local village, however, did not seem appropriate because Grantham was insignificant as a place and the college served a much wider constituency than the community. But it was fitting to retain the word Messiah because of its long use for the institution and the affectionate memories it evoked for former students.[31] Continued reaction to the change of name led Hostetter to send a questionnaire to the alumni, who responded with a large majority in favor of the change. The trustees then reaffirmed their earlier action and the new name was incorporated into the charter on January 15, 1951, thus making official the name that had, in fact, been used unofficially for two or three years.[32]

These developments leading to four-and five-year programs on the college level caused Messiah College to discontinue its membership in the Pennsylvania Junior College Association.[33] In the following year, the college became a member of the Pennsylvania Association of Colleges and Universities, whose annual meetings Hostetter faithfully attended.[34]

Meanwhile, at Hostetter's urging, the college in November, 1951, began a self-evaluation study which led eventually to a visit from the Pennsylvania Council of Education and the granting to the college the right to confer the A.B. degree.[35] In the following year (1954) the Council permitted Messiah College to confer the Bachelor of Science degree in nursing, offered in cooperation with the Harrisburg Hospital School of Nursing.[36] These later accomplishments set the stage for the college to develop a four-year liberal arts curriculum, first offering majors in history, English, the natural sciences, and biblical literature. In turn, this movement toward the liberal arts led the college in 1958 to drop its affiliation with the Association of Bible Institutes and Bible Colleges, primarily because that association insisted on a major in Bible, thus in effect requiring liberal arts students to pursue a double major.[37]

In all of these evaluations, Hostetter took the leading role. Typical was the reevaluation process involved in preparing for reaccreditation from the Accrediting Association of Bible Institutes and Bible Colleges in 1954. Hostetter noted in his diary that a committee was appointed to do the task, but it referred a vast amount of the work back to him. Three days later, after putting the finishing touches to the evaluation, he added: "This item has caused me a great deal of hard work in recent weeks."[38]

By 1954 Hostetter was leading the college in laying the groundwork for accreditation by the Middle States Association of Colleges and Secondary Schools. This move, he pointed out, was necessary because the academic world was increasingly relying on regional accrediting agencies rather than state or other organizations for accreditation standards and evaluation purposes, and because the financial assistance that Messiah College was now beginning to need from foundations and other philanthropic organizations was generally limited to regionally accredited schools.[39] Over the next several years until the evaluation team visited the campus, Hostetter regularly attended the meetings of the Association, where, as he once noted in his diary, he picked up good ideas on organization and administration.[40]

In the process of evaluation that now got under way for the greatest academic challenge in the college's history, several stubborn potential problems emerged. One was faculty salaries. These from the beginning of the college had been extremely low, and not much improvement over the years had been made in them. When Hostetter became president, faculty were receiving from $75 to $85 a month, and even that amount was not always guaranteed. Thus in 1916 the trustees made clear that they could promise to pay the contracted salary only if between sixty-five and seventy-five full-time students enrolled; smaller enrollments could mean as much as two months' pay forfeited.[41] Four years later, Hostetter could offer only $95 a month to Canadian J. B. Cressman who had a recognized M.A.[42]

These low salaries had always been a subject for major criticism by the accrediting agencies, including that of the Bible Institutes and Bible Colleges, as noted earlier. Although it would be unfair to say that Hostetter was unconcerned about this situation, the financial limitations within which he had to work and his view of faculty service militated against significant salary advances. Hostetter considered that work done for Christ and the church would always need to be carried on at considerable sacrifice, and that a Christian, in fact, served better as he worked sacrificially. He himself set the pattern: although president, he drew a salary roughly equal to most of his faculty; in at least one year, five members of the staff received as much as or more than he.

The old salary levels, however, quite clearly would not be acceptable to the Middle States evaluation team. Thus for the 1958-59 school year, the trustees agreed to a revised schedule that significantly raised salaries, giving the lowest paid instructor $2,000 and the highest paid professor $4,000 a year (a small bonus of $200 was allowed a faculty member for a wife who did not work outside the home, and another bonus of $50 for each child under sixteen).[43] Relatedly, teaching loads had remained heavy, in spite of repeated criticism from evaluation teams. Now with the pressure of regional accreditation, a full load was reduced from eighteen hours to sixteen hours.[44]

But the biggest issue in preparing for Middle States accreditation very quickly became the continuation of the academy. Hostetter had suspected this from the beginning, and thus had made a special point of speaking about the issue with Taylor Jones, executive director of the Middle States Association, as early as the fall of 1954 at a meeting in Hershey. Jones had categorically stated that the academy and the college would need to be accredited together.[45]

But the academy was the weak sister of the institution. Decreasing enrollments (from 1946 to 1958 a decline of 32%) meant that the academy was a financial liability to the college. Also, the presence of the academy on the same campus as the college gave the latter an immature appearance. A related problem was the need to use faculty to teach on both academic levels, thus taxing their energies and endangering the integrity of their college teaching.[46]

The first attempt to solve this problem was the gradual separation of academy and college activites, including chapel exercises, campus days, and field days. But this obviously did not solve the basic problem. Thus the college administration asked the trustees to consider discontinuing the academy. This request began a long process of soul-searching activities by committees, circulating of questionnaires, issuing of reports, and exchange of debate at General Conference. A committee formed by the trustees and, of course, including Hostetter, sent out a questionnaire to parents and alumni, to which the response rate was a disappointing 21.3%. That in itself was suggestive, the committee thought, of the interest in the academy. Of those who responded, most indicated that they would probably not send their children to the high school. On the other hand, strong support for its continuation came from the five bishops and some parents, including a dying mother who appealed to Hostetter that her last days would be made more difficult if she knew that her daughters would not be able to attend high school at Grantham.[47]

In spite of such sentiments the committee recommended to the trustees discontinuing the academy, and the trustees passed on the recommendation to the Board for Schools and Colleges and General Conference of 1958.[48] Those bodies, however, were not prepared to move precipitously, partly because of vocal support for the academy at General Conference in that year. Thus another committee was formed, this time by General Conference (and again including Hostetter), whose task was to study the possibilities of providing Christian day school opportunities and report back to the next General Conference.[49]

This committee held three meetings, in the first of which members committed themselves to accreditation for the college and determined that this commitment should underlie all their proceedings. They sent out two questionnaires—one to alumni, and another to the pastors in the Central, Allegheny, and Atlantic regional conferences. Two-thirds of the pastors were in favor of continuing the academy on campus; the alumni were divided. Returns from both questionnaires, however, confirmed the committee's opinion that prospects for healthy enrollments in any academy promoted by the church were poor. The committee thus firmly recommended a gradual discontinuation of the academy by dropping the lowest grade each year.[50]

This recommendation was passed by General Conference, although vigorously debated. As a result, grades 9 and 10 were dropped in successive years. Because of a very limited enrollment, grade 11 was not offered in the third year; thus in the spring of 1960 the academy graduated its last class. The academy ended just at the time of the visit from the Middle States evaluation team. From the minutes of the study committees and from his diary, it is clear that this was the end toward which Hostetter had worked all along.

In July, 1959, Hostetter interviewed Calvin Linton (the chairman of the Middle States team that would visit the college) in his office at George Washington University in Washington, D.C. Hostetter practiced some of his charm and diplomacy on Linton. "I told him," his diary records, "when we heard the dean of one of the schools of a city university was to be our chairman we concluded a heavy burden of proof would be necessary to show that a college of 165 students was worthy of accreditation." Linton assured him otherwise. Hostetter came away optimistic, and well impressed by Linton's "calibre, scope of understanding and general breadth."[51]

But Hostetter's optimism was not well founded. The team visited the campus from February 28 to March 2. They were critical on a number of levels and raised many questions about

the religious emphasis of the college (Hostetter proudly noted
that on this and other issues he found the students "very loyally
standing by the college"). In their final report the team stressed
the need of the college to upgrade the faculty level of training
(more Ph.Ds were necessary), to provide greater depth for the
majors offered, and to obtain more books for the library.

In his turn Hostetter was not pleased with all of the members of
the team, particularly with the one, a college president, who
interviewed Hostetter at length in Hostetter's office, chain-
smoking all the while until the room became blue, and being
critical of the college's statement of faith. After receiving the
written report, Hostetter wrote to Taylor Jones, as he notes in his
diary: "I took up each member of the team and gave him a
personal appraisal of the work each one did." Hostetter did not
deny that some of the criticisms were well made, but he insisted
that some conclusions were based on insufficient evidence.[52]
Three weeks later he debated with himself about sending another
letter to Jones but decided against it.[53]

In point of fact, the visiting team did recommend provisional
accreditation, but their criticisms were sufficiently pointed that
the Association denied the recommendation. Hostetter brought
the bad news to the faculty whose minutes for May 2, 1960 read:
"Doctor Hostetter, in his masterful way with matters of deep
moment, reported the decision of the Middle States Association
that Messiah College was denied accreditation this time."

In mid-May he and president-elect Arthur Climenhaga talked
with Taylor Jones in the latter's office in New York city. Taylor
was encouraging, promising them a special examination whenever the college was ready.[54] Of course, this could not happen
before his retirement a few months later, and thus the prize had
escaped him. Three years later, however, the college did achieve
accreditation, obviously in part because it benefited from the
experiences of the first visit, and because Hostetter had led the
institution considerably far along the road to its accreditation
destination.

Altogether, this academic progress represents a slow yet in
some ways deliberate growth from an institution with essentially
Bible school characteristics to one that was primarily liberal arts
but which retained, however, much of the conservative, evangeli-

cal flavor of the earlier years. This is as obvious in extra-curricular activities as any place, the conduct of which, at least in part, was governed by church relations concerns.

Slides and movies are an example. During Hostetter's years, the college did not directly prohibit slides, but they were used at first with caution. Thus Hostetter, in responding to a request in 1936 from Landis Miller to show his slides in a lecture on "Communism in Prophecy: Russia and the United States," told Landis that he could use his slides if he came early enough for him [Hostetter] to check them.[55] Two years later, faculty were informed that the economics teacher would show some slides in class but without a public announcement.[56]

The use of slides in the classroom and in public lectures, however, was accepted more quickly than movie films. Films were such a delicate issue that, until the early 1940s, requests for their use appear usually to have been referred to the trustees, who with few exceptions routinely deferred or denied the requests, even for educational films (as, for example, in the case of the Anti-Saloon League's offer to show "Ten Nights in a Barroom").

A turning point in the use of films came around 1942 when the trustees finally granted permission for faculty to use motion pictures for educational purposes, subject to supervision and censorship of the Administration Committee, of which, of course, Hostetter was chairman.[57] The college purchased a projector and by the end of the next school year in May, 1943, had shown twenty-two educational films (mostly on science and industry).[58]

Even documentaries, however, were treated with caution, as the previewing function of the Administration Committee suggests. One of the first films shown at Messiah College was on the life of Alexander Graham Bell, the inventor of the telephone. Hostetter did not learn of plans to use the film until a day or two before it was to be shown. He had a long session with the student representatives who had ordered the film, reminding them that they knew movies produced in Hollywood could not be shown. He finally relented, but only after he had previewed the film and had parts of it blackened out.[59]

Entertainment films made slower progress. After some reluctance, Hostetter and his Administration Committee in 1946 allowed "Heidi" to be brought to campus, but when they discovered on previewing the film that Shirley Temple, the popular child star of Hollywood, played in it, they divided evenly on whether or not to show it, their decision finally being to tell the students that there was opposition to the film, but apparently allowing it to be run.[60] Two years later, however, the same committee took action not to approve the showing of "Tom Sawyer" or any other popular novel, although religious and non-religious films would be considered.[61]

This position was gradually relaxed, but even at the end of his presidency, Hostetter was insisting that films shown at the college be selected with considerable care. When this did not happen he was disturbed, as one evening when he attended the hamburger social given by the losing team in the Christmas card-selling contest; everyone had a "lovely time," which, however, was spoiled somewhat for Hostetter by "one picture that was shown that had better not have been shown—it passed the censors too easily."[62] And attending movies off-campus continued to be generally prohibited to students, although he allowed several Canadian students to see a film of the wedding of Queen Elizabeth, providing they went to Philadelphia rather than to a local theater to view it.[63]

A similar development took place with dramatic productions. At the beginning of his presidency, Hostetter was openly opposed to them. In a letter to Hannah Foote of Beulah College, who had obviously been inquiring what Messiah Bible College did on the issue, he reported that his faculty has taken "definite action" against plays and pageants and the wearing of costumes, which, he claimed, militates against the plain clothes of the Brethren in Christ.[64] A year later, in a letter to the president of Moody Bible Institute, he indicated that he and his colleagues have taken a stand "against the modern dramatic craze and endeavor to train our young people for more vital types of Christian service and activity."[65]

Until the late 1940s, the college held the line rather well on dramatic productions, particularly where there might be public relations implications. The result was that performances were largely confined to class nights (to which parents and friends of graduating students were invited). In 1949 Hostetter made a survey of colleges similar to Messiah (Wheaton, Houghton, Eastern Mennonite, and others), found them all opposed to the drama, and thus was more rather than less disposed to maintain a conservative stance on the issue.[66] Yet he had mixed feelings. When class plays were done well and within bounds, he was pleased, and wrote notes of commendation to the faculty advisers.[67] In the same month in which he conducted his survey of Christian colleges, he attended what he called in his diary a comic opera on "Stephen Foster's Music" given by college freshmen for the sophomores, and apparently enjoyed the performance. "It is quite a problem," he confessed, "to know just what course we should follow in respect to the question of drama in our college program."[68]

In the next year, following a study of its policy, faculty adopted a modified position on drama, which was made still more liberal in 1953.[69] And by 1955 a Platform Arts Club had begun to perform dramas for a general audience.[70] Nevertheless, considerable care was still exercised in the dramas chosen, and Hostetter seems never to have rid himself of some apprehensions about the possible negative effects of their production. In late May, 1958, after attending a class program which featured a play centering on the death of Christ and placing emphasis on Pilate and Pilate's wife, he wrote in his diary: "The stage settings were magnificent . . . . [But] it was a pretty strongly heated love play—somewhat too amorous."[71]

The same pattern was followed in sports. Hostetter's earlier position was well stated in a letter to Norman Brubaker, a member of the local congregation, in which he very reluctantly allowed some community young men to use the gymnasium for exercise. But he informed Brubaker that he was "anxious to avoid building up an athletic consciousness on the part of both students and community in relation to our gymnasium," and thus requested Brubaker to discourage attendance at the games the young men would play.[72] In fact, Brubaker, was rather fortunate, because as late as 1950 the use of the gymnasium for similar purposes was being denied to other groups, including the Mechanicsburg Ministerium Association for their basketball program.[73]

The college's sports activities were intramural for most of

Hostetter's years at Grantham. Permission had to be obtained
even to play basketball with Goshen College students when they
were once in the area.[74] When some students in 1943 played
Carlisle high school boys in a "get-up" basketball game, they were
sent home for a week, and those who were only spectators were
penalized by being confined to the campus.[75]

But gradually some flexibility occurred. By 1946 the Administration Committee was granting students the right to play outside
groups, providing that at least half in each group were alumni or
members of the Brethren in Christ or related churches.[76] Several
years later, in 1954, the same committee, at the request of Athletic
Director Ray Hostetter, permitted the college intramural baseball all stars to play a game with the Lisburn baseball team,
champions of the local Bi-County League.[77] In 1956 students
were allowed to play three basketball games with authorized
institutions, and this number was increased to five. in the following year.[78] But a committee, which included Hostetter, in 1958
refused a request for a regular schedule of extramural games on
the ground that the college was not ready for such a schedule.[79]

Despite the impression this may give, Hostetter did enjoy
sports. Whenever he was able, he attended the school's field day
events, where he was an enthusiastic spectator. At the youth
conferences which he served as a speaker, he took part in the
games, at one playing baseball so vigorously that he injured his
arm. He took pride in his sons' athletic achievements, noting in
his diary for one field day that Glenn had broken the school's
record for cross-country running.[80]

And in the fall annual picnics he usually joined the students in
their baseball games. An entry in his diary for September 23,
1953, refers with obvious delight to one of these picnics: "I
umpired a softball game. The best pitcher for whom I umpired
was Ruth Eckert. Faye Wise also did some good pitching. Other
pitchers not as good were Carl Martin, Robert Musser, David
Brubaker. It was a pleasant afternoon." But Hostetter was also
conscious of the views of his denomination, and he insisted that at
a place like Messiah College, the major part of the school's work
was to equip students for Christian service; the minor part, at
best, was sports.

VII

"Keeping the Atmosphere of the College Wholesome"

*T*he conservative style of the college, whether on the religious or social level, was largely accepted without much difficulty by the students. In part, this was because they usually came from home and church backgrounds that, if anything, were still more conservative than what they found at Grantham; but in part, it was also because they had a staff and faculty who related well to them, as trite as that may sound. Such was certainly the case with relations between Hostetter and the students. Few college presidents, the evidence suggests, have been more admired by students than this president.

"Father figure" perhaps best describes the students' impression of Hostetter, an impression created by a variety of activities and attitudes on Hostetter's part. Thus, especially in the early years, he assisted many students to find jobs and live-in arrangements in the community, and over the years he and his wife helped to pay a number of students' school expenses.[1] He learned both the first and last names of each student; one of the ways in which he accomplished this was to look up and down the row of students at chapel time, trying to fix a name to each face, and making a note to himself when he was unable to do so (leading some students to think that the president was taking attendance). And still as a father figure, he gave students practical advice (often in chapel service) on sex, keeping their rooms clean, washing their clothes, and taking baths.[2]

The attention that he gave to students in need, particularly in the earlier years of his presidency, further confirms this image. His correspondence, for example, contains letters to parents reporting that he had visited their son or daughter in the hospital and explaining in detail the student's illness. When Mildred Stump was hospitalized at Carlisle, he visited her several times in the hospital, wrote letters to her father, arranged for her to go back to Indiana, and personally took her to the train. A few months later, when he was about to travel through her state, he wrote to Mildred to say that he was planning on stopping to see her.[3] Similarly with Phoebe Jantz, whose parents requested Hostetter to take their daughter to a doctor for a medical examination of her back which had been injured before going to Grantham. Hostetter did so and then wrote to her parents that after a long conversation with Phoebe, he was sending her home. He assured them that whatever he did for Phoebe he did "gladly and at no time felt that it was a burden to have her here."[4]

To judge from student letters and memories, he was adept at giving appropriate words of encouragement—to homesick students, to older students having difficulty getting back into the routine of class life, to students who had lost members of their families, to students needing confidence that they could indeed do college work.[5] Ralph Palmer is an illustration, as his letter to Hostetter shows:

> I shall never forget the kindness and concern shown me on your part when I first came to Messiah College, a poor country boy with many fears, doubts and wonderments about the future and what it held for me. I shall never forget the experience of entering your office for the first time to discuss with you the possibilities of enrolling at Messiah College. The experience of a common farm boy speaking with a college president was quite different than what I had anticipated. The interest you showed [in] my personal problems left a lasting impression but the thing that I am sure I shall never forget was what followed our much like a father-son talk. It was when you arose from your chair, walked to the opposite side of the desk where I was sitting, and invited me to kneel with you in prayer so that we might talk to our Heavenly Father about my concerns. As we arose from prayer I left your office light-hearted . . . .[6]

Palmer's experience suggests some of Hostetter's counselling practices. He had an open door policy for students, too much so for the sake of his other work, it would appear in hindsight. Busy man though he was, students seem always to have felt that they had as much time with him as they wanted; as a faculty member has observed, he never gave those signs, one so often sees, that the interview should now be ended.[7] As in the case of Palmer, the sessions usually ended with prayer, particularly if students were in difficulty of some nature. "Shut in with the President in his office and behind closed doors," one student has recalled, "was not a terrifying experience but rather a pleasure."[8]

Given these qualities as a counsellor, it is not surprising to find students after graduating returning to him for advice. In 1937 Harold Engle wrote to him from Greenville College for direction in his future career in medicine; Hostetter replied with instructions about keeping one's heart open to the Lord's leading, and with assurance that he had Harold on his "definite" prayer list for young people.[9] Carlton Wittlinger wrote from Taylor University in late 1937 to say that he would be at Grantham over the weekend and that he wanted to talk to Hostetter about one of the most important decisions of his life (an obvious reference to becoming engaged to his future wife Fay).[10] And from Garlin, Kentucky, Feyline Ballou asked questions concerning Christ's second-coming, adding in her letter, "due to the fact that I have the utmost confidence in you I can talk to you as I have."[11]

Many of these same qualities are reflected in the spiritual leadership he gave the students. He spoke frequently in chapel; in the pulpit he was warm and often humorous with a "never ending supply of stories and jokes," as one student has said.[12] He could find time in a chapel service to read a humorous valentine poem from the girls inviting the boys to a party, and on one snowy day in December, 1951, instead of preaching, he read snow poems, including Lowell's "The First Snowfall" and part of Whittier's "Snowbound."[13]

Usually, of course, Hostetter's messages had a more directly religious content. Above all, students found them practical and inspiring. Writing of her recent memories of chapel services, one student expressed well what many others have written or spoken: Hostetter's messages were so practical that "I was filled with a longing to experience such a life with Christ [as Hostetter described]. Your messages were reinforced by your daily life. I knew you were preaching that which you yourself were pursuing. This only intensified my desire for a true Christian life."[14]

This spiritual leadership Hostetter effectively used with students at altar services during revival meetings. He tried to moderate a tendency toward emotionalism that had carried over in these services from earlier years and that was a part of the home congregations of many of the students. In the winter revival of 1953, for example, he was called at midnight by a student to come to the chapel to help pray for another student. When he arrived, he found a group of boys "praying passionately." Hostetter remained with them for nearly three hours.[15]

Still in other ways, Hostetter moved among the students in familiar and benevolent fashion. Dressed in work clothes, he joined them on campus days to clean up the grounds and buildings (one year, when a student's hands began to bleed from pulling weeds he took the student into his house to wash and bandage her hands).[16] He also liked to go to student parties when he had time to do so. Typical was the party for winter term students which he attended in March, 1951; it was a pleasant two hours, his diary notes, with pictures and games (especially pleasant, one supposes, because Hostetter won all the crockinole contests in which he played).[17]

This good relationship with students helps to explain how his firm approach to discipline was not usually negatively received. Particularly toward the end of the school year and the advent of spring, he would press his staff to begin to tighten up on enforcing the rules; and he would warn students (usually in chapel) that they could jeopardize their entire year by one bad act at the end. His favorite story to students at this time of the year was of S. R. Smith who one day carefully washed his new car to drive to Harrisburg. The car was still shining clean until on his return he hit a mud puddle at the entrance to the campus. With much the same effect he gave a chapel talk in late May, 1955, in which, according to the diary, he "reviewed the year and recognized (1) Fermentation as a scientific process that works out the dirt, (2) Fomentation as the result of undisciplined persons agitating. Suggested this was the first year that digitalstoxicosis (holding hands) gained epidemic proportions. Made the effort to discourage the practice." Some students still remember that chapel talk for the long, unknown (and thus successfully used) word.[18]

He was famous among students for the almost uncanny ability with which he could identify trouble. When some students in the late 1930s one night made a loud racket with tin cans outside the dean of men's residence in Hill View (later Smith Hall), Hostetter had all their names by the next morning.[19] On one Halloween some boys placed a pole across the entrance to the campus and smeared it with molasses; unfortunately for them, Hostetter was the first to come along in his car, and in removing the pole dirtied his suit. He soon knew who the culprits were; their penalty was to pay the dry cleaning bill.[20] He had a way, one of his teachers has observed, of showing up at the corners of the campus whenever questionable deeds were about to be perpetrated.

Several stories of how he handled discipline problems still circulate widely among his former students. One involves a farm wagon, which some students during the night took apart and then reassembled in the lobby outside the chapel in Old Main. Nothing was said until chapel, but of course, everyone was waiting to see what would happen. Hostetter got up with his characteristic smile playing about his mouth and eyes and said that circumstances of the day reminded him of young Saul being sent by his father to find the asses that were lost. He had always assumed, Hostetter continued, that the animals which pulled wagons had four legs, two long ears, a tail and went "hee haw." He ended with the words of Saul's servant who reported, "Behold we have found them." And then he sat down. The students who had placed the wagon in the lobby were identified by their displeasure with this allusion to them as asses, but removed the wagon without further word from anyone.[21]

One day Hostetter appeared in chapel with a paper bag in his hand. He held it up for students to see and to guess its contents. No one guessed correctly, so he revealed the mystery by saying that it contained the gum that had been laboriously scraped from underneath the chapel pews. (It would be interesting to know how effective this object lesson was.)[22]

A fashionable joke among students was to set an alarm clock to go off during a chapel service. How Hostetter handled one such occasion can be told by Hostetter himself through his diary, although the story is still current. While he was speaking on intercessory prayer as an expression of religious life, "an alarm clock placed in the pulpit began to ring. I quit speaking and waited until it ran down. I then asked who thought that was a good joke to stand. No one stood. I then asked those who thought such an act was bad taste and deserved the reproach of all to stand and every student and staff member stood to his feet." Eight days later the culprit came trembling to the president's office. "What shall we do with him?" Hostetter asked himself.[23] He was not certain whether to accept the student's apology or to give the matter over to the personnel staff to handle, but he finally decided on the latter (probably because the student had considerable potential for such escapades).[24]

While Hostetter expected rules to be obeyed, he had a good sense of where the limits of discipline lay with his students, and spent considerable time counselling them in order to head off trouble. In the 1954-55 school year some agitation developed over the kind and quantity of food the college served. So he went over one evening to have a long talk with the two students who had been spearheading the trouble; both, according to the diary, "responded quite well." Shortly afterward he took some time in the student assembly to explain by charts how students were getting good food for the money paid.[25] Similarly, he spent the most of one day in early 1950 in talking to some men students, trying to relieve tensions that had developed over a disciplinary action that had been taken against them. "Lord give us wisdom, sympathy and understanding," he prayed in his diary. "It is very important that we maintain standards and at the same time keep the atmosphere of the college wholesome."[26]

He did his counselling and disciplining without rancor, sometimes with humor, and frequently indirectly because he understood that the kind of students who came to Messiah were sometimes punished enough simply by their conscience. Once he came across some girls playing monopoly after midnight (long past the time the rules required them to be in bed). One of them in later years wrote to Hostetter: "I shall never forget the kindness with which we were reprimanded. We were not scolded or spoken to too harshly but we were very sorry for our actions and resolved never again to be guilty of such a misdemeanor."[27] A student who, with others, was making the swinging bridge across the

Yellow Breeches sway violently also later reminded Hostetter how "seeing us from your home, you came down [and] very gently and kindly told us of the inadvisability of our actions."[28]

He came home one night from a trip to find two students in difficulty for having brought a neighbor's goat into the dining room and milked it (because the kitchen staff had not allowed them to have milk on their apple dumplings). Their penalty was to leave school quietly the next morning and to work three days on a chicken farm. But while one of them had a car, they had no money to buy gas. When Hostetter came across them, he got them to tell their story, which he found amusing (at least the goat part), then gave them three dollars from his wallet and some gas from the school pump, and told them to take their punishment like men.[29]

Hostetter's correspondence contains many letters from former students who wrote to ask forgiveness for some wrong that remained unconfessed. They found in Hostetter a ready and generous forgiver. One student asked forgiveness for one night "raiding" the kitchen (a friend who accompanied him had a key). Hostetter replied in typical fashion: "I assure you that you are heartily forgiven for this offense, and you can count the matter as being placed under the blood," and then went on to invite him to the homecoming taking place in a few days.[30] To a former student who sent him $1.25 because he had once cheated on his time when working for the college, Hostetter wrote: "It is such honesty and frank confession in our lives which is necessary if we would be true disciples of the Lord Jesus. God bless you. Please be assured the matter is completely settled."[31] A student who had cleaned his office confessed that she once read some papers on his desk. Hostetter granted her "free and full forgiveness" and went on to say, "Satan would stir these things up in our minds from time to time, but please remember when God forgives He also 'forgets'."[32]

A father himself, Hostetter empathized with parents whose children received disciplinary action. He appears to have been careful to keep parents informed of their children's position and attitudes in such circumstances; he encouraged them to have patience, and often in later years used the difficulties he had had with some of his own sons to show that he understood what they must be feeling.

One of his last letters in this respect was written a few months before he retired as president, and concerned a student who was being sent home for various reasons, including smoking. He reported to the parents that he had counselled three times with their son. "Please do not give up in faith and in effort for your dear son," he wrote. "We have four sons in our home and although they grew up on a college campus, they had some of the difficulties which boys have . . . . Today, . . . the four sons have Christian homes and happy families."[33]

With relations such as these, it is understandable that Hostetter became a model for many of his students. In fact, hero worship is not far from their expressions. "Your life was so in tune with our Lord," William Hoke told Hostetter, "that I saw in you a person that spoke to me of Christ."[34] Another former student praised Hostetter by telling him: "Your Christian character has challenged me to a life of humility and service. As I met you in the classroom, in the chapel, or in your office, you always left me with this impression, 'He has been with Jesus!' "[35] And in 1940, the *Clarion* staff in dedicating the yearbook to him, declared that Hostetter "represents for us in a most intimate capacity the perfection of our Christian ideals . . . ." Such adulation was harvested in abundance by Hostetter both during and following his years as president.

Part of the praise came, however indirectly, in requests by many students and former students that he perform the ceremonies for their wedding. The honorarium they gave him for doing so he returned to the couple as a gift from him and his wife.

A parallel relationship existed with his staff and faculty. Undoubtedly this was in part owing to the ease and frequency with which he praised them, publicly and privately, often in personal letters. They were, he kept saying, his most valuable assets, without whom he could not effectively be president. Virtually always, in his correspondence at least, he addressed them as co-laborers. Such commendation must have gone far to offset the small wages the faculty and staff received.

A letter in 1954 to George Lenhert, superintendent of buildings and grounds, is typical of the many that he wrote. He had intended to write to express appreciation for the excellent job Lenhert was doing of keeping the campus and building looking clean (particularly since he assumed Lenhert heard from people only when he did something to displease them—in that their offices were alike). But then he came on campus to see Lenhert sweeping the steps and sidewalk in front of Old Main, a job that his subordinates should have done. That, Hostetter said, made it "doubly important" that he write to express his appreciation for Lenhert's work.[36]

The faculty retreats in the 1950s at Kenbrook camp are good illustrations of the easy relationship between Hostetter and his faculty. According to his diary, he enjoyed the relaxed atmosphere that allowed him to joke freely and to play volleyball and horseshoe with his staff, and they to tease him about his snoring ("rocks and salts!" he reports them saying).[37]

Apologies to and defense of his faculty were part of Hostetter's approach to his office. A fine example of the first is his asking forgiveness of the Administration Committee for taking a case involving the disciplining of one of his sons out of the hands of the committee. It was inadvertently done, he explained, but nevertheless wrong of him to do so.[38] Like all presidents, he found frequent opportunity to defend his staff. His customary response to criticism of them was that the college hired people for what they could do, not for what they could not do. When students complained that because of poor teaching they were not getting much out of a course, Hostetter reminded them that the college had a library where they could easily make up for what they said they were not receiving in class.

Hostetter's relationship with his staff may be illustrated in his interest in the Harvey Sakimura family. The Sakimuras were of Japanese descent who had lived in California, but because of the war had lost their home and florist shop, had been interned in makeshift army barracks for two years, and were working on a farm in Michigan when Hostetter heard about them. He stopped to see the Sakimuras on one of his trips through Michigan, and arranged for them to come to Grantham to work as the college caretaker of lawns. But this was still wartime, and Hostetter received threatening letters and telephone calls about the Sakimuras' presence at the college. But he stood firm and the Sakimuras remained. Perhaps this in part explains why he took a special interest in the family, each Christmas taking them a basket of fruit and being lavish in his praise of Sakimura as a gardener.[39]

A few of Hostetter's faculty have suggested that in the latter years of his presidency, Hostetter's relationships with his faculty were less easy than earlier, and that this was because in a college that was gradually developing into a more mature and liberal arts institution, a less direct hand in the conduct of affairs would have been preferable. Despite such reservations, Hostetter's relationships with his faculty would still have been the envy of most other college presidents.

In a quite literal sense, he was a teacher among his teachers. With the exception of about six semesters, he taught class continuously throughout his twenty-six years at Grantham, usually about two a semester, but sometimes more. Although this was partly determined by financial considerations, it was also his choice. "I have felt," he wrote in late 1959 to his successor-elect, "that teaching ties one closer to the college."[40]

He taught a variety of courses in Bible, theology, and Christian education. To believe his diary, all of them were his favorites (clearly he enjoyed teaching), but some stood out more than others, especially Pastoral Theology, Ethics, the Psalms, and the Prophets. "It was a great joy to teach Jeremiah again" he commented in his diary in March, 1950. "What a stimulating character was this faithful O.T. prophet!"[41] In a later year, in a course on the Minor Prophets, he was moved as he studied Hosea with his class, many of them ministers or ministers-to-be: "We had a stirring time with Hosea. This great book with its message of God's great love and the nature of true repentance moved me deeply."[42] "Stimulating" is how he frequently described his classes in Ethics, where one of his major concerns was to make students understand the differences between "flimsy popular philosophical theories and morals" like those of John Dewey and Rousseau, and the eternal truths of the Bible.[43]

But the Psalms were his greatest delight. His diary contains many expressions such as, "It is refreshing to me to review these inspiring Hebrew hymns." In fact, he so much enjoyed his course in the Psalms that he planned for years to write a book on them in his retirement, but his hope was never fulfilled.[44]

His teaching method was lecture with some discussion. As he warmed to his subject, he would walk back and forth, chin in his hand. Stories and chuckles would lighten the pace. Intellectual curiosity for Brethren in Christ students was frequently first aroused in one of his classes, as Eber Dourte has testified:

> I was a farm boy. I rarely read books (we didn't have time). In Ethics class when he began to expound on the Epicureans and the Stoics I found myself in new territory. And when he put them up against the Scriptures and showed their difference, well, that was wonderful. One of the most inspiring things that ever happened to me was Dr. Hostetter's introducing Dr. Leslie Morrison's *From Chaos to Character* in Ethics class. It was a new level of philosophical thinking for me. Dr. Hostetter led us into that for a great and growing experience for me as a boy from the farm.[45]

Long after they had left the college, some students were still using the notes and materials they obtained in his classes for their own work in Sunday schools, Vacation Bible schools, or the ministry.[46] Hostetter himself estimated that his many years of teaching the course in Administration of Religious Education was "vitally related" to the growth and spread of the Vacation Bible school movement in the denomination.[47]

The greatest fault in his teaching was his frequent absences from class because of administrative or church and committee obligations. For Hostetter, however, the absences were not unmixed evils, for in his travels he virtually always took student papers and exams along to read, in one case even on a trip to Haiti and Santo Domingo, during which a Mennonite Central Committee staff member who was accompanying him helped to correct and mark the answers.[48]

All of this is a rather striking picture. Given a different time and locale (such as a larger, secular college) would he have appeared as impressive a college administrator and educator as these chapters make him out to be? Perhaps not. But for his place and people his giant stature seems well earned.

Not least as a factor in measuring his stature was the ability with which he held the lines on students without causing their resentment, while at the same time nudging the college's constituency toward accepting the new and expanding visions of the college. Many church colleges during the years of Hostetter's presidency knew the tensions inherent in a situation where students wanted more and the constituency hoped to maintain the status quo. Wherever such tension was successfully resolved there one could find the administrative and personal grace and skill of a C. N. Hostetter, Jr.

His retirement from the presidency at the end of June, 1960, resulted from no sudden decision on his part. He had begun already in the early 1950s to think about the time of leaving office. Two factors were especially important in persuading him to resign well in advance of retirement age. One was the experience of his friend Ernest Miller, president of Goshen College, who Hostetter knew left his presidency against his will. Hostetter spoke on several occasions with Miller before the latter's resignation, and wrote him a warm, encouraging letter after the event. Miller's case persuaded him that he must not hold the reins of office too long, and should resign while people regretted his going.

He also determined to resign because he wanted time to concentrate on some other activities while still in good health. There was, as we shall see, much work to be done with the Mennonite Central Committee, and he wanted to travel in the church, as well as to do some writing.

With such thoughts in mind, he submitted his resignation to the Board of Trustees in 1957. They refused to accept it, arguing that the Greater Messiah Development campaign could not proceed without his leadership. But they did agree that his resignation would become effective in 1960.

Hostetter's leave-taking of the presidency appears to have been without trauma or second thoughts. He spent appropriate time in introducing his successor, Arthur Climenhaga, to his office. In June, he and his wife began moving their household goods into the new house on campus built on land that the trustees had given to them. His last work in his office was to dictate a letter of thanks to all who had contributed to a fund to endow a chair of Theology in his honor (to be called the C. N. Hostetter, Jr., Chair of Theology).[49] Late in the afternoon of the same day (June 30), in a short ceremony on the lawn by Old Main, he handed over the keys of his office to the new president. His long years of service as president had come to an end.

VIII

"Skillful Moderation"

*A*s this study has already suggested, Hostetter's career as college president was only one, although the major, side of a many-faceted churchmanship. The guiding passion of his life was to serve God through the church. He could do that well through the oldest of the denomination's schools. But that position alone could not hold his enthusiasm for service. The numerous other ways in which he ministered in the Brethren in Christ Church is the subject of this chapter.

First, his ministry on the local level. On coming to Grantham in 1934, the Hostetters became members of the local congregation, and he was accorded "full powers" in his office as minister, which meant taking his turn in preaching with the other ministers of the church.[1] In 1936 the congregation, in rejecting the idea of a salaried minister, created the office of supervising pastor with provision for some offerings, and elected Hostetter to the office.[2] In the next year the members decided to replace their nonresident bishop, C. N. Hostetter, Sr., with a resident bishop, and voted Hostetter into that position.[3] He served as bishop of the district until 1957, all the years without pay (except for an occasional offering), in the fashion of all Brethren in Christ bishops in those years.

The Grantham District was a small one. Its center was the local congregation meeting in the college chapel in Old Main. In time, Hostetter came to have oversight of two other groups, although neither was closely tied to the Grantham congregation, somewhat in contrast to other districts in the denomination. Rana Villa near Shiremanstown began in 1929 as a community church, but over the years Brethren in Christ people from Grantham, including college students, had provided most of the leadership. The small congregation technically came under Hostetter's charge in 1939 as a home mission assignment, but was loosely considered as part of the Grantham district until dropped by the district in 1956.[4] Moore's church, several miles to the east of Grantham, had started as a Sunday school in 1946 following services held in an abandoned church building by two Messiah students, Elbert Smith and Cleon Haight, and was brought into the district in the following year.[5]

He carried for his bishopric a pastor's heart. Thus when confessions had to be made (in earlier years, the church believed that repentance should often be followed by public confession), Hostetter would characteristically stand by the one confessing, sometimes with a supporting hand on the person's arm or shoulder. Similarly, on one occasion at a funeral when only two relatives of the deceased attended, he left his seat in the audience and went to the front of the chapel to sit by them in a gesture of comfort and support.[6]

Hostetter's strong attachment to his district may be read in many diary entries. On his way home from California in 1949, he sent each family a personal message, even though this meant getting off the train at Tuscon and later at El Paso until he had bought enough cards for each home. Shortly after he returned home he preached in a Sunday morning service in which, he noted, the Lord gave him a burden for the people and "many spoke of the blessing received."[7] "I do not preach very often to the folks at Grantham," he once wrote, "but I do enjoy preaching here—the older folks are responsive and the young people challenge me."[8]

This does not mean that there were no problems for Hostetter as bishop; quite the contrary. A "liberal" and a "conservative" element existed side by side, and had their representatives on the official board. As a result, the official board meetings were often strenuous sessions, at least to judge by his diary. Hostetter did not object to this; in fact, he thought it wholesome for feelings to come out on this level, but it did, as he once said, require "skillful moderation."[9] In one board meeting, some members attacked plans for the Sunday school program and preparations for General Conference to be held that year at Grantham. "God gave me wisdom," Hostetter confided to his diary, "and delivered me from the sin of Moses who lost his patience as a leader and said, 'Must I bring you water out of the rock?' "[10]

One of Hostetter's continuing concerns as bishop was the relationship of the college-church group with the people of the community. There had for some years been some distance between at least some members of the two groups, fed, it appears, by something of a "holier-than-thou" attitude which some in the community perceived attached to the college and plain people in the "church on the hill."

The congregation's participation in the local fire company was a case in point. Hostetter led his church board in a meeting in July, 1949, in a discussion on the question of whether Brethren in Christ could be part of the company because of some of its activities. The board, according to his diary, agreed "to encourage our people to take an active part in the Fire Co. so as to help eliminate the features that do not interest the church people, or those that are objectionable to them."[11]

Two years later, he noted that virtually no one from the community was attending the tent meetings sponsored by the congregation. That led him to devote one Sunday evening to a talk on the problem; "I spoke an hour and ten minutes and tried to say some very frank things."[12] He kept at the issue and was rewarded by change, however slowly, so that at the July 4 picnic in 1962 he could, in his diary, rejoice in the attendance and add; "Our church is getting a stronger hold on the community. Thank you, Father, for this!"[13]

Some in the congregation thought that building a new church off campus and in the village would be the solution to the community relations problem. Hostetter did not favor this idea and considered it as much an anti-college feeling as a concern for community. But he did not oppose the decision to form a committee in 1947 (of which he was a member) to study the needs of the community and to determine what possibility there was of raising the money for a building. A member of the congregation encouraged the move by offering to donate land for the site. But upon investigation and after free discussion encouraged by Hostetter, it became apparent that the congregation as a whole was not interested in the move.[14] Hostetter breathed easier with this failure, and then less than two years later arranged for the college to donate land on campus for the new church and for the college to pay half the cost of construction and maintenance.[15]

This suggests Hostetter's strong concern for a close college-congregational tie, which he himself symbolized in his offices of president and bishop. The tie between the two groups was symbolized in other ways: the sharing of the college chapel in Old Main, the attendance of students in the congregation's services, college faculty and staff holding membership in the congregation and filling many of the teaching and official positions, and the financial support of the college by the congregation (for many years it usually gave more only to the missions program of the denomination).

The tie may also be seen in their joint revival services, and most notably when Hostetter served as evangelist, which he did four times, first in 1936. He seems to have taken these revival services even more seriously than the many he held elsewhere. The one in the fall of 1955 is typical. On Sunday, October 30, he spent the day in meditation and prayer, and in the evening began the revival by preaching on "The Glory of the Gospel," but was disappointed because "the message did not catch fire as it should." Through the week, he met with the students for their 6:15 a.m. prayer meetings, and then frequently spent the rest of the day in his room "waiting on God." He began to fast.

But still there were no results. So he began to examine his own life: "God laid a great burden on my heart and searched my heart very closely this afternoon. I have had pride and self-seeking in my life. Oh God cleanse my heart from all of this so my life may be a channel thru which God's mighty power can be transmitted." By the end of the week the revival "broke," as the Brethren used to say. "This forenoon," Hostetter wrote in a different tone, "I prayed and waited on God again. Oh how near the Lord came! Do control my life in its entirety by thy will. Forgive me where I have taken my own way."[16]

One of Hostetter's joys as bishop was to host the annual General Conference when it came to the Grantham district. His file for the General Conference of 1954 shows him engaged in the detailed planning and physical labor that went into the preparations. He chaired the committees and personally carried on a large volume of correspondence—to obtain bed and mattresses, to ask about a supply of meal tickets from Roxbury, to request people to serve during the conference, to requisition tents for sleeping, and afterward to send many letters of thanks to people who had helped to serve. After the conference he helped to take down the tents, clean up the campus, and rearrange the furniture, recording at the end of the day: "I worked harder carrying mattresses and beds to the 4th floor of Girls Dorm than I have done for a while."[17] That a college president and bishop should be doing such work seems not to have been a question with him.

In 1957, with the amalgamation of the many districts into five regional conferences, Hostetter ceased to be bishop. He was himself a participant in bringing about this new arrangement. With three other bishops he met with the General Executive Board in 1954 to help determine the date for the new organization to be effected, and to recommend that in the meantime the denomination move toward pastoral support and better local organizaton.[18] When the new regional organization was about to be put into effect, it was Hostetter who, in an article in the *Evangelical Visitor,* justified and explained the plan to the denomination, and who also warned pastors not to misuse the opportunities provided by their new or prospective salaried position.[19]

In 1962 the Bishops' Nominating Committee nominated Hostetter as bishop of the Allegheny Regional Conference. His diary by its simple recording of the fact suggests that he would have accepted the appointment, but because of later developments, each bishop was returned to the conference over which he had been presiding.[20] As in his resignation from the college presidency, however, he does not appear to have regretted leaving the bishopric or missing the reappointment that seemed to be his in 1962.

A major role for Hostetter in the denomination continued to be with the Home Mission Board. The position of secretary to which he was appointed in 1925 he filled until 1946, when he became chairman.

As secretary, Hostetter took care of many details of the home missions program, apart from the responsibility he shared with others of supervising missions in a designated area (all without salary, it goes without saying). Among his correspondence are numerous letters on such details as reminding workers to send their quarterly reports to the *Evangelical Visitor,* arranging for tents, furnishings, and workers for summer revivals, and giving advice to young or inexperienced workers. He helped to make decisions about construction of church property, arranged for fire insurance on mission property, obtained railroad rate favors for mission workers, advised them, if necessary, on how to get to their work (as in a long letter to Martha Sentz of Pennsylvania before she set out for Paddockwood, Saskatchewan), and obtained visas for workers to cross the Canadian-United States border.[21]

Each member of the Home Mission Board had oversight of a number of mission churches, usually in proximity to where he lived. Hostetter's charges were for many years those in Pennsylvania that lay west of the Susquehanna River and included congregations in the Altoona-Blandburg and Saxton-Breezewood area, as well as Granville and Canoe Creek. From 1945 onward the congregations were Altoona, Janesville, Canoe Creek, Ganister, Blandburg, Liberty Valley, and later Hunlock Creek.[22]

These charges took considerable amounts of Hostetter's time. He attended their council meetings and attempted to be at all their love feasts. He frequently served as their evangelist, spoke at their Bible Conferences, homecomings, and anniversaries, officiated at reception and baptismal services, and dedicated their buildings.

Not least were the trips he made to mediate differences of opinion among the members. In one, he had to settle a dispute arising out of leadership problems (the minister wanted to control everyone, including the Sunday school superintendent); in another, he had to deal with some who thought their pastor was stubborn and not filled with the Spirit (one member wrote to Hostetter that if he did not "send a Holy Ghost man [for pastor] that's on fire for God and preach the fire down from heaven that it can splash out on to the congregation and get us back where we once was *[sic],* all you will need to do is lock the door and put the key in your pockets as the spirit of God is being lifted").[23] At a council meeting of the same congregation in 1952, he stood "flat-footed" in defense of the pastor when the latter was sharply attacked for accepting members on an associate membership basis.

But he became attached to this congregation. This was partly because he could talk frankly to them and yet retain their respect, as he wrote to fellow board member Albert Engle after a meeting with them in 1952:

They gave me quite an emotional farewell on Sunday morning. The interesting point is that most of the people who expressed their appreciation publicly particularly emphasized the "spanking" that Brother Hostetter gave them. Tears flowed freely and the folks were generous in their praise. However, remembering how many times we had to speak in terms of very frank and pointed corrections, it was encouraging to note the responsive attitude from these folks.[24]

The custom during those years was for two or more members of the Home Mission Board to accompany each other to mission churches when an especially difficult problem arose, the second member thereby providing moral support and adding to the strength of tone by which the Home Mission Board spoke. In this role, Hostetter visited mission churches beyond his own territory, often with Abner Martin; Martin, in turn, travelled with Hostetter. Martin, an older, patient, and soft-spoken minister made a good companion for Hostetter. The two became close friends, sharing many confidences, and, in their correspondence, even giving each other advice on raising chickens. Referring to the new mountain churches in central Pennsylvania, the *Evangelical Visitor* in 1958 declared that "much of the privilege of leading these babes in Christ into the fold of the Brethren in Christ came through the counsel and guidance of Brother Abner Martin and Brother C. N. Hostetter, Jr."[25]

Not all problems for the Home Mission Board, unfortunately, were confined to Hostetter's and Martin's geographic area of responsibility. Wherever they occurred, Hostetter, as secretary, tended to be somewhere close to the center, helping to solve the issues. Several representative cases will illustrate the frequent counselling and mediating nature of his work.

In one mission station, a worker had served as superintendent for years, but now was being difficult in her relations with other workers. The board decided to replace her with a man, but invited her to remain at the mission. She quickly informed Hostetter she would not stay, and refused to answer the letters he sent her. She did not leave the city, however, and this led some people to criticize Hostetter and the board for a cavalier treatment of a faithful servant of the cross.[26]

Chicago Mission had similar difficulties. One worker who had been at the mission for twenty-five years, was now becoming a hindrance to the work and needed to be moved. Hostetter gave her a choice: either move to the Messiah Home in Harrisburg or go to live with relatives on the West Coast; in either case, the Home Mission Board would pay her expenses. This approach, however, was not effective, for some time later Hostetter reported to the members of the board that despite many sessions he had spent with the worker, she insisted on staying in Chicago. Worse yet, she was going from door to door soliciting money and sympathy for herself.[27]

Another worker was reassigned to the Chicago Mission under the mistaken impression that mission superintendent Sarah Bert would accept her, regardless of her reputation as a "trouble maker." Hostetter now had to make the most out of a bad situation. He wrote to the worker to extend best wishes on her return to Chicago, but suggested that she would need to make a complete readjustment so that "fellowship is sweet and unconstrained among all the family." If she could not do this, she would need to retire from the work, which she could do without disgracing herself or "putting a blot" on the mission by going back to school. Messiah College would help to finance her school expenses.[28]

In a third case at Chicago mission, Sarah Bert herself became something of a problem for the Home Mission Board because she found difficulty, after many years of strong and effective service, in giving up the leadership of Chicago Mission to her replacement, Carl Carlson. Even after the change in leadership was officially made, she exercised the office de facto for some time. This required great patience on the part of Hostetter and especially for Carlson, but Sarah Bert's character was so strong and her regard in the denomination so high that neither one of them had sufficient determination to move too far against her will.[29]

A perennial trouble spot for the Home Mission Board was the mission at Arcadia, Florida. By 1933 the situation had deteriorated to the point where the board decided it was necessary to visit the troubled congregation, and thus sent Hostetter and two other board members to investigate. According to the report of the three men, they talked freely to people who had been inconsistent in their Christian life and at the center of conflicts, advised and exhorted to unity and harmony, and decided to continue the work.[30]

The most persistent of Arcadia's problems centered in one member of the congregation who had been critical of the church leadership almost from the beginning of his association with the group. He intensified his criticism when, after being served with an injunction by the local court from tearing down a building which had been seized for what was claimed as a non-payment of taxes, he was censured and disfellowshipped.

But the man was not the kind of person to take such action lying down. For years until his death in the mid-1940s, he campaigned to make the board and the local pastor apologize for their action. His campaign included the printing and circulation of broadsides, airing his grievances over the local radio and threatening to do the same in each of the areas where board members resided, and vowing to take the board to court. As secretary, Hostetter was the chief recipient of the protagonist's letters, which he largely ignored, revealing on one occasion to Board Chairman M. G. Engle, that he rarely got past the first paragraph or two.

After several years, the General Executive Board heard the case, and shortly afterward, Hostetter had a meeting in Carlisle with the man. Neither effort was successful. In an attempt to be conciliatory, Hostetter admitted that the nature of the case troubled him, thus seeming to suggest that there may have been error on both sides. The former Arcadia member later used that statement to attack Hostetter both publicly and privately. He wrote to Hostetter, challenging him to make the matter public. "An innocent person has no fear," he said. "They don't have to cover their back tracks .... They don't need to fear for all men to know the truth about their past lives." After some words about repentance, confession, restitution, and forsaking of sin, he demanded of Hostetter: "Go Thou and do likewise." Hostetter made a final effort at reconciliation in 1944 by meeting with him in Florida and by writing a letter in which, with obvious purpose, he called the man brother twelve times, but all to no avail.[31]

From 1925 to 1952, the Home Mission Board issued ministerial licenses, a responsibility that had potential, often realized, for other kinds of difficulty. The case of Charles Eshelman in the 1920's is illustrative.

Eshelman had been called to the ministry by his home district, but when at the time of his examination he declared that he would not follow the district's wishes to grow a beard, the district officials refused to proceed with his installation. Without their support, Eshelman could not obtain the license for which he had applied. Even kind Abner Martin took a hard line: since the sisters of the church had to "get in line," Eshelman should too. M. G. Engle agreed with Martin.

But Hostetter came to Eshelman's defense. He argued that if Eshelman were given a license he could at least do the evangelistic work to which he felt called, and perhaps this in time would lead to ordination.[32] But when the district officials got wind of this suggestion, they made it clear that they would be "dismayed" if the license were granted over their strong objections. Someone in the district sent out the rumor that at one time Eshelman had been placed under some kind of probation. Hostetter traced the story down, determined that it was false, and made certain that all involved in the case knew the truth.[33]

The outcome of this maneuvering and of Hostetter's championship was that Eshelman received his license. Two years later, after Eshelman had moved to Grantham, Hostetter successfully pressed the Grantham district bishop, Wilber Snider, to give Eshelman ordination, emphasizing that Eshelman by this time had surely proved himself in evangelistic work to be worthy of that privilege.[34]

Finances were a constant problem for the Home Mission Board: the Brethren for many years talked about missions more than they gave money to support them. The problem prompted Hostetter as early as 1926 to project a plan to make mission churches financially independent as soon as possible, a plan that eventually was followed in principle. Reclassify missions, Hostetter suggested, in two kinds: pastorates and missions. Pastorates would be those abler than missions to help themselves; the leader would need to supply the rest of the financial support.[35] The implication was that in time the mission pastorates should become completely self-supporting and take their place in the denomination as a regularly constituted congregation.

Apart from any other consideration, and following some old-fashioned thinking, Hostetter was convinced that congregations became healthier by supporting their own work, however difficult that may be for them to do. Such thinking was behind the letter he wrote to M. G. Engle in 1939 concerning the relatively new work at Blandburg and Rainsburg: "We must begin more and more to have every congregation stand on its own feet. If we can help the folks to finance their building projects and then leave the responsibility for paying them and improving and keeping them in order very largely to the local congregation it is the proper thing to do."[36]

This may have been a move in the right direction, but it was far from solving the larger problem, which especially during the depression years was extremely acute. In 1932 finances were so low that no workers were added to the program, except for the new work at Saxton. Few buildings were constructed. In 1932 four building projects were started—at Granville, Saxton, Kentucky, and Gladwin, Michigan—and to none was the board able to offer financial assistance (Hostetter used this situation to turn down a request from California for help on a project there).[37] Three years later Hostetter was still having to write refusals for similar requests, as for example, to Saskatchewan members who wanted help to build a chapel at Howard Creek (North Star).[38]

For several years, the board looked unfavorably at paying evangelists, arguing that it took all the money they had to pay the workers' allowance. This forced some mission workers to conduct their own revivals.[39] But even the workers' allowances were in jeopardy. As Hostetter once explained in a letter in 1937 to fellow board member Wilber Snider, the $20 monthly allowance (apparently unchanged for five years) was paid to a mission pastor if there was enough money in the treasury, less if there was not.[40]

Given the financial problems of the Home Mission Board, Hostetter as much as any of the members preached a conservative fiscal policy. His insistence on mission churches becoming self-supporting as soon as possible was part of this conservatism; he was convinced that missions would not become so if they came to rely on the church for all their support. Even when the Home Mission Board was most desperately in need of finances, Hostetter resisted borrowing money, a position in which he was firmly supported by M. G. Engle.[41]

He also objected to frills in the buildings and lifestyles of the mission workers even in better financial times, as the interesting case of the restrooms at the Bethel church in Kentucky illustrates. Some friends of the church had offered to pay for installing inside toilets in a remodeling project under construction in 1952. Hostetter and another member of the board opposed the offer because the church would respond less well to the needs of home missions if they knew that a home mission church had inside restrooms.[42]

Undoubtedly because he was so keenly aware of the financial needs of home missions, he and his wife gave liberally toward their care. His correspondence shows that they made frequent gifts of cash both to the home mission funds and to individual workers particularly in need of assistance.[43] Especially in the depression years he served as evangelist among them without remuneration.[44] And he took special interest in former home mission workers who in retirement had no means of support. When Walter Taylor died in mission work at Houghton, Ontario, after years of sacrificial giving and service, his wife Melinda was left without financial means—too poor, in fact, to buy a tombstone for her husband's grave. Hostetter took up her case by pressing the Beneficiary Board to admit her to the Messiah Home in Harrisburg, and, when finally obtaining their consent, making out the formal application for her entry and care.[45]

Workers, Hostetter insisted, had to be first class people; there was no room in the home missions program for misfits who could find nothing better to do.[46] He did not always meet his ideal. Undoubtedly to obtain quality workers, he frequently took the initiative in contacting individuals to take assignments. Paul and

Esther McBeth went to Arcadia, Florida in 1931 as a result of such a contact.[47] Albert and Margie Engle were persuaded to go to Kentucky because Hostetter had gone to their home to ask if Engle was "married to Grantham," or if he would consider a missions appointment.[48] Others, such as Ralph and Stella Winger, who stood at a missionary conference to dedicate their services to mission work, could expect to receive a follow-up letter from the secretary of the Home Mission Board.[49]

As usual, he saw the college as the training ground for and supplier of mission workers, home and foreign. He tried to maintain a keen sense of missions on the campus, and was in large measure successful. In 1957, five years after leaving the board, he observed in his diary after a Missionary Career Day at the college that "the task of World Wide Missions continues to be a number one challenge to students on our campus. Oh God, make us a center from which Christian influence can radiate with effectiveness."[50] He kept a running account in his diary of the number of foreign missionaries who had been students at Grantham, recording in April, 1955, for example, with his usual tone of pleasure that Fred and Grace Holland were the 111th and 112th missionaries who were alumni of Messiah College.[51]

His encouragement of young people serving in the church while still students is nowhere better seen than in his arranging for them to be at the mission churches in the holiday seasons and over the summer. This provided workers for the missions and home mission experience for the students. But as students they sometimes had much to learn. The correspondence between Hostetter and Engle in Kentucky (where many students in the 1930s and 1940s obtained valuable training) is instructive. Engle wrote from time to time of the students' immature preaching (one used the expression "I bet" too frequently for Kentucky congregations) and inappropriate actions (the men of one quartet who spent several weeks with him liked to go around without shirts, but Engle earlier had censured Kentucky men for coming shirtless to church). While Hostetter would report to Engle that he spoke to students about such complaints, he also defended them. On the charge of immature preaching, he wrote a typically diplomatic letter to Engle:

I realize that our male quartet was low on preaching ability, but I did feel that they could be of use to you and therefore urged them to go forth into the field. Your people of course have the disadvantage of having an experienced hot-shot evangelist in their midst [Albert Engle]. Fifteen years ago when you and I started in evangelistic preaching we had no experienced man to put us in the shade. The disadvantages of that work are offset for the boys [of the quartet] by the blessing and help that comes to them from contact with you as an experienced worker in the Lord's service.[52]

Hostetter's position in the denomination made it possible for him to arrange for moving personnel in and out of the various institutions with which he was connected. This was especially true for the college and home missions. In 1927, for example, as we have just seen, Hostetter suggested the Albert Engles' leaving staff positions at the college and going into mission work in Kentucky. And it was he who brought them from Kentucky back to the college again in 1944, because, as he wrote to Engle, some of the younger staff have some immaturity in their thinking about the church. "We need," he added, "some definite and positive and wise teaching along these lines for the benefit of our whole program."[53] Five years later, as another example, he moved a college staff person into a home mission assignment to make way for a more professionally qualified person, but he considered that in so doing he had made the best change for both the college and the missions program.[54]

Hostetter clearly enjoyed his work in home missions, time consuming and problem-filled though it was. Part of his pleasure was working with what he thought were board members of high quality. "It is a joy to work with these brethren," he wrote after a board meeting in 1949. He commented in much the same way next year, after noting that in their recent meeting the board faced many problems in their discussions (financial support, new building projects only partly finished, worker assignments, and more). "We have an excellent Home Mission Board—you can discuss matters very frankly and you feel as though the corporate judgment of the group can be trusted."[55]

Hostetter's commitment to and pleasure in his home mission work may be illustrated in the Missionary Institute following

General Conference in Ohio in June, 1949. Such institutes or conferences and numerous speaking engagements on missions were virtually a way of life for Hostetter. This one was special, in a certain kind of way, because he had given up leading a Mennonite Central Committee-sponsored tour of Europe for college students to participate in the Institute. He wrote in his diary that the Institute gave him a vote of thanks for staying home from Europe to be with them. "I replied that I did not think any 3 days in Europe could mean what this institute meant for me personally."[56]

His worth to the home missions program may be measured in part by much of the above narrative; it may also be measured by an episode that occurred at the General Conference of 1949 (held that year in Stayner, Ontario), which has given a fame of sorts to that conference. The Nominating Committee included in its report the recommendation that Hostetter be taken off the Home Mission Board and placed on the General Executive Board (in prestige, one of the most important boards in the denomination). That recommendation sparked one of the longest debates in the history of the General Conferences, led by members of his own board and lasting long into the night. In the end, he remained on the Home Mission Board. His diary gives no clue concerning his feelings on the matter; one can speculate, however, that he was pleased with the decision.

When finally he left the board in 1952 it was probably because by that time he had become involved in a major way with the Mennonite Central Committee, and considered that the time had come, after many years, to end his service with home missions. That he was chairman of the Nominating Committee for that year meant that he could make his withdrawal with greater ease.[57]

Over the years, Hostetter served on a number of other boards and committees. These included the Transportation Committee (for which for many years Hostetter helped to arrange clergy fares for travel and special rates for persons going to General Conference), a committee to develop a ministers' pension plan, the Publication Board (beginning in 1959, where his ability to work with financial figures was an asset), and the Board for Schools and Colleges (by virtue of being president of Messiah College).

He was also a member of the committee that published the

denomination's 1935 hymnal *(Spiritual Hymns)*. For this hymnal he was asked to write a song that would be appropriate for an occasion such as General Conference. The result was "We Join to Worship Thee O God." Years later he explained his creation to a student: the hymn was prepared "thinking of the church assembled in Conference, seeking the guidance of God in business and administrative decisions. It was designed to open our hearts and minds to the will of God by grateful praise and a sensitivity to the leadership of the Spirit."[58] Later, in 1964 and at the request of the Commission on the Sunday School, he wrote "Forward Christian Workers" (to the tune of "Onward Christian Soldiers") for the centennial anniversary of the Brethren in Christ Sunday schools.

His contribution to the next hymnal (published in 1963) was to prepare the worship section. This work he shared with Ray Pannebecker, president of Bethel College at Mishawaka, Indiana, since the hymnal was a joint enterprise with the Missionary Church. The two men agreed that the readings would be set up to end with a congregational response, to be varied in length (with a preference for short responses), and to use the authorized version except for archaic words.[59] November 1, 1961, found him behind schedule and thus hard at work on the project, and very much in need of divine guidance, as his diary suggests: "Oh Lord, help us prepare or rather select Scripture readings that will minister real grace to the hearers. The reading of God's word in the houses of God must be made a rich and thrilling experience. Help us select the Scriptures that will enlighten, instruct, inspire and edify!"[60] That statement serves also as an illustration of what Hostetter thought constituted meaningful worship.

The Church Review and Study Committee of the 1950s was for the history of the denomination one of the most significant committees on which Hostetter served. The committee's formation came out of the background of considerable soul-searching by the denomination, beginning in the late 1940s, about its slow growth. Recent membership in the National Association of Evangelicals (NAE) had convinced prominent leaders, including Hostetter, that historic Brethren in Christ policy and practices needed to be reexamined.

The catalyst for such thinking occurred in 1950 in Indianapolis when the eight Brethren in Christ attendants at the NAE convention met informally in one of their hotel rooms after an evening program. (The group represented a good cross-section of the denominational leadership.) There they began to talk about the spirit and enthusiasm of the convention and to contrast that with the lack of life and growth they thought they saw in their own denomination. They talked late into the night, with Hostetter acting informally as chairman. Two issues perceived as related received the most attention: the tradition of non-salaried ministers, who, because they had to earn their own living, could not give themselves to their pastoral work as they should; and how to assimilate members into the church, including youth and new converts. John Hostetter, one of the attendants at Indianapolis, used his General Conference sermon a few months later to call the church to evangelism and spiritual renewal, and away from its emphasis on tradition and legalism, as he saw it.

In this context General Conference created the Church Review and Study Committee in 1950, with Hostetter and five others who had attended the Indianapolis meeting making up one-half of the committee, and gave the committee the broad task of making a "review and study of the state, function, and work of the general church."[61] By the next General Conference (in 1951), the committee had prepared its initial report and recommendation. The stage was set for them by Hostetter in his General Conference sermon, which he titled "St. Paul's Charge to the Elders." He called for a pastorate that was adequately supported financially and exercised care for the flock. Perils to an effective pastoral ministry, he emphasized, were self-interest, ritualism, lukewarmness, and traditionalism. Traditionalism, which exalts the old and opposes the new, accepts change for oneself but denies it to others, he saw as one of the greatest dangers; in that, the modern church has its parallel in the New Testament church which desired to hold on to circumcision. Hostetter closed with a stirring challenge for a new spirit of evangelism and sacrificial service to the church.[62]

The recommendations introduced by the committee led to prolonged and vigorous discussion. The most controversial was the one on dress in which the committee proposed, in effect, to drop from official church statements any specific descriptions of dress, and to allow greater freedom in interpreting and the wearing of the prayer veiling. The recommendation proved too strong for that General Conference, and the question was recommitted for study.

The subsequent history of the work of this committee need not be traced here; that has been done elsewhere, notably, in Carlton O. Wittlinger's *Quest for Piety and Obedience.*[63] Besides, Hostetter's role in the work of the committee cannot be traced with any precision. It is important to note, however, that Hostetter was at the center of the group that, beginning with the 1951 General Conference, led the church throughout the 1950s in a dramatic shift from earlier, more uniform and traditional practices to a more individualized and flexible approach to church life. At the end of the decade, dress, including the wearing of the necktie, the prayer veiling, and the wedding ring, were no longer governed by specific statements. Life insurance and musical instruments in worship no longer lay under any prohibition. An associate membership existed for persons who would earlier have been ineligible for reception into the church. For membership, rebaptism by trine immersion was no longer necessary if the earlier baptism had been a believer's baptism, even though by pouring or sprinkling. A commitment to a salaried ministry had been made and in many places adopted into practice. And a large-scale reorganization of administration had been achieved, including dissolving the many small districts and rearranging the denomination into five regions, each with a conference and a bishop (thus relieving Hostetter of his Grantham bishopric, as noted above). These changes were reflected in a new *Manual of Doctrine and Government* completed in 1961, parts of which were assigned to Hostetter to write.

What was Hostetter's role in these developments? On the whole, he was supportive of the direction of the change, although he was not the one to push most of them. His most valuable contribution, as members of the committee have suggested, was his ability to understand where the denomination as a whole stood on the issues, and thus to sense how far the committee could push for change. That sort of balance on Hostetter's part, it is conceded, kept the committee from the kind of radical action that very conceivably could have torn the denomination apart.

Moreover, Hostetter's presence on the committee was a reassurance to the more conservative elements in the denomination, and lent credibility to the work of revision.

Enough evidence exists to give some idea of Hostetter's movement on at least some of the issues with which the Review and Study Committee wrestled. One was dress. As we have seen, Hostetter had always publicly taken a conservative view on this question, and had given many talks in college chapel and elsewhere on the prayer veiling and modesty of dress. Even as the committee was preparing its report for the 1951 General Conference, he gave two addresses at the college on the value of the church's teaching on separation in dress, emphasizing that it was not based on negative attitudes but on biblical assumptions, and that the Scriptures do give definite teachings to govern dress regulations.[64] Even after the prayer veiling and dress had been debated twice in General Conference, Hostetter suggested to Arthur Climenhaga that he publish in the *Evangelical Visitor* the results of his work on the prayer veiling (based on his M.A. thesis at Taylor University): "It seems to me opportune and necessary at this time for Christian scholarship to place before our people basic facts supported by Scripture and history in relation to the prayer veiling."[65] Undoubtedly by that suggestion, Hostetter was hoping to counteract a too rapid movement to abandon the covering.

But Hostetter not only eventually went along with the direction of the committee but became personally convinced that a more liberal stance was historically and biblically correct. Already he had been condoning a more liberal position in the home mission churches where the rules were more flexible, as when in responding to an inquiry from Henry Ginder in 1945 he explained that women in the mission churches are not required to wear the traditional head covering, providing they have something on their heads other than the usual head dress.[66] On another occasion he wrote to the superintendent of a city mission cautioning against forcing the prayer veiling on high school girls, recommending associate membership instead.[67]

By the mid-1950s he had lost much of any dogmatism he may have had in his teaching on the subject. In November, 1956, he reported in his diary with an apparent touch of humor that he preached in the morning service on "Preparation for Communion" and emphasized the proper place of symbolism, including the symbolic value of the prayer veiling, but "when I got home mother said it was weak and apologetic and no conviction about it."[68]

The reason for this shift seems clear from correspondence in 1967 that he had with Mennonite sociologist J. Howard Kauffman, who had written to Hostetter to inquire about the historical practice of the prayer veiling. In his reply, Hostetter said that he had made a "pretty careful study" of the historical evidence for wearing a specially designed prayer veiling: "I read practically everything that I could lay my hands on that would relate to this doctrine of the covered head in worship . . . . I failed to find any information that would support the practice of a distinctive and specially designed 'prayer veiling.' " He ended by saying that he had not publicized his supporting evidence but it had played a part in his denomination eventually approving the covered head as a principle of worship but not requiring a particular style.[69]

Hostetter himself continued to dress as he always had done—in plain black suits with upright collar. The only exception was a light colored suit which he bought for world travel in 1960, but that too was plain cut.

On wedding rings, a related issue, Hostetter was in advance of many in the denomination. By the time the Church Review and Study Committee began to air the question at General Conference, he was marrying church members who wanted to include the exchange of rings. He himself did not take part at that place in the ceremony, but by prearrangement he paused while the bride and groom exchanged rings.[70]

On the issue of church membership for people divorced and remarried before their conversion, Hostetter took a relatively liberal position, and was one of the committee members who pushed for acceptance of the principal of associate membership for such people. Again, precedence had been set in the home mission work, although obviously without the knowledge of the denomination generally, and Hostetter in at least one instance had personally sponsored membership for a divorced couple at one of the southern mission churches.[71]

By the time the review committee began to work on this issue,

Hostetter had a case in his own district. A woman in the community who had been the "innocent" one in a divorce had remarried and then become converted. When she applied for membership in the Grantham congregation, Hostetter put her off. But she protested that if Jesus had forgiven her she could not see why others did not also, and why she could not be accepted by fellow Christians. Hostetter took her letter to a meeting of the committee and read the letter with tears in his eyes. As reported by one member, Hostetter asked in words something like the following: "What are you going to do with people like that who are born again and have no condemnation? Surely the church can find a way to minister to such people."[72]

At the General Conference of 1963 Hostetter sponsored a recommendation that would give associate membership to persons converted after divorce and remarriage and who have a living husband or wife. In an impassioned speech he told how he himself had held a traditional view of marriage until recently when a woman (the same one of the letter?) had related to his wife how she had hastily and unwisely married when eighteen years of age and had been left by her husband a few months later. She eventually remarried and she and her present husband now had a happy home of four children. Even if she wanted to, she could not go back to her first husband. She was certain that it was God's will that she and her present husband continue their home.

Hostetter went on to remind the members of conference that for years the church has insisted that if such a couple wish to become members they may do so only if they cease to have sexual relations (although such a requirement is not written into the constitution and by-laws). That, Hostetter said, is placing an undue emphasis on sex in marriage, and such a view is unbiblical. Of course, he conceded, there is danger in the step he was sponsoring; there is danger in dynamite too, but we still use it.[73]

He noted afterward in his diary that the debate on the recommendation was long and failed by a vote of 158 to 143 to obtain the necessary two-thirds majority.[74] Later in his ministry at Palmyra he was essentially to ignore this negative vote by performing wedding ceremonies for people for whom his recommendations had attempted to provide.[75]

Although the Brethren in Christ with few exceptions held

together through these significant changes, for many the changes were startling, even traumatic, and extremely difficult to accept. Hostetter performed an important function in helping such members to somehow live with the new ways of the church. In part this was done by both his and his wife's continuing to dress plain, and thus showing that plain people could still be part of the church in a meaningful way. He also did much counselling and corresponding with conservative people about their difficulties in accepting change, as a letter in 1963 to an old acquaintance from his Refton days illustrates.

The Refton member had challenged Hostetter on his statement that the changes that had come into the church were good; that was a wrong view, because the Bible never changes. Hostetter replied that, in fact, he had not said that all changes were good; some were the result of drifting away from God. On the other hand, Christians must watch that they do not get so upset by other people not following the Lord that they, too, fail to follow. He went on to warn his friend of the danger of falling into legalism, as Paul warned the Galatians: "Frankly, let me say in confidence and with charity that this is a snare that has caught many of the dear people in the New Mennonite and some in the Old Mennonite Church where with little or no spiritual life they think they will be saved because they obey." That was a telling point because his friend had roots in the Mennonite Church.[76]

This review of Hostetter's committee and board work reflects the respect with which he was held in the denomination, both for his ideas as well as for his abilities as a committee member. Usually he was one of the less vocal members in committee sessions, often waiting until others had expressed their views but then proposing action that seemed to be the course to take. Some committee members sometimes found this frustrating, thinking that Hostetter did not want to commit himself until he knew where the others stood on the question at hand. This criticism in at least some measure undoubtedly overlooks Hostetter's instinct for the middle ground.

Just as impressive an indicator of denominational regard was his election as moderator of General Conference. Before the administrative reorganization in 1957, no higher accolade could be given than to be chosen moderator; the office constituted, in effect, the leadership of the church. Thus it is all the more impressive that he should have been elected to the position four times—in 1941, 1948, 1952, and 1955.

Even more striking was the church's selection of Hostetter to deliver three General Conference sermons—in 1943, 1951, and 1961. No other person in the history of these keynote addresses has been so honored. That fact was not lost on Hostetter; as he prepared for his third sermon, he prayed in his diary: "Do not allow *little proud* thoughts [to] hinder me. Please destroy them and let me TRULY SERVE!"[77] Entitled "Lessons from the Churches in Asia," the sermon came immediately following his trip to the East for the Mennonite Central Committee; thus he was excited to share what he had found, particularly the vitality of Christians in the East. "God graciously helped me," he wrote after the sermon. "Many expressed their thanks. Joel Carlson said it was better than anything he ever heard Harold Ockenga or Paul Rees speak. Take the glory to thyself, oh Lord, and make me a better servant of Christ and the Church."[78]

As moderator of General Conference, his instincts for moderation usually served him well. He was familiar with parliamentary rules and thus kept the conference body from becoming tied up in procedural knots. Tense situations he would often relieve by a bit of humor. His concern that all voices be heard earned him a reputation as a fair-minded moderator. But the same virtues at times led to a slow pace in moving conference business. As one former moderator has observed, Hostetter was too fair to crack the whip when such needed to be done.[79] He himself never considered that being moderator was his greatest strength. To listen, however, to the tapes of the General Conference of 1955 (the only year for which his moderating is tape recorded) is to be more rather than less impressed with his ability as a moderator.[80]

On the floor of conference, speaking as one of many members, Hostetter's voice carried great weight. As in committee meetings, he was not as vocal as some members, but when he did speak it was with a sense of where the mind of the conference lay. Again, to some, this seemed occasionally like fence sitting; Hostetter, they suggest, should have been more aggressive on some issues.

The immense respect his word had may be illustrated by an episode in one conference in which the members had become confused about the meaning of a motion and thus about how they should vote. One member stood to ask how Brother Hostetter was going to vote. He admitted that he did not understand the question himself, but he was certain that Brother Hostetter did, and he wanted to vote with him. Despite the laughter that followed, that member of conference had somehow expressed a fact of Brethren in Christ church life.

Beyond his work on boards and committees and at General Conference, Hostetter continued without reduced pace to serve his denomination as an evangelist, as well as one of the most widely used speakers at special services. Part of his attraction as evangelist was his appeal to young people, which seemed to grow with his age. Frequent mention is made of this appeal in reports in the *Evangelical Visitor* of his evangelistic services, as, for example, of the meetings he held at Cheapside, Ontario, in 1945: "A prominent feature of the revival was the response of many of our young people . . . . They absorbed the simple and clear gospel messages. It was indeed a satisfaction to see these in their early youth sincerely face the real issues of life and dedicate themselves to God."[81]

Part also of his continuing attraction as an evangelist was his manner during the altar services. In character with the rest of his personality, he took a counselling approach to seekers, praying quietly with them, an open Bible before him. A "kindly" manner is how his fellow evangelist and old-time friend, E. J. Swalm, has described his altar work. Others remember him "weeping with those who wept" and enjoying the testimonies that followed.

For reasons not altogether understandable, Hostetter in time came to think that he had lost something of his usefulness as an evangelist, a feeling probably caused in part by an increasing difficulty in giving an altar call. This feeling seems to have begun around 1950. After a series of revivals from 1949 to 1952 which he thought were less than successful, he came to Free Grace at Millersburg in January, 1953.[82] Although the pastor, Luke Keefer, told him that this was the best attended revival since the one conducted in 1920 by T. Avery Long, Hostetter was worried about the meetings, so he stayed in bed one morning to read *How to Give the Invitation,* by John R. Rice and Hyman Appleman. "My heart was deeply stirred," was his response in his diary.[83]

In August, 1956, he was evangelist at the Roxbury camp meeting. He hesitated to accept the role because of his perceived continuing inadequacy in giving an altar call, and only did so after Henry Ginder promised to help him at that point in the service. It was as Hostetter expected. After the Monday evening service he confessed in his diary: "I have difficulty 'drawing in the net.' In that area I have always been weak and limited. Oh God help me in this meeting!" He had been able to get through only because "the Brethren Ginder, Keefer and Byers helped excellently at the altar call."[84]

This sense of not succeeding in his revival meetings (or the possibility of not doing so) seemed to haunt Hostetter to the end of his evangelistic career. In a revival meeting at Cross Roads in 1962, he reflected over his last two meetings and this one, and commented that they "had so little and barren results that I cannot continue in his way unless Thou dost help and use thy servant."[85] Two months later he was at Locust Grove, going through, he thought, the same kind of experience. "Dear Lord," he prayed in his diary, "teach me anew how to be a fisher of men! Thou must help thy servant if he is to catch men."[86] Similarly at Martinsburg in the following year, he wrote: "Oh God, give us souls in these meetings! I cannot go on simply talking to people with no one responding."[87]

And yet the evidence is that the evangelistic services he conducted were generally successful, as the church measured success in such matters. Such entries in the diary as above seem often to conflict with reports of the same meetings in the *Evangelical Visitor*. The reader of the two sources may be pardoned for thinking that Hostetter was holding too high a standard for himself.

Interesting insights into Hostetter's character occasionally come through in other diary entries made during these revival meetings. In 1957, while holding one of his several meetings at Bertie in Ontario, he visited a home in the community in which the family was poor and large and a small child had just died. "I was moved," he wrote, "to give him [the father] $5."[88] Similarly, while holding a revival at Wainfleet, again in Ontario, he called on a man severely burned by a gasoline explosion. "As we visited in their home I was impressed to give him $5. While we were at prayer I placed it on the table under some dishes."[89]

Hostetter was in demand as a speaker not only as an evangelist but also for the dedication of church buildings, parsonages, college buildings, and similar church-related structures, both within and without the denomination. (A file folder covering fifteen years in the 1950s and 1960s contains material on thirty such dedications, but it is clear that the file does not include all those in which he took part.) He participated, usually by speaking, at the ordination for numerous ministers, many of whom were his former students, and one his son Lane. He was often called on to speak at Sunday school conventions, Bible conferences, love feasts, and, until their demise, harvest praise services (often held in barns).

Not surprisingly, he was in great demand at the denomination's youth conferences, from Canada to California. As late as 1960 he was a speaker at three youth conferences in one summer. College president and bishop though he was, he entered into the youthful spirit of these conferences, bringing messages on the young people's level and joining them in their recreation. In the Kansas Youth Conference in 1951, he played shuffleboard and one day went boating with eleven-year-old Jared Hoover, who, Hostetter reported, handled the boat well.[90] Two years later, at the youth conference at Cedar Grove, he played baseball so vigorously that he injured a leg.[91] At Lock Haven in 1960, at the age of sixty-one, he was one of the fielders for his baseball team; he recorded in his diary with some pride that he scored a run each time he was at bat.[92] His appreciation for the Brethren in Christ young people he met at these conferences is reflected repeatedly in his diary. "A splendid lot of boys and girls," he wrote in one place. "They challenge us to give them their best . . . . They must be challenged by something beyond themselves. Help us do it effectively!"[93]

In the summer holiness camp meetings of the denomination, Hostetter was one of the principal figures, usually as Bible teacher, sometimes as evangelist. His first experience in a camp meeting came around 1926 when he was evangelist for the annual holiness camp meeting at Tabor, Iowa, conducted by the Hepzibah Faith Missionary Association (a position obtained for him by one of the group who had heard him in evangelistic services at

Abilene in 1925). Particularly in the 1950s and 1960s, after the Brethren in Christ had begun their own, Hostetter served virtually every year in at least one camp meeting, and in several years, three.

But was Hostetter truly a holiness man? the question has been asked. He was, given certain qualifications. Early in life, on his seventeenth birthday, he claimed a sanctification experience at Grantham, as noted in chapter two. In a letter to Abner Martin in 1927, he wrote of the world needing "soul stirring doctrine on the New Birth and the Sanctified Spirit Filled Life."[94] Later in the 1950s when the Church Review and Study Committee turned its attention to the doctrine, Hostetter gave Luke Keefer (one of the leading proponents in the denomination of second work holiness) unqualified support in his writing of the article on sanctification for the *Manual of Doctrine and Government* (with the result that Keefer's article remained virtually unchanged from its original form).[95] Hostetter himself did not hesitate to speak about the infilling or empowerment of the Holy Spirit, terms widely used among the holiness advocates.

But Hostetter's approach to the holiness position, in character with many of his attitudes and beliefs, was moderate rather than radical. He tended to use terms such as "infilling" and "empowerment" rather than "second definite work of grace," as his sermon notes and writing indicate. Nowhere is there any indication that he thought or talked about the eradication of the old man (or the sin principle), as the most radical of holiness preachers sometimes did (thus going beyond the official statements of the denomination).

Furthermore, Hostetter emphasized the practical rather than the emotional and inward-looking nature of the work of the Holy Spirit, at least to judge by the materials in his files. That work, he claimed, was to cure selfishness (the principle of community of goods still stands, although the practice may vary), give power (for virtue, knowledge, self control), bring love, give courage to withstand evil, and magnify God rather than self.

The problems of holiness people, too, tended to be of a practical nature, as he pointed out in a seminar on holiness at Elkhart, Indiana, in May, 1967. Holiness people need to beware of Pharisaism, of a "holier-than-thou-attitude," of paying too much attention to externals which divert from the truth. "Holiness professors, like Anabaptists," he told his largely Mennonite audience, "have had trouble in maintaining the Biblical perspective on separation from the world. Among Anabaptists sometimes resistance to social change has been mistaken for nonconformity to the world. Among holiness people the same desire to be separated from the world has set off a rash of negative mandates against social change and new conventions, such as radio and television. Such legalism mars effective testimony."[96]

As for the demonstrations that accompanied the camp meetings, Hostetter appears to have had mixed feelings. He was opposed when he thought that they were carried to extremes, since this seemed not only to be saying more about the individuals involved than it did about the Holy Spirit, but also because, when carried to extremes, demonstrations hindered the work of the Spirit and were offensive to some who attended. Thus of one camp meeting in which he served in 1961 he wrote in his diary that there was "much shouting and demonstration. This serves a good end in that it releases the tensions of fear that bind some, but this uncontrolled emotion becomes a hindering stumbling block to some people." These latter included a few local pastors who "find real problems in tying in their pastoral program with the emotional tone of the camp meeting. Oh Lord, lead us through this impasse!"[97]

But when the emotionalism was not overdone, Hostetter had no objections; in fact, he considered it natural and useful. At Roxbury in 1955 he noted that there seemed to be more demonstration than in some years, and, he added, "God is working." Those who remember him at camp meetings recall his quiet smile while sitting on the platform during demonstrative periods.

John Rosenberry, one of the leading holiness preachers in the denomination and who shared with Hostetter in a number of holiness camp meetings, has put Hostetter's position well in the following comment:

> His teaching on holiness never contradicted the teaching on the "second work of grace" experience, although there was a progressive part to his teaching which recognized progress after the second-work experience. I don't think he was a

great second-work preacher, but he understood and appreciated the doctrine of sanctification written in the Bible.

He was not a demonstrative man. I have seen him smile during demonstration, and also raise his hand at times. Apparently he enjoyed it. C. N. was never a part of the emotionalism, but he never resisted the demonstration.

John Rosenberry has also given us a good insight into Hostetter's altar work at these emotionally charged camp meetings: "C. N. would be at the altar to counsel and to help people. He was not a great altar worker, but he was effective as he reasoned and counselled with people. It gave our camp meetings a good balance, which we needed and I appreciated."[98]

Except for some of the more emotional moments, Hostetter obviously enjoyed the camp meetings, a sign of his genuine interest and ability to fit in with various kinds of church life and people. All the camps had an early morning prayer hour, and these Hostetter usually attended. "My favorite prayer period," he wrote of the Roxbury camp in 1961, "is the 6 to 7 period in charge of John Rosenberry. This provides an excellent opportunity to pray through on problems and needs."[99] (It may be added that Hostetter was fascinated by Rosenberry, sometimes saying that Rosenberry understood more psychology than any one Hostetter knew.) Along with praying, Hostetter fasted when he thought his messages were not being effective.

Divine healing services were also a part of these camp meetings. "A mighty message on healing . . . scriptural and closely reasoned," he wrote of Luke Keefer's sermon at Roxbury in 1955. Hostetter himself preached such sermons ("God spoke to my heart and blessed the message," he wrote of one). Several diary entries show him taking handkerchiefs that had been anointed at the service to sick people in their homes.[100]

In fact, Hostetter in time came to so much enjoy Roxbury that he and his wife built a cabin on the grounds in time for the 1956 camp meeting. In early June he wrote in his diary: "Folks speak with much appreciation of our cottage. The design seems to appeal to them. Lord we thank thee for enabling us to erect this cottage!"[101]

The stature of churchmen is surely measured in part by ability, but in part also by an understanding of and appreciation for the various elements comprising the life of the denomination. On the latter, as on the former, C. N. Hostetter, Jr., in the judgment of those who knew him, stood tall.

IX

"We Cannot Compartmentalize Man"

*C*N. Hostetter, Jr., was strongly committed to the biblical peace position of the Brethren in Christ Church.
As much as anyone, he helped to confirm the commitment of the denomination to nonresistance during and after
World War II, and in so doing to move his fellow Brethren in
Christ to a closer relationship with Mennonites and the Mennonite Central Committee (MCC). A sign of this closer relationship
was his own significant involvement in that organization.

Although he gave literally hundreds of addresses on peace and
nonresistance, he wrote little on the subject—at the most, a few
articles and a pamphlet of twenty-three pages. The latter, entitled
"Rethinking our Peace Position," brought together two sermons
on nonresistance (as the Brethren in Christ preferred to call the
doctrine) that he preached at the Lancaster Brethren in Christ
Church in 1951. The pamphlet circulated widely in the denomination and some in Mennonite circles, and is illustrative of his
mature thinking on the subject.[1]

In the pamphlet, Hostetter spoke out of the context of the
Korean war and the consequent pressure placed on Brethren in
Christ young men to serve in the army. After insisting that the
conscientious objector would die for his country and is against
evil (only his reasons and methods are different), he explains why
the Christian cannot go to war. War violates the principle of truth
(it is planned deception), and the sacredness of life and property.
War is contrary to the task of the church, which is to love (how
can one love and win an enemy by killing him?), and contrary also
to the teaching of the New Testament and the practice of the early
church. To the argument that God permitted, even encouraged,

war in the Old Testament, Hostetter replies that this only seems true at the first glance: actually, God would have done the fighting for the Israelites had they trusted him. Best of all, the Old Testament points to a better way—the greatest and final revelation—in the person of Jesus whose entire ministry was one of love and peace.

The New Testament, Hostetter categorically asserts, teaches that love is the supreme law, that peace is the Christian's obligation, and that enemies are to be dealt with in kindness and good will. This New Testament view was held by the early church until the time of Constantine, when the church began to be captured by the state for the latter's own ends. "Numbers of our good fundamentalist brethren," he said in making the modern application, "have never freed themselves from the captivity of the state which started way back there."

He concludes the pamphlet by answering several commonly asked and so-called "tough" questions. War, he agrees, will never be outlawed, but that doesn't mean we should not oppose it. If all were conscientious objectors (a hypothetical situation), God could save us (although it is not certain that he would), but if he did not, think what 150 million vital, dynamic Christians could do: they would "break up from underneath any kind of unjust tyranny that would be imposed on us from above." A few million may be put to death at first, but that would happen in war in any event. Finally, if someone were to attack his wife and family, he would try to restrain the attacker, but he would not go so far as to take his life.

Here and elsewhere, Hostetter insisted that the basis for the peace position is Scripture, not liberal ideas. Moreover, the position made its best witness, not in demonstrations (which he lived long enough to see in Washington, D.C., and elsewhere), but in the testimony of good personal relationships and in service to people in need.

When the United States entered World War II, the Brethren in Christ moved to establish close ties with the Mennonites. In the joint programs set up to meet the problems caused by war, Hostetter played a particularly significant part in the Civilian Public Service (CPS) camps set up around the country as an alternative to war duty. He entered this program through the

Goshen College door. At the beginning of the school year in 1941, he conducted a week of Bible study and prayer on the Goshen campus.[2] A few weeks later he received a letter from Orie Miller, executive secretary of MCC, saying that his brother Ernest, president of Goshen College, had reported favorably on Hostetter's work among the students, and requested that Hostetter give essentially the same service to the young men in the CPS campus. He had recently visited the camps, Miller continued, had been impressed with the need for someone to conduct Bible study and prayer, and had spoken with some of his colleagues about whom they should ask to do it; all agreed that Hostetter was the man for the appointment.[3]

Hostetter consented and in November of the same year made his first visit to a CPS camp. These visits continued throughout the war, mainly in the East but as far west as Colorado. He found much dedication in these camps, but also considerable frustration with what many thought was insignificant work and a too lengthy removal from the main stream of life. So Hostetter listened and counselled and encouraged.[4]

Soon reports by the camp director of Hostetter's work began coming back to the MCC office at Akron, Pennsylvania: "very appreciative letters," Henry A. Fast reported.[5] One camp director has suggested the source of this appreciation: "He could soothe the CPS fellows. These boys at that time thought they were going through a period of awfully bad luck. Some visitors would come to the camp and be shocked when they didn't find everything and everybody perfect. But C. N. was not shocked when he found conditions less than ideal; he was immediately sympathetic, and the fellows could sense his sympathy."[6]

He also taught several courses, usually on the New Testament church, for the Mennonite colleges, which were cooperating to provide a sort of continuing education program for the young men in the camps. This work took him, among other places, back to Goshen College for summer school teaching in 1943, and to the CPS unit at Howard, Rhode Island, near the end of the war.

While at Howard for several days, he took a night train to Maine to spend some hours with CPS man Wilmer Heisey, for what the latter has called one of the great experiences of his life. Heisey had been stationed alone in Maine; for thirty-one months he saw only two Brethren in Christ, one of whom was Hostetter. Hostetter arrived at Bath (where Heisey travelled to meet him) at 4:30 in the morning, with the temperature below zero. Heisey has recalled what next happened in these words:

> He sensed where I was. He didn't confront me as others had with the question of how I was getting along in my spiritual life. We found a room and he told me bedbug stories! We overslept and missed church in the morning because they thought he was a priest and so sent us to a Catholic church. We ate in a restaurant, then went to a hotel in the afternoon before they turned on the heat. He told me stories about Bob Worman, and read me a couple of chapters from *Screwtape Letters.* We went to church at night. The next morning at the railroad station he talked to me just briefly on a matter of social relationships. Then he got on the train and left.
>
> I just shook my head and said, "I can't believe it." He just so completely gave himself to me. He never once did that which people are wont to do.
>
> Then when he got home he wrote my mother a letter which said something like this: "I visited Wilmer. He is getting along fine." And my mother sent it on to me. That was the master stroke of a wise man.

Not all Brethren in Christ young men during the war took the conscientious objector stance. In fact, the trend to combatant and noncombatant involvement became sufficiently marked that General Conference in 1942 took the very strong action of declaring that anyone who accepted any military service, combatant or noncombatant, "automatically declares himself to be out of fellowship with the Brethren in Christ Church and suspends his membership."[8] This action, however, was too strong for significant sections of the denomination; thus General Conference was forced to reconsider the issues at its next meeting. It appointed an ad hoc committee of ten with Hostetter as chairman to bring back a statement at the same conference. Following a strenuous all-night session, the committee recommended and General Conference accepted dropping noncombatant participants from those to be disfellowshipped.[9]

Although General Conference had ruled categorically against combatant service (and, in effect, reconfirmed its actions in 1948), Hostetter and the Grantham district took a more redemptive attitude to its young men who violated the official church position. It appears from a study of the district records that no combatants were dropped from the church membership lists; at least, those involved were not informed if action had been taken against them.

The main problem arose when combatants returned home to take up church life again. John Zercher is illustrative of the problem. During the war he had risen to the rank of captain, and after to a major in the reserves. The district decided to place Zercher under probation for a year and a half before full membership privileges would be restored. During this period, Hostetter spent much time in counselling Zercher, giving him books to read on nonresistance and persuasively presenting the peace position. He insisted that Zercher write a confession of error before being allowed to resume full membership rights. According to his own testimony, Zercher composed a number of statements, none of which were quite satisfactory to Hostetter. Not until he had resigned his commission in the army reserves and written an acceptable confession was he received back into full fellowship, in early 1949.[10]

To the young men who went to the CPS camps from Grantham district, Hostetter and the home people offered encouragement by supplying small allowances, paying the cost of clothing upon induction into the camps, and sending letters and Christmas presents. Hostetter himself served on one of the congregational committees responsible to see that these services were provided.[11]

Hostetter's involvement in the CPS program and his strong support of the peace position within the denomination undoubtedly explains why General Conference in 1945 chose to place him on its Relief and Service Committee (soon to be called the Peace, Relief and Service Committee), replacing Orville B. Ulery who was gravely ill. He served as chairman of this board until his resignation in 1947 because of other assignments. A year later, however, he was back on the committee in an ex officio position, by virtue of having taken Jesse Hoover's place as the Brethren in

Christ representative to the Mennonite Central Committee. Thus
began a long and fruitful ministry with an organization that
would increasingly come to absorb his attention and talents.

Almost at once he was in Washington, D. C., to take part in the
first of many appearances over the years before federal agencies
and congressional committees. With MCC personnel in April, he
went to protest the continuation of conscription provided for in
the bill that later became the Selective Service Act. In this trip and
three later ones (all within four months), Hostetter and his colleagues held conferences with the National Service Board and
presented testimony against the bill to both the Senate Military
Affairs Committee and the House Armed Services Committee.
Although they were not successful, Hostetter reported that at
least the act contained one good feature: it replaced the CPS
camps with a Voluntary Service (VS) program (technically speaking, however, the service was not voluntary).[12]

In 1950 the Mennonite Central Committee, at the urging of
Executive Secretary Orie Miller, increased the number of seats on
its Executive Committee from six to seven and appointed Hostetter to the extra seat. "Another job with heavy responsibility,"
Hostetter reflected in his diary.[13] Three years later he was elected
to a still more responsible position—the chairmanship of the
Mennonite Central Committee. To understand how this latter
appointment became possible, it is necessary to note how, beyond
his work with CPS during the war, he came to be known and
respected in Mennonite circles.

He continued to be used as a spokesman for MCC at Washington, D.C., on matters of the draft and the position of conscientious objectors, partly because of his proximity to the nation's
capitol, partly because he was effective as a spokesman: self-
assured, sincere, intellectually respectable, he was described by
one witness.[14] He made at least two trips to Washington in 1951
and two in the following year, accompanying such MCC leaders
as Harold S. Bender and J. Harold Sherk. He enjoyed these
contacts with federal officials and congressmen, apparently finding them less formidable than he had anticipated. "These gentle-
men were most courteous to us and gave us a respectful hearing,"
he remarked of such senators as Lyndon Johnson, John Stennis,
and Wayne Morse, before whom he testified in January, 1951.[15]

Part of Hostetter's growing visibility in the Mennonite world came from his continuing activity with the Council of Mennonite and Affiliated Colleges, organized in 1945 as a consequence of the colleges' cooperation during the war. Messiah College was the "affiliated" institution, and Hostetter by virtue of his presidency was a member of the council, serving, in fact, as secretary from 1946 to 1950 and as chairman from 1950 to 1954. The council met periodically, usually at the annual conventions of the Association of American Colleges, as well as during the annual foreign students conference sponsored each year by the Council.

The foreign students, mainly from Europe, were brought to one of the Mennonite Colleges in the United States, including Messiah College, for a year of study. Hostetter's interest in this activity is evidenced by personally handling such details as travel and visa arrangements for those students coming to Messiah College, and by trips he made to Washington, D.C., to facilitate admission of foreign students to all the Council's colleges. These trips on one occasion took him to the Pentagon and on another to the War Department, where, despite what must have seemed unholy ground for such a strong pacifist, he found the officers "solicitous" and "anxious to help."[16]

His interest in this part of the Council's work is also shown in his driving the college's foreign students virtually every year to the annual foreign student conference. "Did we not have a very merry time?" a student from Germany later recalled of the trip that she and four other foreign students took with Hostetter in 1952.[17] Of the same trip, Hostetter recorded in his diary that at Hannibal, Missouri, the black student with them was denied service. When Hostetter failed to convince first the waitress, then the proprietor's wife, and finally the proprietor that she should be allowed to eat with them, Hostetter walked out with his students to find another restaurant.[18]

The Council of Mennonite and Affiliated Colleges also sponsored an annual summer tour of Europe, primarily for students, part of the experience including working in reconstruction camps in Germany, France, and Italy. Hostetter led this group in 1950, sharing responsibilities with John Engle, and, while students were in the camps, joining MCC personnel in investigating MCC's continuing role in Europe and assisting in further planning for a

Bible school at Basel.[19] In the detailed diary that he kept of his trip
may be read the wonder of an American abroad in Europe for the
first time.

The group left Grantham on June 15, and traveled by plane to
Luxembourg. From there Hostetter led twenty-four students
toward the Netherlands, and John Engle the remaining toward
Paris. Hostetter's diary forms a running commentary on his
activities and impressions. As they drove through the towns and
countryside he was impressed by the thrift, productivity and
cleanliness of the Dutch: "No dirty cheap streets like in America,"
he observed, and thereby reflecting his own thrifty and tidy
inclinations. From Amsterdam the group visited the historical
Mennonite countryside, including Menno Simons' monument
near Witmarsum. But the Reikjmuseum held the greatest attraction for Hostetter; he was so "thrilled" by the Rembrandt paintings that he returned a second day to the art gallery.

At Brussels, Belgium, he was equally impressed by the Rubens
paintings and, in another way, by a Nazi concentration camp—"a
gruesome story of inhumanity and cruelty." Paris was a different
story: "drinking everywhere, plenty of love making in the streets,
. . . a large number of book shops . . . and high quality books."
Here, too, he was obviously delighted with the art in the Louvre
(although he questioned the need for so much nude statuary), and
attended the Paris Opera House to hear the "Damnation of
Faust" ("a masterpiece of music and drama").

From France, Hostetter traveled with his students through
Switzerland, which, he could not help but observe, like the
Netherlands "shows the mark of a stable industrious people." In
Italy, outside of his contact with the Waldensians, Hostetter
seems to have enjoyed most his visits to the art galleries in Milan,
Florence, and Rome. "I was amazed at the wealth of content," he
wrote of the Vatican Museum. "The sculpture was grand, more
modest than at Florence. The paintings of Raphael, Michelan-
gelo and Leonardo de Vinci are wonderful. The Sistine Chapel
was most impressive . . . ."

From Naples and the ruins of Pompeii the group made their
way north, coming to Oberammergau in Germany to attend the
passion play (given the first time since 1934). After staying in
Mennonite homes around Thomashof, the students split into

three groups, each group going to a work camp. Hostetter accompanied one to Donaueschingen, where homes for refugees were being built. He helped the students on the project for two days, excavating dirt, unloading blocks and bricks, and keeping up with the young men as they handled 100-pound bags of cement.

On July 29, Hostetter met the MCC study commission (composed of himself, Orie Miller, Harold Bender, Henry Fast, C. F. Klassen and others) at MCC headquarters in Frankfurt. The work on this commission took him to Mennonite homes and churches, childrens' homes, refugee camps, board meetings, and again to the Waldensians in Italy.

He found the European Mennonites interesting and sometimes puzzling. One German Mennonite, "a jolly fat wine drinking Mennonite with a Kaiser Wilhelm mustache" insisted unsuccessfully that Hostetter drink a glass of wine with him, although Hostetter did bend enough to touch glasses. He thought one German minister's "high silk hat, swallow tail coat and peccadillo collar" set the minister up as "an A1 aristocrat." He was interested in the difference between the German Mennonites: "The south Germans are not professionally trained, most of them are self-supported and are . . . warm and cordial. . . . The North German preachers show strength and skill, less warmth toward Americans but much appreciation to MCC." At the meeting of the Dutch Board of missions at the Single church in Amsterdam, he was struck by the number of ashtrays on the table, and also by the chairman, a woman, who presided "with dignity and precision." He thought he saw indifference and lethargy in the spiritual life of the Dutch Mennonite Church and ascribed this to "liberal theology." At a conference in France he was amused at how men and women greeted with a kiss members of the opposite as well as their own sex: "They do it modestly but heartily, the men greeting the sisters in the same way."

The Findings Committee, of which Hostetter was a member, compiled twenty-nine recommendations for the study committee. Hostetter listed five that he thought most significant, including MCC rendering a spiritual program in Europe with a reduced staff, conducting the main mission activities among the Mennonites through MCC, maintaining contact with the Waldensians, and supporting the European all-Mennonite Bible School. Thus Hostetter played a significant part in important decisions made by MCC in relation to its program in Europe.

These decisions were made at MCC headquarters in Basel. From there, Hostetter traveled through France on the way to meet his students at the work camp where he had left them. (He stopped at Geneva and decided to see a musical revue. "The program was not quite what I had anticipated," he comments, "but it gave me an insight into the tourist pleasures of Geneva.") At the work camp he found morale good and everybody happy. On his travels he had bought gifts for his family—pocket knives, Swiss clocks, and more—an activity he practiced on later trips abroad; these he took considerable time in packing before flying with his group to London.

In England, he took some students to see "Julius Caesar" at Stratford (the play "emphasized the truth in my mind that 'they who live by the sword perish by the sword.' "). He spent the next day at Oxford, but in the evening could not resist returning to Stratford to see "Measure for Measure" (a comedy with a good moral lesson, he noted).

After he had boarded ship on August 31 to return home, he noted in his diary that he had visited eight countries (some several times), traveled 4,000 miles with students in a bus, 2,000 miles by car with the MCC study group, and 1,000 miles by train in England, Germany, Switzerland, and the Netherlands. He finished his entry by observing: "What an interesting experience. I hope I can return again. Lord grant that I may serve thee better as a result of this experience!"

The trip made Hostetter a confirmed world traveler. He encouraged travel abroad for others, and gave them some tips: travel to learn, including about European Mennonites (don't read comic books while you travel), and to spread good will and the Christian spirit; be an optimist, look for good, and watch your manners (don't say, "I consider our church at home much more beautiful than this old dump," or "What, no ice water? Well, I'm sure I would never have stopped here [had I known]").[20]

This trip advanced Hostetter's standing with the Mennonites. All were agreed (especially his students who rated his leadership as "superb," "excellent," "exceptionally good") that he had conducted the tour in excellent fashion; his own estimate to the presidents of the Council was that it was probably the best trip to date.[21] And from the trip he gained further visibility among Mennonites because on his arrival home he began almost at once responding to invitations to speak in their churches about his experiences in Europe.

In fact, however, he had been meeting Mennonite audiences before the trip. In October, 1947 he was back at Goshen College to conduct another week of Bible study and prayer, and in the spring of 1950 gave one of the addresses at the opening of the new Union Building.[22] At the World Mennonite Conference in 1948 (held at Goshen and Newton, Kansas) he chaired the session on young people's work.[23] In 1949 he spent a day with Mennonite Publishing House staff at the Laurelville Mennonite Camp as their devotional speaker.[24] Following an MCC meeting in November, 1951, he spoke at the invitation of Harold Bender to the Mennonite Historical Society on "The History and Principles of the Brethren in Christ Church." ("You have been a most welcome visitor to our campus," Bender wrote in sending the invitation, "and our faculty and students will gladly come to hear you.")[25] In May, 1951, he preached several times at the Eastern District Conference of the General Conference Mennonite Church.[26] And in 1952 he gave the commencement address at Hesston College in Kansas. These and other appearances before Mennonite audiences made Hostetter increasingly well known in Mennonite circles.

In turn, Hostetter brought Mennonite people to Grantham. Orie Miller was one of the principal speakers at the Bible Conference in 1943, and through the years had a standing invitation to return to the college any time he could fit a speaking engagement into his schedule.[27] Donovan Smucker gave the college's commencement address in 1951.

All of this suggests that when P. C. Hiebert, the long-time chairman of MCC, retired in early 1953 and his replacement needed to be found, Hostetter was not an unknown and untried figure among the Mennonites. Various Mennonite groups had had opportunities to see him in action, both on the platform and as an executive, including chairing two Executive Committee meetings in 1952 during Hiebert's absence.

This in itself, however, does not explain why he should have received the chairmanship. In fact, at first thought, it is somewhat surprising at least for members of his own denomination that this should have occurred at all, considering that Hostetter was Brethren in Christ and not Mennonite, and that the group he represented was one of the small ones in MCC. There were, however, factors in his favor, including his growing visibility among the Mennonites. Moreover, it was important at that time to have the right "mix" in MCC official positions. The (Old) Mennonite church already had two strong men on the Executive Committee in the persons of Orie Miller and Harold Bender. Similarly, a chairman selected from the General Conference Mennonites would have given that large group, in some estimates, a dominant position on the committee, at least in the eyes of the Mennonite Brethren. And it was not appropriate to assume automatically that Hiebert's successor would come from his own group, the Mennonite Brethren, partly because Hiebert had held the position from the beginning of MCC. "In this predicament," Henry Fast has observed, "it appeared like a Spirit-guided compromise to nominate and elect Brother C. N. Hostetter of the Brethren in Christ to serve as chairman. But as a matter of fact, he had already so commended himself to the respect and love of the membership that I believe everybody was happy and grateful over his appointment to this honored and responsible position."[28]

There is in addition, however, an intriguing thesis, that behind Hostetter's selection may be seen the skillful yet brotherly hand of Orie Miller. This view suggests that Miller knew Hiebert would soon be retiring and that he considered Hostetter to be a worthy successor. He thus had as one of his own objectives in increasing the size of the Executive Committee in 1951 the bringing in of Hostetter to the smaller, more active group, where he would more likely move to the chairmanship. This thesis is lent a small amount of credence by an entry in Hostetter's diary which reveals that at the meeting in which Hiebert announced (nearly a year before Hostetter's appointment) his intentions to resign, Miller approached Hostetter to ask whether he would consider accepting the chairmanship. Hostetter records that "I deferred and suggested that Orie become chairman . . . . To this Orie did not fully concur."[29]

Hostetter's appointment as chairman of MCC has been seen with less wonder by Mennonites than by Brethren in Christ. Henry Fast's expression that Hostetter had "so commended himself" supports the view that in the various ways described, Hostetter had proven himself to the Mennonites of MCC circles to be the logical appointee to the chairmanship. To go from there to conclude that no one else was really in the running for the position was understandably a human response to make.

Hostetter's diary hints at the excitement at the moment of his election, both for himself and for his colleagues. He must surely have known that he was much in the running for the office. He recommended to the nominating committee, however, that Orie Miller be elected chairman and William Snyder be appointed executive secretary in his place. But the committee brought in a single slate in which all the officers were recommended for appointment, except for Hostetter, who was nominated chairman, and Snyder, who now took Hostetter's place on the Executive Committee. "It was a rather tense moment," Hostetter wrote. "The Committee had said nothing to me prior to the announcement. P. C. Hiebert was elected a life member of the Ex. Com. and MCC. There were many expressions of support. A marked feeling of unanimity was in evidence."[30] His statement to his colleagues undoubtedly had something to do with that feeling: "I may not be able to hold the torch as high as Brother Hiebert," he said in obvious reference to Hiebert's physical height, "but I hope it will shine as brightly. My concern is that the hand bearing it will not be seen."[31]

Hostetter's major contributions as MCC chairman, it is generally conceded, lay less in conceiving and pressing into action creative ideas and bold new designs, and more in creating the atmosphere in which these could be generated and carried out— of being the "oil in the crank case," as one MCC staff member has observed.[32] Thus in moderating a meeting, he typically began with a Bible study—prepared, sincere, always a reminder of the importance of the work at hand. As various members of MCC have said, Hostetter's opening devotions set a tone of seriousness of purpose for the meeting, encouraged a brotherly spirit in discussion, and gave a sense that members would be doing God's work, not theirs, in the hours ahead. For the same purpose, he promoted the MCC practice of working toward a consensus. To do this he encouraged all members in a business session to speak their minds, frequently by calling on less forward members to express their opinions.

Then, too, on the occasions when views clashed and tension built, he had an effective way of telling a joke to relieve the tension. His jokes, often of a Pennsylvania-Dutch origin, became famous among the Mennonites and at this writing are still circulating among MCC personnel.[33] William Snyder obviously had this facility in mind when he and Robert Kreider substituted for him in leading an orientation session for TAP (Teachers Abroad Program) because Hostetter was out of the country. ". . . Life must go on," he wrote to Hostetter, "and we will do our best though I don't think Bob has as many humorous stories as you do."[34] And after Hostetter had retired from the chairmanship, Winfield Fretz wrote to complain that "my public speaking arsenal is a bit rundown due to the fact that you did not replenish it this year with your usual classic anecdotes."[35]

In character with his style was Hostetter's attempt to reconcile groups and individuals. In those years, there was less of an ecumenical spirit among Mennonites than now exists, as the dynamics of Hostetter's election suggest. Hostetter looked for ways to reduce the potention friction in this situation. To illustrate, in 1954, a year after his election, Hostetter became concerned about the feelings of the Mennonite Brethren toward MCC, now that their leader, Hiebert, was no longer chairman and his attendance at MCC meetings was irregular. He wrote to Orie Miller to suggest that another Mennonite Brethren, Waldo Hiebert, be placed on the Executive Committee, a suggestion that was accepted at the next annual meeting in December.[36]

Another illustration of Hostetter's attempts to reconcile opposing views and thus to facilitate the work of MCC was his approach to what he considered an unhealthy feud between Orie Miller and Harold Bender. By other accounts, he read too much into the frequent clash between brilliant men of strong opinions and personalities, but on the other hand it is true that their opposing viewpoints at times tied up the work of the Executive Committee. Bender was primarily interested in the European nature of MCC's work and emphasized the need to find ways to preserve the faithful; Miller, on the other hand, thought more in global terms, such as the missionary implications of MCC activities.

By late 1954, Hostetter had become frustrated as chairman with the situation. After a meeting of the Executive Committee on December 18, 1954, he wrote in his diary that he was "annoyed by the feud between Harold Bender and Orie Miller. It seems as tho Harold is supercritical of Orie except when someone from the G. C. [General Conference] attacks Orie, then Harold is there to defend him."[37] Although Hostetter's language is perhaps too strong, it undoubtedly represents the frustration he felt at the moment.

When in his opinion the situation did not improve he talked privately and frankly with both men at a meeting of the Executive Committee in October, 1955. Curiously, in his diary at that point he reported only his conversation with Bender: "I . . . very frankly counselled him about his struggle for power with Orie Miller. He received it kindly."[38] Apparently Hostetter supported his admonition to Bender by reporting opinions from the younger members of the committee that were similar to his own. After reflection Bender wrote two weeks later to assure Hostetter that "there is no feud between Orie Miller and myself, at least so far as I am concerned, and there never will be." He and Miller were not as close as they had once been, Bender admitted, but that was far different from any kind of a feud. He concluded by urging Hostetter to use his influence with the younger members to correct such opinion, which Hostetter agreed to do.[39]

Although Hostetter was not the creative originator of new ideas and methods for MCC, he had special interests in several of the sections of MCC. One continued to be peace. From his first coming to MCC in 1948 until 1964, he was a member of the Peace Section. In part because of this interest, although undoubtedly most because he was chairman, he repeatedly represented MCC in Washington, D.C, on peace issues, as, of course, he had done before his appointment to the chair. In February, 1955, he testified against the continuation of conscription before the House Armed Services Committee (taking some care to record in his diary that "Chairman Vinson was very courteous to me").[40] Following the testimony Hostetter wrote to the Peace Section to say that he wants to push a "strong united voice against Universal Military Training and Service . . . the program that is slowly creeping in and subtly gaining support," even though it meant "subordinating to second place our own requests [as conscientious objectors] for privileges and rights."[41]

In September of next year, he was in Washington, D.C., for a dinner of the National Service Board of Religious Objectors (NSBRO) with General Hershey and representatives from the White House. All these officials spoke well of the 1-W program carried on by NSBRO (at that point, over 6,000 1-W men had worked in forty-three countries). Hostetter made the response to these officials, and came away calling the affair "a great day!"[42]

His position as MCC chairman and thus as a leader in peace and relief activities took Hostetter to Washington for activities outside of MCC. In May, 1961, following his trip abroad for MCC, he became that organization's representative on President John Kennedy's Food for Peace Council. The purpose of the Council, as explained by its director, George McGovern, was to develop public information on and enlist support against world hunger, and to advise him as director.[43]

Hostetter met with the Council in Washington at the end of June, 1961. At a reception in Blair House, he observed that "the liquor flowed freely, but I settled for ginger ale." He attended several sessions, the most interesting one a panel that included editor Norman Cousins and columnist Drew Pearson. Cousins' remark that the United States should feed the hungry, not because we have a surplus or want to win friends, but because people are hungry, impressed Hostetter, and probably was the source for a similar expression that he sometimes used himself.[44]

Not much, however, seems to have come out of this Council, undoubtedly largely because of Kennedy's untimely death and McGovern's departure as director. Hostetter attended another meeting in September, 1963, and was appointed as one of two Pennsylvania members on the regional level of the Council, but the diary and other sources do not reveal much more than this.[45]

At the same time, Hostetter became involved with Congress in planning for the new Peace Corps. When the United States government took the first steps toward initiating this program, it explored the idea of working with voluntary agencies such as

MCC. MCC in its turn considered that perhaps its PAX program could be strengthened and increased by cooperation with the Peace Corps. The problem, of course, was to arrive at a satisfactory working relationship, a matter of particular importance for groups with an Anabaptist background.

This was the focus of Hostetter's testimony before the Senate Foreign Relations Committee on June 23, 1961. He professed himself much in favor of the Peace Corps idea; everything about his background supported such an effort. But certain elements of the proposal if allowed to stand would mean that MCC could not work with the Peace Corps. MCC could not sign a contract with the government; this would give a political complexion to MCC activity. Neither could MCC agree to the policies against proselytizing (with its implied restrictions on Christian testimony) and against restrictions on selective measures for choosing workers.

When MCC perceived that the government would not bend on these concerns, it withdrew its interest in a direct relationship to the Peace Corps. In the end, that body decided against a contractual relationship with any volunteer agency, thus confirming the wisdom of Hostetter's and MCC's point of view.[46] Out of this context, however, MCC developed the TAP (Teachers Abroad Program), which was seen as something of an alternative to the Peace Corps' project.[47]

Refugee problems also brought Hostetter to the capital for testimony. He spoke for MCC in July 1955 on the refugee problem in Vietnam before Edward Kennedy's Judiciary Subcommittee.[48] In 1966, as the war in Vietnam began seriously to escalate, he and William Snyder sent a letter to President Lyndon Johnson protesting American policy in that country. MCC knew from experience, they pointed out, that the American approach to the situation created refugees and intensified the war, rather than pacifying the area. The United States should decide its policies, not on what is good for the United States, but on what is good for the Vietnamese. The next day Hostetter and six other MCC representatives met in the White House with one of Johnson's aides to discuss proposals to end the fighting and to impress on the administration that MCC service in Vietnam would continue entirely apart from the American military presence in that country.[49]

A strong and almost life-long missions man himself, Hostetter had a keen interest in relating peace and relief work to missions. The relationship was not an easy one to make in those years. The various missions boards of the constituent members of MCC acted largely independently of each other and warily viewed such centralizing efforts as MCC seemed to be. Moreover, missions boards tended to consider MCC work as being social in nature and not enough connected with saving souls. For its part, MCC thought that in many situations missions and relief work could and should be supportive of each other. A question for both sides was how to consider relief work at a given location, particularly if such work developed into a call for a continuing relationship with Mennonites in the form of a mission or church.

Hostetter took a leading part and acted as the bridge in coming to terms with these questions. In September, 1957, he, H. A. Fast, and Waldo Hiebert worked as a committee to plan a study meeting with a workshop format to consider questions raised in communications from the Eastern Mission Board of the Mennonite Church.[50] Out of their work came a session on MCC relief and missions with members of the mission boards at the annual meeting of MCC in January, 1958. Hostetter served as chairman of this study session and presented a paper on "The Scope and Function of MCC." "The relationship of relief service and missions," Hostetter said, "is important and closely bound to the task we desire to do together and to the individual concerns of the constituent groups. As in all cooperative efforts, it is necessary to discern fundamental principles and to give these our best support. At the same time, respect and consideration must be shown to differing viewpoints and minority concerns."[51]

Despite this conciliatory tone, other papers focused sharply on areas of disatisfaction. This led to a "conjoint" meeting of the MCC Executive Committee and representatives of Mennonite mission boards four months later on May 16. Out of the discussions at this meeting came a decision to have an ongoing relationship among the boards, and between them and MCC. Thus occurred the birth of COMB (the Council of Mennonite and Affiliated Mission Boards), which proceeded to meet at stated intervals and to be the primary point of clearance for MCC mission concerns.[52]

Among the first of the issues the new group wrestled with was the nature of the peace mission of MCC to Japan, how to administer relief in mission areas where mission boards were at work, and the possibility of a peace mission in South Africa. This last resulted in a decision early in 1960 to send Henry Hostetter, Executive Secretary of Brethren in Christ foreign missions, for several months on an exploratory peace mission to South Africa and to visit the various fields in Africa where MCC constituent mission boards carried on missionary work.[53]

Hostetter himself was clear that MCC work, in the strict sense of the term, should be in relief and not missions. He discouraged MCC beginning and sponsoring congregations as such: how are we going to baptize the members? he would ask when pressed on the point (an obvious allusion to the various modes of baptism—sprinkling, pouring, immersing—practiced by MCC's constituent bodies).[54] When Ronald Lofthouse, the newly appointed chairman of MCC (Saskatchewan), wrote to Hostetter about MCC's apparent lack of interest in continuing to sponsor the Montreal Lake Children's Home in northern Saskatchewan, Hostetter replied that "MCC was organized not to replace the church but to do the things that the churches could not do alone."[55] He insisted, too, that in areas where MCC worked with emerging indigenous churches, MCC should refrain from a paternalistic, ownership attitude. Thus when the Indonesian churches expressed a wish for a closer relationship with the American churches through the mission boards and MCC, Hostetter insisted that these relationships must be fraternal "in light of fruitful evangelism already going on in Indonesia."[56]

The issue of missions versus relief work, however, was in a sense a non-question for Hostetter: both were essential to the life and ministry of the church. He tended, however, to emphasize one or the other, depending on his audience. When with his fellow Brethren in Christ and his colleagues in the National Association of Evangelicals (NAE), he stressed social concerns. Both groups, because of their evangelical backgrounds, emphasized the gospel ministry and were inclined to view social work as smacking too much of liberalism and standing in the way of saving souls. Thus in a presentation to the NAE convention in 1966, after showing that by precept and example Jesus taught his followers to feed the hungry and relieve the suffering, he insisted that twentieth-century Evangelicals make the same error as the Jerusalem church did when it separated evangelism and relief by neglecting the Grecian Jewish widows. "Hundreds of you," he continued, "must do something more for relief . . . . The church or congregation that does not have Christian relief in its budget is failing to do its duty . . . . [That church] is as much remiss as the church that does not support missions."[57]

On the other hand, within MCC circles Hostetter tended to emphasize the need for the gospel witness. This was undoubtedly owing to his well-founded understanding that in doing work of a social nature it is easy to be active for action's sake, and thus to minimize the spiritual foundation of MCC work. He must also have taken into account that there were those both within and without Mennonite circles who thought that MCC had already reached that state of inferior grace.

Thus in his leadership role in MCC, Hostetter repeatedly reminded his colleagues of the need for the gospel to accompany and indeed to be the basis for their social work. It was somehow natural, when at the 1966 annual meeting of MCC (Canada) he was asked what changes he saw over the years in MCC, that he should single out for his reply the changes in MCC's efforts to witness. "Whereas we earlier separated relief and mission work rather sharply," he pointed out, "we now expect our volunteers to give an unapologetic Christian witness in all the relief and service work they do."[58] One reads into the statement a sense of personal accomplishment.

But this in a certain measure misrepresents Hostetter's overriding point of view, which was that Christian witness and Christian social concern must go hand in hand—in fact, must be part of the same package, to use a metaphor appropriate to MCC. Thus in a devotional address to the MCC annual meeting in 1963, he insisted that "we cannot compartmentalize man, but must recognize that his nature is a unit, a living personality. We must be aware of his total need." He followed that remark with a caution that social work should not be used to catch sinners in the gospel net:

Evangelism and relief work are difficult to combine, lest we reap a harvest of 'rice Christians.' To use relief or Christian social service as a 'bait' for evangelism was not Christ's way and is unworthy of His followers. Jesus fed men because they were hungry . . . . Because of the difficulties man may conclude that evangelism and relief must be totally separated. But the nature of man and the teaching of Scripture show that these are not only related; they are interrelated.[59]

This helps to explain why, following the first meeting of MCC and the mission board representatives referred to above, Hostetter should write to William Snyder his conviction that there should be personnel doing MCC work and mission work at the same time; what better way to strengthen ties of mutuality between mission boards and MCC. That could surely be done without preempting each other's role.[60] It was thus in character that the reports which he wrote while travelling for MCC overseas should usually comment on missions, or missions potential, arising out of the work of MCC.

Such views complemented his conviction that relief work calls for flexibility and openness to change. To the supervisor of a young medical worker with MCC in Asia, he once wrote that the young man must take a realistic view of matters; he must remember that "most service in the Orient must be done *with* and *under* nationals and that in nearly every hospital he will find: (1) great limitations by lack of help; (2) inefficiency and slowness of administration; (3) practice of oriental situational ethics that seem questionable to a westerner." But still he must attempt to serve.[61] To the director of relief work for the NAE in Vietnam, Hostetter once wrote: "I know of no work in the world that requires more flexibility than the ministry of Christian relief," and then went on to encourage him that the mark of a strong leader is one who is not afraid to bend for fear he will break.[62]

The mental health work of MCC was another program that had considerable interest for Hostetter; this was another way of ministering to other kinds of needy people. Because of its proximity to Grantham, he was most directly involved with the Brook Lane Psychiatric Center near Hagerstown, Maryland, the first of such hospitals sponsored by MCC. In 1953 he became part of a committee that developed a master plan for the institution, including buildings, and social and hospital services.[63]

Whether the administration of the hospitals would be centralized or decentralized became an issue needing resolution. Typically, a study committee was formed to resolve the question, and typically also Hostetter was a member. The outcome of the study, and one which Hostetter pressed, was a decentralization of the program, each unit having its own local board of directors, with a subcommittee of MCC (the Mennonite Mental Health Services) to coordinate the work of the individual units.

As in other areas of MCC activity, Hostetter urged a holistic ministry in mental health work. Some associated with the mental health program wanted to run the hospitals strictly on a professional basis, arguing that while the patients should be ministered to in warmth and love, their confused state of mind would only be worsened by mixing religion with their treatment. Hostetter, with others, resisted that point of view, and supported the building of chapels, the hiring of chaplains, and an open integration of faith and mental health therapy.[64]

He also insisted, thrifty though he was, that if the mental hospitals were to do their work effectively they needed the best in equipment and professional services. This, in addition to his view of the need for integration of faith and medical treatment, was well expressed in his dedicatory address at the opening of the Prairie View Hospital in Newton, Kansas, in 1954:

> The ministry of healing for mental illness is not simple and easy. To make Prairie View Hospital's service effective, we need to use the resources of the best in human knowledge, efforts and skill plus the aid of divine grace with its supernatural healing power. Without supernatural grace man's best knowledge, efforts and skill frequently wander in the wilderness in the search for mental health. The gospel of Christ has a relevant and dynamic contribution to make in the search for mental and emotional health.[65]

In the formation of MCC (Canada), while not playing a leadership role, he lent important encouragement and support. That was needed because to some in both Canada and the United States it appeared that in forming the new organization, the sense of unity and direction in peace and relief work would be weakened. In late November, 1964, he and Robert Kreider traveled to Kitchener to assist in the formation of MCC (Ontario), with interest in insuring that organization's good relationships to MCC (Canada). A few months later, he returned to give several addresses at MCC (Canada)'s first annual meeting at Elmira (because, as Jacob Klassen wrote in his invitational letter, Ontario Mennonites needed to be convinced of MCC (Canada)'s loyalty to MCC).[66] Klassen wrote again after the event: "It was good for the delegates to the meeting to be aware of the close working relationship between the new MCC (Canada) and the larger Mennonite Central Committee. I think your presence there was an assurance to the Ontario brethren that we want to continue to work together very closely. From the comments I heard following your evening message, I can say that you made a 'home run.' "[67] In the same year, Hostetter became an ex officio member of MCC (Canada) and in the two years that remained of his chairmanship attended its annual conference.[68]

In these and other ways, Hostetter carried on the chairmanship of the Mennonite Central Committee. As the leading official spokesman for MCC, he traveled widely in the Mennonite and Brethren in Christ communities, especially after trips abroad. At Akron and elsewhere he led or assisted at many commissioning services for workers. He attended the meetings of many, if not all, of the sections of MCC and, as already observed, usually was placed on ad hoc committees that had difficult work to handle. He was frequently at MCC headquarters at Akron; for two months in mid-1959 while both William Snyder and Orie Miller were out of the country, he served as acting executive secretary. Staff personnel found a good listening ear in Hostetter, at least in part because he did not try to assume or direct too closely their functions.[69]

His interviews with Carl McIntire, a right wing religious leader and outspoken critic of communism, must have been among his more interesting activities. When in 1961 the Mennonite Central Committee sponsored a visit of several Russian Baptist churchmen to the United States (as one effort to renew contact with Mennonites in Russia), McIntire, who saw the Baptists as communists in church clothing, was vocally critical. He picketed the places where the Baptists spoke and condemned one Mennonite leader over an Elkhart, Indiana, radio station. MCC arranged a meeting between McIntire and three MCC leaders (Hostetter, Harold Bender, and Elmer Neufeld) for October 5 at McIntire's headquarters in Collingswood, New Jersey. Not much progress, however, was made. Hostetter noted in his diary: "I was interested to see how this man's mind operates who had made heresy hunting his chief life vocation. I left with a depressed feeling."[70]

A second interview three years later followed picketing by McIntire and his group at the Philadelphia airport of another MCC-sponsored delegation of Russian Baptists. This interview went better; Hostetter's notes speak of an exchange that was frank, courteous, with mutual respect for differing viewpoints. (Edgar Metzler, one of the MCC representatives at the meeting, has recalled how different it was to talk with McIntire in his office than on the picket line.) But McIntire was pressed hard for making remarks about the Russians without speaking with them, thereby "doing a great disservice to persecuted Christian brethren." "We also pointed out," Hostetter recorded, "that his procedure showed much more concern about trying to stop Communism than to obey Christ's great commission and confront Communists and all men with the Gospel of Christ." McIntire's parting smile and thanks, Hostetter thought, were sincere.[71] "This was the kind of thing C. N. wanted to do," Metzler has observed of the reasonable, forthright tone of the meeting.[72]

Following his trip to Europe in the summer of 1950 for MCC and the Council of Mennonite and Affiliated Colleges, Hostetter made several other trips abroad, most of them for MCC. These trips were among the most important services he performed for that organization.

In 1957 he attended the Sixth Mennonite World Conference at Karlsruhe, Germany, as an MCC representative, and coupled that assignment with a schedule of meetings and tours of MCC work in Europe. On the way to the conference he spent a day again at Stratford where he saw a production of "King John" (he thought the acting superb but did not care for the plot), chaired a meeting at Amsterdam which decided to proceed with an international organization employing conscientious objectors, visited PAX work at Kaiserslatten and Eikenbach, and attended a meeting at the Beinenburg Bible school near Basel where there was much frank talk and improved understanding about Mennonite mission work in Europe.

On August 9 he arrived at Karlsruhe where the next day he read a paper on "How to Produce Faith and Discipleship in our Young People" before what he called scholars and theologians. He called for a better understanding of youth—of their emotions and aspirations—and for an adequate scriptural teaching. "There were many comments of appreciation from Dutch, Germans, and Americans," he noted of his presentation. The following day he chaired a meeting which drafted a statement for the conference condemning the armament race and the atomic bomb.[73]

After the conference he met with a committee working on finding lost persons in Russia, visited the PAX unit in Vienna and toured relief, refugee and educational centers in Germany. Starting for home he went to Paris, where almost immediately he headed for the Louvre to spend three hours looking at the sculpture and paintings, and returned there the next day before going home. He attended services with two PAX men in the city and inquired of their supervisor and officer in charge of the UNESCO voluntary work camp if the Paris "atmosphere is a good place [for] these boys where the fences are truly down and the fellows very much on their own."[74]

Hostetter's next travel abroad came in 1960 and 1961 in an extended trip of seven months to Asia and the Middle East. His instructions asked him to serve as pastor to MCC workers, evaluate MCC aid and educational programs, check MCC workers assigned to other relief agencies, determine where more medical personnel could serve, and explore new frontiers for MCC in Asia.[75] He performed a similar, though more minor, service for the World Relief Commission (WRC) of the NAE, of which also he was now chairman. The assignment came immediately following his retirement from the presidency, and thus served as a means to adjust more gradually to his new circumstances in life.

He left Grantham on September 20, stopped at Honolulu, and arrived in Japan on September 25. After making some initial contacts for a return to that country, he flew to Korea, where his first major work was done. Here he visited five MCC feeding stations, a project for widows, and schools and colleges; he had personal interviews with each worker, conducted Bible studies, gave addresses and devotional studies in churches and conferences (including Bob Pierce's World Vision pastors' conference), and held conferences and board meetings with agencies through whom MCC and WRC were working.

His diary gives something of the impression that Asia's great need made on him as he met it for the first time here in Korea, seven years after the cease fire of the war in that country. One of his first activities was a visit with MCC director Jacob Klassen to what he called a haven for beggars and the feeble-minded. "What a road!" he wrote. "What needy people! What little of this world's goods some people have! I tried to take a few pictures!"[76] A few days later he attended a school for orphan boys, read some of their biographies, and commented: "How tragic are so many of their stories. What broken hearts some of these orphans carry!"[77]

His pastoral style in Korea and elsewhere is reflected in his diary. On October 1 he accompanied the entire MCC personnel for a weekend retreat up into the mountains several miles from Taegu. "After a Korean dinner in which I ate my first roasted grasshopper we had a worship fellowship and I spoke on Phil. 2, Joy in Service, and then slept Korean style on a heated floor with mat for mattress and another mat for cover." At the Kyong San school several days later, he met with the staff and faculty in the evening. "We sat around the low tables in the chapel.... After the dinner of Korean food we played games. I was penalized by being asked to sing a song and I sang, 'The more we get together.' A very fine spirit was felt throughout the evening."

The Korean assignment had potential for difficulty. Relations between NAE and some elements of the Presbyterian Church in Korea were not good; Hostetter was obviously connected with NAE in his role as chairman of WRC. MCC personnel in Korea, who wanted to relate to all elements, were apprehensive that they might be caught in the middle. Hostetter's handling of this delicate situation is reported by MCC Korea director Jacob Klassen:

> William Snyder allayed my fears by saying that C. N. Hostetter, Jr., brings resolution into situations in which he moves. And how right he was .... Bob Pierce of World Vision was there in Korea at the same time. Hostetter knew

Pierce and so we came together and met the World Vision people in Korea for the first time. He also related easily to the leaders of the Presbyterian Church and also to the colleges and their presidents, which enhanced relations between them and MCC.

My wife Katherine said that when C. N. left it was like saying goodbye to Dad .... For us as a family and as an MCC unit in Korea those were perhaps the most memorable weeks of our three year term, because C. N. was counsellor, pastor, friend.[78]

From Korea he flew back to Japan where he visited Brethren in Christ and Mennonite missions, and spoke at a retreat for their missionaries. He was clearly impressed by the Japanese—by their industry, and not least by their customs. Of the service in the hotel where the missionary conference was held he wrote: "The floor lady in charge of our party took a very personal interest in me—ready to help me walk up and down the stairs, put on my robe, etc., etc. Such service I am not accustomed to .... I took a last hot bath tonight. These certainly do prepare one for a good night's rest."[79]

From Japan he flew to Taiwan where he visited Mennonite churches and missions, a Mennonite hospital and schools for the blind and orphans, and Church World Service officials and projects. Here in Taiwan he finally mastered the chopsticks, but confessed that "still my style needs brushing up to a better level of adroitness."

Hong Kong was his next stop. Almost at once he was put into a rickshaw by his Chinese interpreter, but this gave him some problems: "I had a feeling of discomfort as I rode wondering if I was making a beast of burden out of a human being. His desire to do it and his pleasure at earning 70 cents Hong Kong (12¢ U.S.A.) offset in a measure my negative feelings."[80] Here as elsewhere he visited hospitals (including one where Norman and Eunice Wingert began relief work), MCC feeding operations, and projects run by the Lutheran World Service, Church World Service, and the Roman Catholic Church (the priest in charge told him that America's problems could be solved if they would just produce more noodles). Hostetter encouraged the Mennonites to open mission work on the island, particularly in connection with a school, and reported that residents thought the Wingerts would be the best persons to lead the project.

On November 27 he arrived in South Vietnam and the next day traveled through communist-troubled country to Djering, where he visited a mountain school to which MCC sent food. The people of the area, to show their appreciation for MCC, conducted a special ceremony for him and the PAX workers. "I was made a member of the Mau tribe," he wrote, "and then they put a brass bracelet on my right arm. They also gave a set of beads for my wife. I was deeply touched by the ceremony and had to shed some tears."[81]

Here in South Vietnam, on the eve of President John F. Kennedy's decision (late 1961) to dramatically increase the number of United States military advisers in the country, Hostetter made numerous contacts with the Christian and Missionary Alliance Church, through which MCC carried on much of its relief work. For these leaders Hostetter had great admiration—their dedication and devotion in the face of deteriorating conditions he thought difficult to match. After preaching in one of their churches (through an interpreter, as usual), he was presented several lacquered plaques and a fan by the congregation. "What finese [sic] these oriental people have in showing their appreciation," he observed of their courtesy.[82] Still, he had some words for the leaders: he supported MCC workers in insisting that relief is only for the needy, and that non-Christians as well as Christians should receive it. To the Akron office he encouraged the view that MCC work should be phased out, but cautioned against setting arbitrary deadlines because of the country's needs and uncertain conditions.

He left Vietnam on December 9, flew to Singapore, and then on to Indonesia. Here he found immense confusion and frustration, created in large measure by the country's bureaucracy. Troubles such as the difficulty in obtaining visas and travel permits he shared with other MCC personnel, a problem he unsuccessfully took up with government officials. Several times in his diary he noted a popular saying: "If you are not confused about Indonesia, then you are poorly informed." For MCC people and Indonesian Mennonite church leaders working under these and other trying circumstances and operating hospitals and schools over the islands with MCC support, he had many words of praise.

Suhadiweko Djojodihardjo particularly impressed him. This most prominent leader of the Indonesian Mennonite Church, he observed, "is a well-trained man who speaks Dutch, Indonesian, Javanese, English, and German. He is keen, well informed, and a man with a depth of spiritual life." He accompanied Djojodihardjo to a community Christmas party attended by Christians, communists, and Moslems. Djojodihardjo gave a message unbothered by a very informal atmosphere: "Dogs wandered in and out at will, lifting their legs at the pulpit and decorations and had a fight in front of the pulpit while the . . . pastor was speaking."[83]

For Indonesia, Hostetter urged on the home office at Akron the need for longer and overlapping terms of service for MCC personnel, and more safeguards in the distribution of food. That, he wrote, would reduce the confusion, but only somewhat.

In Thailand, where he next went, he visited PAX men serving on an agricultural project, a hospital and school operated by the Church of Christ, and a leprosarium for which he requested an MCC medical doctor. From there he flew to India, visiting Mennonite schools, hospitals and missions, Indian seminaries, and the work of the United Missionary Church and the Wesleyan Methodists. He met with the Brethren in Christ Church in their council, where he preached the conference sermon and gave ordination to two young Indian ministers.

Following a brief trip to Nepal to visit PAX men at a United Mission hospital, he returned to India to attend a large convention of the Mar Thoma church, invited there by one of their leaders, Bishop Theophalis, whom he had met in Korea. Before leaving India he visited the Taj Mahal, where "a great day seeing this beautiful memorial" was slightly spoiled by his guide: when Hostetter referred to the memorial as a building, the guide sharply rebuked him by saying it is "the spirit of a beautiful woman preserved in marble."

He flew on to West Pakistan for a day with two PAX men assigned to an irrigation project, who were doing such good work that people were asking for a Mennonite church to be started among them. In Jordan, he visited all the work with which MCC was related—orphanage and schools, nursing and medical services, clothing and food distribution, and sewing classes. He was impressed with the leadership of Walter and Rachel Martin, Brethren in Christ friends from Pennsylvania, and with the difficulties they had in working with a people who suffered great injustice at the hands of international statesmen. And now in the Holy Land all those places he had talked about in his Bible classes suddenly came alive. He waded out into the Dead Sea, led a communion service at the Garden Tomb, and toured Jerusalem.

In Greece, he spent several days with fourteen PAX men on an agricultural project at Tsakones, and found the local priest and villagers "lavish in their praise of the personnel and their work." On the return home he stopped in Germany, where he spoke at a conference of PAX men at Regensburg, and in England, where once again he went to Stratford, this time to see "Much Ado About Nothing," but was dismayed because "the love scenes were TORRID." He arrived back at Grantham on April 7 and began immediately to prepare for an address he was to give the next day at the Allegheny Regional Conference.[84]

As this account has suggested, Hostetter returned home favorably impressed with much that he saw—the dedication and performances of MCC workers and directors, the doing so much on so little, the surprising strength and vitality of the mission programs and the national churches. He became more cognizant of the problems in relief work, and more convinced than ever of the need for MCC and Mennonite missions to work together.[85]

These views he proceeded to air in committee meetings and in two months of deputation work in Mennonite and Brethren in Christ churches. "I look forward," William Snyder had written even before Hostetter had arrived home, "to your interpreting in a large way the program that you have seen and to bring freshness and concern to the various conferences."[86] Hostetter did not fail Snyder in his expectations. In Canada, he travelled from Ontario to British Columbia, and then after a brief rest across the United States to Kansas.[87]

In the year following his return, he also spent considerable time with MCC personnel, evaluating in light of his findings the cost and value of MCC programs, and served on a committee to study MCC's work as it related to mission outreach and young church development.[88] And, at the 1962 Mennonite World Conference in Kitchener, he gave a major address on "Our World Wide Ministry for Relief" for which he drew, in part, on his experiences of his recent tour.[89]

Other trips for MCC followed, usually including an accompanying assignment for WRC. In November, 1962, Hostetter and Edgar Stoesz traveled two weeks in Santo Domingo and Haiti to investigate the continuing role of MCC in those countries, including what help might be given to churches and other relief agencies, such as Church World Service, and whether to expand into a permanent Mennonite body in Haiti. To the last issue, Hostetter and Stoesz essentially said no, citing one worker who claimed, "Haiti needs Christ but I am not sure she needs the Mennonite Church." Instead they recommended for virtually everywhere increasing assistance to hospitals, schools, churches, and Church World Service, particularly in the form of MCC workers. They encouraged transferring the hospital operated by MCC at Grande Riviere du Nord to the Haitians as soon as possible, but with continued help after termination, an opinion much in line with MCC general policy.[90]

Less than a year later, in the summer of 1963, Hostetter traveled again for MCC—to Algeria, Greece, and Jordan. In Algeria, MCC work was carried on through the Christian Committee for Service in Algeria (CCSA), composed of seventeen Protestant churches or church-related agencies. Hostetter visited the places for which MCC had major responsibilities, including a medical dispensary and a farm for demonstration education in agriculture. He recommended a continuing presence in Algeria, despite cut-off dates proposed for MCC's education farm, arguing that Algeria's closeness to Europe makes it an ideal place for European Mennonites to serve in, that Algeria could be a base of missions to Moslems, and that the welfare needs of the country were considerable.

In Greece, he inspected the MCC agricultural project at Aridea and had an interview with a member of the country's Department of Agriculture, who agreed that the government should take over the project as MCC phased out in the near future. Back at Athens and touring the city, he records seeing, among other wonderful sights, a group of country young people "do some lovely folk dances."

His major work was in Jordan. There his task was once again to visit the relief and educational work of MCC, and also to investigate the feasibility of establishing mission work in the country. The sum of Hostetter's suggestion on the former was to encourage the beginning of a Mennonite hospital and as much as possible to reduce direct relief and place greater emphasis on self-help, with assistance on self-help projects from MCC. As for a mission program, he recommended a pastoral ministry begun within the framework of MCC and then perhaps expanded as circumstances might warrant.[91]

While in Jordan he frequently visited places in and around Jerusalem connected with the life of Jesus. These visits later became the basis for a series of short articles in the *Evangelical Visitor* on musings in the Holy Land.

In July, 1966, he was back in Haiti, again for both relief agencies that he served. For MCC his work appears to have been primarily pastoral. For WRC, he contacted many of the evangelical missions in the country and recommended that this was not the time to increase its aid to Haiti, because the United States government, through whom WRC obtained some of its supplies, was reducing its help, and because the Evangelical Fellowship could not provide leadership for distribution.[92]

Hostetter's last trip abroad was in 1967, following the Eighth Mennonite World Conference in Amsterdam. He attended the conference, took a part in a panel discussion (with Djojodihardjo, among others), and reported on missions in Zambia and Rhodesia. He also found time to return to the Reijksmuseum, where he spent an afternoon in a "leisurely way" and being "thrilled anew with Rembrandt's great works."

From July 30 to August 28 he was in Africa, touring missions and talking to MCC personnel in TAP and PAX—in many ways, mainly a pastoral visit. After three days in Kenya and Tanzania, he flew to Burundi, where he had difficulty getting into the country and out. When he went to the airport at Bujumbura to fly to Zambia, he found his flight had been overbooked. He was one of six forced to remain behind. The next flight out was four days later. To keep his appointment, he made a 600-mile trip through rough and dangerous African roads to Kempala in Uganda, where he thought he could obtain a flight. Instead he had to take a train to Lusaka and from there to Choma in Zambia.

Here began a seven-day visit in which he talked with all the missionaries in the Brethren in Christ Church in Zambia and Rhodesia, and toured all the missions except one. The "swing toward evangelistic involvement" of the missions program pleased him. On the other hand he was "amazed and impressed" by the work of the hospital at Macha. "What a wonderful week" he wrote of this part of his trip.

From there he flew to Kinshasa in the Congo to attend an MCC worker's retreat. The Congo was unsettled; nevertheless he insisted on traveling three hours through the country and several police roadblocks to visit Jack and Marilyn Wolgemuth stationed at a hospital in Kimpese.

Conditions in Nigeria, the last stop on his tour, were even worse. He was warned not to go, but because contact with most of the MCC workers in the country had been lost, he insisted it was his duty to keep to his plans. He succeeded in reaching only six workers at Ilorin, and that only by driving for 200 miles each way over rough roads and through military roadblocks. Two of the TAP persons were in bed with hepatitis. For two days, as his diary notes, "we talked over their problems, found ties of acquaintance . . . . We had good Bible study together. The six were thrilled and relieved that we could get to them." On August 28 he flew out of Lagos for London, understandably feeling "a sense of release and safety in getting transit from the conflicts of Africa."[93]

Hostetter's approach to his work on these trips abroad for MCC and WRC are worthy of some description. He liked to think of himself as a facilitator and as an interpreter between MCC workers overseas and the administration in headquarters in Akron. On his copy of the mimeographed report of his 1963 trip to Algeria, Greece, and Jordan, he scribbled some notes (obviously for presentation at an MCC meeting) in which he pointed out the tendency for communications to become clogged between the home office and workers abroad; his role, he explained, was to unclog the channels and to encourage communications. For this reason he avoided making administrative decisions "on the spot." Instead, he explained, counselled, listened.

This self-estimate is substantiated by other evidence. The lengthy reports that he wrote to Akron were largely descriptions of what he found, rather than categorical statements calling for change. The reports appear usually to have been prepared with care and after consultation with the MCC staff whom he was visiting. One MCC administrator, a director overseas, has observed that Hostetter did not travel abroad with preconceived ideas and that when he wrote a recommendation it was not only Hostetter's but the workers' as well. Thus the people in the programs were not later caught by surprise. "We didn't complain, 'Why didn't he say that when he was here?' or 'Who told him that sort of thing?' No, it was 'Here we go!' C. N. really heard us and he took it to the Executive Committee, and there it is, in black and white!"[94]

His pastoral and affirming roles in these tours should be reemphasized. An administrator who accompanied him on one of his trips has recalled that virtually the first thing Hostetter would do when he met a group of MCC workers would be to reach for his Bible and say, "Let's have a Bible study." When questioned about this practice, he said that people are best brought together around the Word.[95] In addition to these Bible studies he gave many sermons and devotional messages, and always he counselled and encouraged, and sometimes corrected.

That such pastoral work was well received is evidenced by the many letters and other responses he received during and after a tour. While still abroad in 1961, William Snyder wrote that various staff people had found Hostetter's work a blessing "in a pastoral way in giving wise counsel to the workers," and added, "I almost felt like cabling that you should stop out there for a year or two to keep up the good work . . . ."[96] Those isolated workers at Ilorin in Nigeria whom Hostetter had made a heroic effort to reach in 1967 wrote the following expressions to their supervisor, who passed them on to Hostetter: "We are happy to report that we had a grand and inspirational time with Hostetter here in Ilorin . . . . Before we retired that night, C. N. led us in a devotional of Psalm 91, concerning God's protection and guidance in our lives, especially here in the uncertain country of Nigeria . . . . it was truly inspirational."[97]

Over the years of his chairmanship of MCC Hostetter had continued to serve as an ex officio member of the Brethren in Christ Peace, Relief and Service Committee. He used his position with that committee to encourage Brethren in Christ support of MCC. "I feel a little disturbed about it," he wrote to members of the committee in 1953, "when I look over our reports in the MCC meetings. I hope, therefore, that the committee can agree to give the entire offering that is received at [General] Conference for this Mennonite Aid program [to refugees]."[98] In 1962, and writing for the committee, he sent a letter to all pastors in the denomination, indicating that the previous year's 25% drop in donations to relief "makes me feel ashamed" in light of the need and Christ's teachings.[99] When relief offerings to MCC did not seem to improve, he suggested to the committee the sending of more people into the churches to educate the constituency.[100]

Actually, he had been encouraging such education over the years, as the appearance of such MCC and Mennonite figures as Peter Dyck, J. A. Toews, Erland Waltner, Harold Bender, and Orie Miller at Brethren in Christ peace conferences and General Conference attest. In turn, he tried to get as many Brethren in Christ involved with MCC as possible. "Since there is some opposition," he wrote to E. J. Swalm, "to the Brethren in Christ participation for the Mennonite Central Committee and the World Conference, I have always felt that to scatter the representation somewhat has value. The more people that are involved in these interrelationships of the Mennonites, the more wholesome the situation and the better the tie."[101]

The Peace, Relief, and Service Committee benefited greatly by having as a member the chairman of MCC. Hostetter had the background to propose new ideas and to suggest ways in which the committee could cooperate with MCC. He also brought from his position with MCC a detailed knowledge of draft legislation, and thus with Kenneth Hoover did much of the counselling for men involved with the military draft. His influence on the committee and elsewhere (along with that of E. J. Swalm's) helps to explain why when the Brethren in Christ were increasingly moving in NAE and NHA circles, they also moved just as noticeably toward MCC and Mennonite groups as well.

For twenty years, Hostetter served on the Mennonite Central

Committee, fourteen as chairman. He resigned as chairman in 1967 because of declining health. He accepted, however, a term as a member of MCC and attended several meetings, but after 1970 was no longer able to accept even that responsibility.

As this chapter has in various ways suggested, Hostetter came to have an increasing close tie to and appreciation for the Mennonites, which complemented a natural and familial inclination in that direction. Thus during the Mennonite World Conference in 1962 at Kitchener, when John Zercher asked Hostetter what group of Christians he was most comfortable with, he replied, "These [the Mennonites] are my people."[102] Even granting the euphoria of the moment that may have conditioned his reply, his statement was essentially true. This helps to explain why his closest friends outside Brethren in Christ circles—Harold Bender, Orie Miller, William Snyder, and others—were Mennonite.

This helps also to explain why he should become involved in other activities associated with the Mennonite world. When the Institute of Mennonite Studies was formed in 1958, he became a member of the Advisory Council, on which he served until resigning in 1964.[103] More importantly, he was active in the events that led to the organization of the Associated Mennonite Biblical Seminaries at Elkhart, Indiana.

The original concept was for a seminary that would merge the General Conference Mennonite seminary program (at that time affiliated with the Church of the Brethren seminary in Chicago) with the Goshen Biblical Seminary of the Mennonite Church (housed on the campus of Goshen College). Hostetter attended the second exploratory meeting in December, 1954, as a representative of MCC and thus as a liaison between the various Mennonite groups. He encouraged the concept of an all-Mennonite seminary by suggesting that the Brethren in Christ would be interested in the seminary because they were not entirely satisfied with present experiences in seminary training.[104]

Very soon, however, the problem of location became such a thorny issue that it threatened to break off discussions. The Goshen leaders insisted that they could not leave their location; the General Conference Mennonites wanted a more neutral campus and one apart from an undergraduate environment. In this impasse Erland Waltner, the leader of the General Conference group, turned to Hostetter, asking him to speak with Orie Miller, who seemed to be the most determined of those wanting to remain at Goshen.[105] Hostetter did so, but without changing Miller's mind. He encouraged Waltner, however, to be patient and to consider that Miller was probably acting out of concern that the move would further separate the conservative wing of his body from Goshen College. He pledged his own support for whatever Waltner deemed necessary to keep the talks going.[106] He was of further help to Waltner when at the end of the year he chaired a two-day conference, which, while not settling the question of location, at least assured that the talks, which had seemed certain to end, would continue. For this measure of success, Waltner gave Hostetter's chairmanship the credit.[107]

Meantime, at the General Conference of 1955, Hostetter had presented the seminary idea to the Board for Schools and Colleges and the Ministerial and Examining Board, both of whom expressed "active interest" in the seminary and urged Hostetter to represent them at further meetings. By the middle of the next year, when a new proposal emerged to launch the associated seminaries by the General Conference group locating at Elkhart and the Old Mennonites remaining at Goshen, Hostetter was able to assure Mennonite leaders that the Brethren in Christ were ready to join in the inter-Mennonite seminary movement at the Elkhart location and to appoint a staff member.[108] Hostetter's statement, claimed Arthur Rosenberger, President of the General Conference Seminary Board, helped to persuade his group to proceed with the Elkhart site in cooperation with the Goshen College Biblical Seminary, which for the time being would remain located at Goshen.[109]

When the General Conference of the General Conference Mennonites approved this plan, S. F. Pannebecker suggested that Hostetter encourage the Brethren in Christ formally to participate with the Elkhart seminary. This would encourage other smaller Mennonite groups also to join and might even cause the Goshen seminary to reconsider its position on location.[110] To promote such participation, Hostetter in November, 1956, was made a member of the seminary board and named to the Joint Planning Commission as the Brethren in Christ member. Several months later, in February, 1957, he was invited to join the Elkhart faculty as Professor of Christian Education.[111]

But this was not to be. The trustees of Messiah College, as already noted, persuaded Hostetter to postpone his retirement from the presidency until 1960. And in spite of continued urging, he could not convince the Brethren in Christ to become a part of the new seminary venture. In June, 1957, he wrote a strong letter to the members of the Board for Schools and Colleges and the Ministerial and Examining Board stating his "concerns about the outcome of our ministry studying in six or seven different seminaries as they are now doing." He did not agree that the breadth and diversity that some argued in defense of this situation was valid for such a small church as the Brethren in Christ.[112] But despite these arguments, General Conference, on the recommendation of the two boards, decided instead to strengthen the fifth year of theological study at Messiah College, and only to approve the Associated Mennonite Biblical Seminaries and Asbury Theological Seminary as preferable for training Brethren in Christ for pastoral work.[113]

Hostetter was disappointed. He wrote to Nelson Kauffman that a majority of the Conference prefer affiliation with the associated seminaries, but a vocal minority favor Asbury because of its doctrinal emphases. Further selling of the seminaries, however, would win friends among the Brethren in Christ.[114]

While he did not join the faculty at Elkhart, he gave one of the dedication speeches on the opening of the seminary and in the summer school of 1960 taught a course on the Philosophy of Christian Education.[115] This gave him a chance to look closer at the seminary. He determined that a good man in evangelism would be needed if the Brethren in Christ were to tie officially into the seminary.[116] Several years later he expressed to Waltner his concern that the seminary's teaching ministry was stronger than its preaching.[117]

Nevertheless, Hostetter remained a strong supporter of the associated seminaries, always nursing the hope that the Brethren in Christ would become officially a part of the organization. It was a hope born out of his growing appreciation for the character and views of his Mennonite brethren.

Above, Hostetter family. Back row from left to right: Christian (Jr.), Ella (his mother), Christian (Sr.), Henry. Front row: John, Richard (Ella Harris's son), Ella.   *Below,* Graduating class, 1922. C. N. Hostetter, Jr., is in middle of middle row.

Teacher's Training Class at Lancaster, 1921. Superintendent C. N. Hostetter, Jr., is at far right.

C. N. Hostetter, Jr., as stereoscope salesman

Fenwick, Ontario, tent meeting, 1924. From left to right: Earl Sider, Elsie Sider, Mary Sentz, Helen (Ready) Mater, C. N. Hostetter, Jr.

In camp while holding summer evangelistic meetings in Virginia in 1932. Hostetter is at left.

Above, *At home in Refton. From left to right: Lane, Nelson, Anna (holding Glenn), Hostetter, Ray*
Below, *C. N. Hostetter, Jr., congratulated at his inauguration by retiring president Enos Hess*

Faculty Meeting (Hostetter at right)

Recipient of D. D. degree from Houghton College in 1945. From left to right: John Wesley Bready, President Stephen Paine, Hostetter

Joint Board of Trustees and Associates (Hostetter at left front row)

Cornerstone Laying, Girl's Dormitory, 1949

Above, Assistant Moderator, General Conference, 1969, at Messiah College
Below, Home Mission Board. From left to right: M. G. Engle, John Nigh, Albert Engle, Hostetter, Alvin Burkholder, Carl Stump, Henry Ginder, Dale Ulery

With former Messiah College students at Luray Civilian Public Service Camp in Virginia, 1942. Hostetter stands second to the right.

Above, At missionary conference in Japan, 1960. Hostetter is in middle of front row.

Left, Mennonite Central Committee Officers. From left to right: Hostetter, unidentified person, Orie Miller

Hymnal Committee at work in summer of 1934. From left to right: Hostetter, Montfer Free, E. J. Swalm, Ralph Musser, Laban Wingert, Vernon L. Stump

Roxbury Holiness Camp Staff for 1955. Left to right: Andrew McNiven, Jacob Bowers, Harry Hock, John Rosenberry, Charlie Byers, Hostetter, Raymond Nissley

Above, Hostetter at an NAE convention. Behind him, from left to right: Clyde Taylor, Herbert Graffam, Arthur Climenhaga, Billy Graham
Left, With Glenn's children
Below, Grandparents and grandchildren (1960)

World Relief Commission (around 1960). Hostetter is third from the left, front row.

With Russian guests (front row) of MCC. Standing in back row from left to right: Harold S. Bender, J. J. Thiessen, Hostetter, Henry A. Fast, and William Snyder

Long-time friend E. J. Swalm congratulates the Hostetters at the banquet celebrating Hostetter's fifty years in the ministry.

The Hostetter family. Left to right: Ray, Lane, C. N., Anna, and Nelson

"A Positive Evangelical Fellowship"

*B*eyond his own church and the Mennonite Central Committee, C. N. Hostetter, Jr., became interested and active
in a variety of other organizations, either religious or
service-oriented in nature. His activities in them further the image
of Hostetter as a person who enjoyed becoming involved and
who was attracted to a wider world beyond his own denomination.

His contact with the National Holiness Association (NHA,
and now Christian Holiness Association, or CHA) was at least as
early as 1937 when he brought Joseph Smith, a former president
of the Association, to campus to conduct an eight-session School
of the Prophets.[1] (The Association had its origin in the 1860s in
the National Camp Meeting Association; it brings together in its
annual convention and committee work such holiness groups as
the Wesleyan Methodists, Nazarenes, Free Methodists, Salva-
tion Army, Brethren in Christ, and individual congregations of
other denominations.) In 1939 Hostetter himself gave an address
at the NHA convention at Asbury College on "Is The Bible Made
Sufficiently Prominent as a Book of Study in our Holiness
Schools?"[2] and in 1940 he spoke at the International Holiness
Convention at Houghton College.[3] By 1940 the college had
become a member of NHA.[4]

Thus Hostetter had been active for a number of years in NHA
before the denomination as a whole decided on affiliation in
1950. In that year, he attended NHA's convention in Indianapolis, and was elected to the organization's Education Committee.[5]
At the 1953 convention, he was placed for a term on the Commission on Evangelism and gave one of the addresses.[6] But while he
had an early and continuing interest in the NHA, he did not

become so integrally a part of it as he did of some other organizations, notably MCC and the National Association of Evangelicals (NAE).

The NAE was organized in 1942; Hostetter first attended one of its conventions in 1947. He was at the Chicago convention in 1949 as part of a study committee to consider Brethren in Christ affiliation with both NAE and NHA. Here he met many "old friends," including Leslie Marston, Harold Sheets, John Mummau and V. Raymond Edman, and heard outstanding addresses, including a "masterpiece" by Stephen Paine of Houghton College on the more evangelical task of NAE in contrast to the work of the National Council of Christian Churches and the American Council of Churches.[7] A few months later, the study committee recommended to General Conference Brethren in Christ affiliation with both NAE and NHA, a recommendation which conference members accepted by a vote of 125 to 30 for NAE.[8]

At the NAE convention of the following year occurred the late night meeting of Brethren in Christ leaders, which, as noted earlier, served as a catalyst for change in the denomination. At this convention Hostetter was elected to the college division of the Commission for Educational Institutions. He served on the Board of Administration from 1952 to 1955, and again from 1958 to 1961. He was appointed in 1953 to the World Relief Commission, the relief arm of NAE, where he played an increasingly important role. In later years he served frequently on the Nominating Committee, sometimes as chairman. And in 1960 he was elected member-at-large to the Executive Committee.

Hostetter valued his association with the leading names in the evangelical world, and was impressed by them. During the NAE convention in 1954, he noted in his diary (obviously with some surprise) that "here is a fine group of men, earnest Christians from Holiness, Pentecostal and Calvinist fellowships with whom it is a joy to worship and work." He thought Paul Rees (long a friend) impressive in his handling of business sessions and in his delivery of sermons: "For clarity of exposition he ranks with top teachers."[9] He never quite mastered, however, the salaries the officers received. Following a meeting in October, 1954, when the salary of one official was raised from $6,000 to 7,000 (at a time when Messiah College faculty made considerably less than half that amount), he observed that "these men do not know very much about sacrifice compared with Brethren in Christ men."[10]

The affiliation of the Brethren in Christ with NAE, Hostetter believed, was a profitable, even crucial one. He made this clear in an article in the *Evangelical Visitor* in 1958, entitled "NAE and the Church." In addition to the great good in evangelism that it was doing throughout the world, NAE, according to Hostetter, was proving to be a great blessing to the denomination: "For the Brethren in Christ this fellowship has helped to fire the hearts of bishops, ministers and laymen, to make our Sunday schools more effective, to improve the functioning of our church schools and colleges, and to fan and fuel the flame of evangelism and personal testimony."[11]

But this valuable association was not always a comfortable one for Hostetter, particularly because of elements within NAE that were strongly nationalistic, sometimes even militaristic. He appears to have first commented on this problem at the 1951 NAE convention in Chicago, which took place at the time when President Harry Truman dismissed General Douglas MacArthur because of their differing views over the conduct of the war in Korea. On the second day of the convention, the NAE president called a special session to request that the assembly send a message to Truman protesting the dismissal. Hostetter described the session in his diary: "MacArthur is most popular with evangelical missionaries, and the NAE convention was almost hysterical. I voted 'no' on the resolution loud enough to attract attention, but I could not get the floor for a speech. The convention even discussed asking Congress to impeach the President."[12] He later wrote to Asa Climenhaga that he was "shocked and much disappointed" over the conduct of the convention, but quickly added that not everyone had acted in such a "childish way." Leslie Marston, Stephen Paine and others "showed themselves poised and balanced and did not go in with the crowd . . . . Many however . . . were very militaristic and anti-government in their outspoken statements."[13]

In this respect, Harold Ockenga was a continual puzzle to Hostetter. He admired Ockenga's platform abilities (especially his skill at speaking masterfully at length and without notes) and his championship of evangelicalism and missionary activities.

This admiration obviously had everything to do with Ockenga's
selection as commencement speaker at Messiah College in 1952.
But Ockenga was a leader of the "God and Country" group in
NAE, and so Hostetter was frequently at odds with him. Thus he
was typically "much disappointed" when, at the 1954 convention,
Ockenga gave a message that was "a call to militarism against
communism."[14]

Ockenga and this theme set the background for a dramatic
episode that occurred in the convention of the following year
(1955). The Commission on Social Action, of which Carl F. H.
Henry was chairman, had arranged for a panel of speakers to
address the subject of "Christianity and War in Our Times."
Harold Ockenga and General William K. Harrison were to be
members of the panel. Hostetter immediately sensed where this
would lead the convention. In mid-December he wrote Henry a
strong letter, pointing out that the two men would present a point
of view not accepted by all evangelicals and therefore the view of
those who believe that war is contrary to the will of God should
also be heard. "The inclinations of evangelicals," he pointed out,
"and particularly of fundamentalists, is to take for granted that
the Bible approves participation in war and classify all opposition
to it as identified with the pacifism espoused by liberals. The
evangelical fellowship should be better informed."[15]

Hostetter's request was not honored, and his fears were confirmed. Harrison gave a ringing challenge to the Christians to do
their duty to God and country by fighting. Dismayed, Hostetter
protested the address to several of the leading members of NAE,
including Kenneth Geiger, Stephen Paine, George Ford, and
President H. H. Savage. They and others were also troubled by
the Harrison address because it was a breach of the tacit rule of
NAE which holds that members should associate on the basis of
what unites, not divides, the NAE body. Geiger especially was
disturbed, claiming, according to Hostetter, that "the repeated
public utterances in support of war in our convention was building up quite a backlog of unrest among the NAE constituents
who do not share that opinion."[16] Savage and others requested
Hostetter to give a response on the next day.

Hostetter counselled with the other Brethren in Christ at the
convention and then returned to his hotel room to sound out

ideas with his roommate, E. J. Swalm. By 4 o'clock the following morning he was awake and in prayer. He spent the forenoon in his room, so intent in "waiting on the Lord and praying" that when he noticed that his Hamilton watch had stopped he was already five minutes late. He rushed out of the hotel, hailed a taxi, and arrived at the convention hall just as he was about to be called to the platform. Savage introduced him and emphasized that Hostetter had been invited to speak on "The Christian and War." "I trembled but the Lord helped his unworthy servant," he wrote in his diary at the end of the day. "I was astonished at the favorable response."[17] Others who were there are unanimous in describing the speech as diplomatic, masterful, and well received. Even the academic dean of Wheaton College later wrote to ask for a synopsis of his address for use in the classroom, and *United Evangelical Action,* the official journal of NAE, published it in its August issue.

A few days after returning to Grantham, Hostetter wrote to Carl Henry at Fuller Theological Seminary to follow up on his success. He began by congratulating Henry on a "forthright and penetrating" address Henry had given at the convention, and for arranging the panel on "The Christian and War," since that was a sign that Henry thought Christians must face the issues of the subject. But he regretted that the issue had been presented in a large gathering. He called on Henry to use his Commission on Social Action to arrange for a less public study session on the question.[18]

Henry replied immediately. He did not approve of what had happened, including Hostetter giving his address (after all, two wrongs do not make a right). He insisted that his commission had acted honorably because it had warned Harrison not to make remarks that might offend a minority, opposite view. But, Henry added, whatever the merits or demerits of the case, he was weary of the matter. Besides, people's minds were made up on the subject, and it was too difficult to get collegiate men to carry on an effective discussion.[19]

Hostetter, however, pursued the issue with Henry. He was prompted to do so when he received a letter from Harold Sherk of MCC relating that Mennonites and the MCC people had been discussing how to speak to fundamentalist groups, such as NAE, about peace questions. Sherk suggested that the best way may be through MCC constituencies which have representatives with NAE. Hostetter was ideally suited for leadership in this work, Sherk added, "because of your own close contact with the NAE over a number of years, and your interest in promoting the kind of conversations suggested, and the opportunities that you have had for bringing this question to the attention of NAE people . . . ." He thought that George Ford's letter in the October 15 issue of *Christian Leader,* which called for a discussion of the war-peace issue in a commission setting at NAE, might provide Hostetter with an opening.

Hostetter clipped Ford's letter from the magazine and sent it to Henry, urging him to reconsider his position.[20] But although Henry's reply was more moderate in tone than his earlier one (he conceded that such a session might be a good idea), he did not think he could get the right men to represent the pro-war side without offering them an honorarium; the Mennonites, he recognized, would have no such difficulty.[21]

Hostetter was somewhat more successful with the Commission on Social Action in 1960. Following some exploratory talks in October, 1959, with NAE officials by Hostetter, Guy Hershberger, and Erland Waltner, the commission, now under Arthur Zahniser, agreed to sponsor a session on "The Christians and Military Service" at the next convention. Hostetter's correspondence in arranging for and encouraging attendance at this meeting clearly illustrates his role as a bridge between Mennonites and MCC on the one hand, and evangelicals and NAE on the other.[22]

But the session on April 26, 1960, was hardly a success. The peace groups within NAE brought John A. Toews from Winnipeg to present their position; V. Raymond Edman, President of Wheaton College, was asked to speak on the other side. Ten persons sympathetic to the peace side attended (five Brethren in Christ, two Mennonite Brethren, and three other Mennonites). The other side was represented by only four—Zahniser as chairman of the commission, the man in charge of devotions, a friend of Edman, and, because Edman did not attend, the reader of Edman's paper. This paper, according to one source, was as poor as the attendance, since it focused not on Scripture but on a Sergeant York who changed from being a pacifist to a soldier.[23]

Another problem for the peace groups developed in the next (1961) convention, when Harold Ockenga gave what Hostetter described as a "brilliant analysis" of communism but appealed only to force to stop it. The speech brought some soul-searching among the peace representatives and led to a caucus in which they discussed the election campaign attitudes of some NAE leaders of the previous year and their anti-Catholic and anti-communist speeches. But Hostetter defended the NAE. The Brethren in Christ, he told the group, were part of NAE because there were important things they could do with that body, and that on the whole NAE officials tried to be scrupulously fair. The caucus ended by agreeing that even peace churches could not afford to live in isolation and that there were positive features in joining other conservative groups in a voice to government and in a "positive evangelical fellowship."[24]

Following the caucus, Hostetter arranged for a meeting of the peace groups with NAE officers to object to Ockenga's statements that communism could be met only by force. The officers insisted that Ockenga's views did not reflect the NAE basic statement of faith, nor was it supported officially by the Association. The last word in this event was had by Hostetter who wrote an article in the April, 1963, issue of *United Evangelical Action* in which he maintained that the best way to meet the challenge of communism is not by force of arms, but by love and the gospel.[25]

He was, in fact, in these years disturbed by what he considered to be the undue attention given to communism by many in NAE. After attending, for example, an Executive Committee meeting in June, 1961, he wrote in his diary: "The NAE program is spending so much time and effort in its anti-communist propaganda that I am somewhat disgusted with the emphasis."[26] He was thus greatly pleased when Bob Pierce (whom he had come to admire) in a speech at the 1962 convention gave a "stirring message" in which Hostetter quoted him as saying: "Don't ask me to spend my time fighting communism or the World Council of Churches."[27]

But Hostetter continued to insist that problems and failures should not result in peace groups withdrawing from NAE. To John Howard Yoder, who was critical of the involvement of peace churches with NAE because of its militaristic propensities,

Hostetter responded with the argument that the groups to which they belonged "have an obligation to the Christian world that we cannot afford to miss by too much abnegation."[28] Following the 1960 session, however, he did essentially agree with Yoder that a different tactic should be followed, one that would be more informal and outside the setting of NAE meetings, but still with NAE and NAE-related peoples.[29]

That new tactic is illustrated in a study conference in March, 1963, that Hostetter helped to arrange between evangelicals and peace representatives. The planning for the conference was done by an ad hoc committee composed of men from both sides (Vernon Grounds, Lloyd Kalland, Kenneth Kantzer, Frank Furrell, Arthur Glaser, Edgar Metzler, and Hostetter as chairman). "We had a very frank discussion and a profitable time together," Hostetter wrote after one of the committee meetings.[30] At the conference, Hostetter himself read two papers and was pleased with the conference as a whole: "a very good program" was his judgment.[31] Given his favorable impression, it is curious that he does not seem to have been closely connected with whatever other attempts may have been made to bring the NAE and MCC-related groups together, although he was active in other peace conferences of mixed groups.

On a more individual level, he was part of an MCC group that met with Billy Graham in August, 1961. Hostetter was consistently impressed with Graham. He heard Graham speak frequently at the NAE conventions; he invariably labelled Graham's sermons with such adjectives as "powerful" or "impressive."

Because Graham was so much a leader of evangelicals, Hostetter and the Mennonites considered it important to dialogue with him on the peace issue. A group of sixteen persons, including Hostetter, met with Graham for breakfast on August 20, 1961. John C. Wenger briefly described the Mennonite faith and Hostetter the work of MCC. Graham, attentive and congenial, expressed himself as being in 99% agreement, and commended John Stott as one of the keenest modern theologians who had come to the pacifist position.

Those who attended the meeting were pleased, and after Graham left, Hostetter pressed the point that this was how peace discussions were probably best conducted—with those who were open—and not by attempting to talk with everyone. He and Elmer Neufeld were asked by the group to plan for another meeting with Graham, but when Graham was approached in early 1962, he informed the two men that his schedule for that year was too full for further meetings. It does not appear that Hostetter was a part of any later interview that may have been arranged.[32]

Hostetter's closest connection to and greatest service with the NAE was through the World Relief Commission (WRC). This relief arm of NAE was established in 1944 primarily to assist in providing European refugees of the war with clothing. After the war emergency conditions passed in Europe, the world crises shifted to the East and so too did the work of the WRC. When Hostetter became a member of the commission in 1953, its center of activity was in Korea, but during his years with the organization, it expanded elsewhere, until it was operating in such areas as Vietnam, Taiwan, Hong Kong, and Haiti.

In time, the WRC also expanded its distribution from clothing to include food and medicine. In 1954 it registered with the New International Cooperation Agency to serve as a channel for the flow of American surplus food and to be reimbursed for ocean freight shipping charges. At about the same time the WRC made an arrangement with the Inter-Church Medical Association to obtain medicines, drugs, and vitamins below cost for relief distribution.[33]

The WRC operated largely as a service agent. Its representatives overseas were usually missionaries and workers serving with evangelical mission organizations. In a departure from this policy, the WRC in 1958 placed its first personnel overseas (in Korea) in the person of Byron Crouse, Jr. In the previous year, becoming more aggressive, it began to cooperate with other church-related agencies, such as MCC.[34] But the philosophy of WRC, at least during Hostetter's years with the commission, remained primarily one of working through established churches and agencies overseas, rather than operating its own program.

Following his appointment in 1953, Hostetter became an increasingly valuable member to the WRC. In 1954 he was placed on its Executive Committee, and in 1955 and 1956 was elected second and first vice-chairman respectively. When the Adminis-

trative Committee, a small group designed to give more concentrated and immediate direction to the executive director, was
formed in 1957, Hostetter was named a member.[35] Finally, in
1959, he became chairman of the commission, a position which
he held until his resignation in 1967.

Thus from 1959 to 1967 Hostetter headed two world relief
agencies—WRC and MCC. There was advantage in this for both
organizations. For MCC, the WRC was a source for some of
MCC's supplies, particularly in Asia. There was also something
of a psychological dimension to the relationship that worked to
MCC's advantage. Such groups as the Mennonite Brethren, the
Evangelical Mennonite Brethren, and the Evangelical Mennonites tended to think that MCC had too many ties with such
ecumenical groups as the Church World Service and the World
Council of Churches agencies. Hostetter's position on the WRC
provided MCC a link with the more evangelical church agencies
and thus gave some assurance to the more conservative, evangelical wing of the Mennonite constituency that MCC relationships
were not entirely one-sided.[36]

And Hostetter made certain that MCC did not suffer from his
role with the WRC. Although he considered that he owed service
to the WRC in the interest of relief work in general, and while he
was convinced that the Brethren in Christ had much to gain from
their association with NAE, he was clear in his commitment, as
well as his denomination's, to the work of MCC. To William
Snyder he spoke on more than one occasion words to the following effect: "Now William, you don't have to worry. The Brethren
in Christ are working through MCC, and our money will go
there. My role in the World Relief Commission is to help and
encourage them in their vision of relief work."[37]

But the WRC gained just as much by Hostetter's connection
with MCC. By the time he became a member of the commission
and particularly by the time he was made chairman, he had
acquired a considerable background knowledge of relief work by
virtue of his association with MCC. The commission was able to
tap this background knowledge and experience, and through him
to make contacts and develop programs that it normally would
not have done. An early example may be seen in 1954 in Hostetter's bringing Wendell Rockey, newly appointed as WRC Execu-

tive Director, from his New York office to Akron, where Rockey spent several days talking to MCC administrators and observing MCC methods of shipping, packaging, and publicity.[38]

Other examples may be found in the way MCC assisted the commission in its attempts to begin and continue work in areas beyond Korea, assistance which the commission from time to time took official action to encourage. The WRC Executive Committee in June, 1960, asked Hostetter to explore and report on the possibilities of the commission's working with MCC in its large relief program, and, as noted in the previous chapter, arranged for Hostetter to combine work for WRC with that which he did for MCC on his world trip in 1960-1961.[39] Four years later the same committee passed a resolution to cooperate with MCC "to see that every portion of the world has some kind of relief provisions especially in times of emergency needs: and to secure personnel from MCC to send into those areas where they may be called or for service representatives to train local personnel as to 'how to do relief.' "[40] In the following year, MCC agreed to share with NAE agencies its experience in operating under government regulations (both home and foreign) and "in making the relief efforts supportive of the broad objectives of church building and renewals."[41] When in the same year it became apparent to NAE that Church World Service, the relief agency of the National Council of Churches, would probably no longer service evangelicals, NAE Executive Secretary Clyde Taylor wrote to Wendell Rockey that this would create the need for an even greater liaison with MCC.[42]

The World Relief Commission's attempt to begin relief work in Colombia illustrates more specifically Hostetter's function as a bridge with MCC. Since 1959 the commission had been attempting to find an entrance into Colombia but had always, as the agency thought, run against opposition from the Roman Catholic relief organization, which appeared to have been set up to exclude Protestant relief aid. Finally, in late 1961 Hostetter arranged for MCC to send Samuel Miller to try to find a way through this stone wall. (At the same time, Hostetter refused a request to write an article attacking the Catholic relief practices, because, as he wrote to one NAE leader, "I cannot serve the role of a 'reporting policeman' and at the same time exercise the

influence that I must exercise if we are to get into Colombia.")[43]
Miller spent several months in Colombia, but found opposition
so strong that WRC decided not to pursue the project.[44]

In 1963 a more successful venture was begun in Burundi by
Norman Wingert, a Brethren in Christ relief worker who was lent
(seconded, to use MCC and missions terminology) to the WRC
by MCC. In India, all WRC relief assistance was channelled
through MCC. This explains the interesting situation in which
the $2,000 raised by Harold Ockenga's Boston Park Street
Church in 1966 and given to WRC for India had to be sent
through MCC.[45]

One of the instances of most direct cooperation between the
World Relief Commission and the Mennonite Central Commit-
tee in Hostetter's years in these agencies occurred in Vietnam.
MCC began relief activities there in 1954, working closely with
Christian and Missionary Alliance missionaries and the National
Church, and eventually linking up with and leading the Vietnam
Christian Service. WRC's relief work included a farm at Hue for
vocational training for refugees and three other vocational training centers. MCC was originally asked to sponsor the Hue farm
but instead channelled that responsibility to WRC.[46] But MCC
helped in the projects in a substantial way, providing in the initial
stages of the program $10,000 for construction of facilities at the
Hue farm, funds for setting up and operating extension vocational training for refugees at the three other centers, and personnel for all four locations.[47]

The administration of this work created some difficulties for
the commission, particularly with personnel leadership and relations with the National Church leaders. By mid-1966 the situation called for close scrutiny. Clay Mitchell, secretary of the
WRC Executive Committee, wrote to Hostetter in August: "It
looks as though we will have to turn to you personally to size up
the situation on the field, or get your ever-willing organization
MCC, to do the job." Hostetter, he claimed, was the only one on
the world-wide committee with "the insight, experience, etc.
required in this world-wide responsibility, so we have to lean on
you continually."[48]

And so Hostetter made another trip to Vietnam, where he was
assisted by Elmer Kilbourne of the Oriental Missionary Society

and WRC director in Korea. The two men talked with National Church leaders, recommended expansion of WRC activities in face of the growing refugee problem, and successfully dealt with the administrative problem. Of Hostetter's work, Kilbourne reported to Wendell Rockey: "If Dr. Hostetter had not been there, none of this could have been possible.... Dr. Hostetter is a wonderful man of God and it was a very inspiring and profitable experience being with him."[49]

Hostetter resigned his leadership of the World Relief Commission in 1967, at the same time that he left the chairmanship of MCC. But his interest in the work of the commission remained. When Elmer Kilbourne was in the United States in early 1969, Hostetter informed him about his resignation and invited him to his home. "I would like to hear about your work in Korea," he wrote, "and visit with you again, if at all possible...."[50] With his retirement the cooperation between the two relief agencies declined, another evidence of the linking role that Hostetter had played between the two world relief agencies.

His association with NAE undoubtedly explains his membership on the trustee board of Christ Church Mission in New York city. (The mission began in the 1880s as a ministry to converted Roman Catholic priests.) The mission also had on its board some of the leaders of NAE, including Clyde Taylor, Clay Mitchell, Paul Fryhling and others, who, it appears, were responsible for bringing Hostetter also on to the board. He served as a trustee from 1958 to 1963, declined reelection to another term, but continued to make small cash donations to the mission.

Beyond these organizations—NHA, NAE, and Christ Church Mission—Hostetter associated closely with several denominations. Among them was the United Zion Church.

The United Zion Church (originally known as the United Zion's Children) formed in the 1850s, when the parent Brethren in Christ body expelled them for constructing a meeting house under the leadership of Matthias Brinser. Informal ties, however, remained between the two groups, which led in the 1920s to a committee to investigate a merger. This committee was short-lived, but another one was formed in 1935. Hostetter was strongly in favor of the committee and the merger. After holding a successful revival among the United Zion members in late 1934, he wrote

in a small notebook: "A desire to bring about a closer union
between our two bodies—Brethren in Christ and U.Z.C.—was
created in my mind."[51] It is tempting to link that thought in some
way to the creation of the committee in 1935.

Hostetter's father and, later, brother Henry served on this
merger committee. The committee sponsored periodic fellowship
meetings between the Brethren in Christ and the United Zion
Church. Hostetter himself frequently attended and took a leading
part in these meetings. Although not a member of the committee,
he attended at least some of its formal discussions on merger.[52]
But progress was slow. Hostetter ascribed this in large measure to
difficulties among the United Zion people which led to forty or
fifty (according to his figures) leaving their church at Annville to
become members of the Brethren in Christ Church at Cleona.[53]
He was a member of the committee formed in 1962 to reopen the
question of merger, this time with both the United Zion Church
and the United Christian Church. When the committee met, its
members agreed that these two small bodies needed to unite with
some other group to remain alive, but bishops in both groups,
according to Hostetter, stoutly opposed doing so with the
Brethren in Christ.[54]

Hostetter's relations with the United Zion Church were on
other levels as well. He had married one of their number. He held
revival meetings for them (at Elizabethtown, Annville, Hahn-
stown, Akron, and elsewhere), and spoke at their Bible conferences, Sunday school conventions, and worship services. He can-
vassed among them for funds and students; by 1956, ninety-five
of their young people had come as students to Messiah College,
virtually the only college they attended.[55]

Obviously, Hostetter was popular among them, his wife and
plain clothes making good entrances for him into their fellowship. But above all, according to one of their leaders, they were
attracted by his apparent humility: "The one word that really sold
C. N. to us was his humility. Our people weren't excited about
education in those days, yet he was like us, though educated. You
couldn't see his high training. He moved among us and you could
understand him."[56]

Hostetter was also frequently among the members of the
Holiness Christian Church (now the Evangelical Christian

Church). He spoke frequently in their congregations and camp meetings as an evangelist and youth speaker. In the early 1950s the denomination approved Messiah College for the education of its ministers and young people, a large proportion of whom did attend the college, attracted there by their acquaintances with its president.[57]

Diary entries for 1953 and 1954 illustrate Hostetter's fondness for this holiness group. In August, 1953, he served as evangelist for their camp meeting at Seifert. "These Holiness Christian men," he observed, "are a very fine group and God is using their testimony." Another diary entry in the same week followed a time of fellowship with the young people after an altar service: "There is a lovely sweet spirit in this camp meeting. God's Spirit is on the place." After his last messages of the week, he wrote: "Many folks wanted to speak to me and I went to Kehler's cabin for coffee. I left for home at 11:30 p.m. They gave me $170—the largest I ever got for one week."[58]

In the next month he was a weekend speaker at the Holiness Christian camp at Pine Grove, where he "had a pleasant period of fellowship with these dear saints."[59] In January of the next year, he spoke on Sunday morning in their Hanover church and afterward went to the home of the pastor for dinner. Here he had, in his words, "one of the most sumptuous *Pa. Dutch dinners I ever ate.* So much food! Fried ham and roast chicken. 5 kinds of cake—3 kinds of pie, 3 kinds of dessert, etc. etc."[60] That meal seems nicely to suggest the mutual pleasure of Hostetter and the Holiness Christian members.

In 1955, Hostetter agreed to be placed on the trustee board of the Pennsylvania Temperance League, although he warned in accepting the assignment that his attendance at board meetings might be erratic.[61] His diary, in fact, suggests that his attendance was spotty. He resigned in 1963.

He was more active in a more local organization, the Cumberland County Tuberculosis and Health Association. Elected to the Board of Directors in 1944, he became Vice President in 1950, refused nomination to the presidency in 1952, and resigned in 1960 before beginning his world tour for MCC and WRC.[62]

His diary indicates that he made decided efforts to attend the Association's board meetings in Carlisle. At the Association's

dinners he frequently served as toastmaster and customarily said
the grace. He sometimes spoke for the Association—once at the
Cumberland Valley High School. Occasionally he presided over
special meetings, as in 1958 at the dinner at Allenberry in Boiling
Springs of the State T. B. Association.[63] In 1951 at the dinner in
Carlisle to launch the annual fund drive, he acted as toastmaster,
paid tribute to the president, Harold Irwin, and presented an
orchid to Maude Phillips, the Executive Secretary for her "fine
work." "The meeting," the diary notes, "went over with a bang
and I received many expressions of thanks."[64]

Why Hostetter should give time and effort to such an organization is not entirely clear. Perhaps he considered this a good way as
a college president to fulfill a community obligation. He
undoubtedly also saw it as part of his wider work of bringing
relief to those in need.

XI

"Work Out Your Will in These Boys"

C N. Hostetter, Jr., was a very public man. As most public men, however, he had a more private life of personal interests and family. These complemented and help to explain his public roles.

As most Brethren in Christ, he was conservative in politics, a Republican by nature. Most of our information about his political views and activities comes from the diary, which limits the number of years in which he expressed himself on such matters. One of the earliest signs of this interest was his attending, with his son Lane, a session of the 1944 Democratic National Convention, held that year in Chicago, where he was studying in summer school. It appears from the diary that he may have voted for the first time (at least on the federal level) in the elections of 1952. He listened for most of two days to the Republican convention of that year, and in September went to Carlisle to register in order to qualify for voting.[1] Like many other Brethren in Christ who went to the polls for the first time in 1952, he voted for Eisenhower, whom some members of the denomination seemed ready to claim because as a boy he attended Sunday school in Abilene for several months. Hostetter was moved by Eisenhower's prayer at the inauguration and asked: "Did he carry some of the influence of prayers he heard in the Abilene Brethren in Christ Church?"[2]

He took, if anything, a greater interest in the 1956 and 1960 elections. He listened to both the Republican and Democratic conventions in 1956, and after following the speeches of both candidates declared that Adlai Stevenson could not beat Eisenhower, at least he hoped not, since it "would certainly be unfortunate to place the leadership of the nation in Stevenson's hands."

After voting the Republican ticket, he stayed up until 1:00 a.m. listening to the returns. When Eisenhower's election was announced, Hostetter declared that he was not surprised; he didn't think the American people would switch from Eisenhower to Stevenson.[3]

Along with all his other pursuits, Hostetter followed economic interests. In 1938 he bought the Treona property (on the side of the Yellow Breeches across from the campus), which contained the former orphanage building, a barn, and acreage to the top of the hill (where college faculty houses are now located). He rented apartments in the building, raised chickens (usually around 200) in the barn, and sometimes grew crops (in the diary he writes of selling 300 bushels of shelled corn to a local grain dealer).[4]

The picture of Hostetter as farmer is an interesting one. The diary reveals him cleaning eggs with son Glenn as early as 4:00 a.m. before going off to college or a church assignment, spreading fertilizer (with C. Z. Musser's spreader), and mowing patches of thistles and weeds. "I was farmer again," he once wrote, obviously with pleasure, after several hours in the fields.[5]

The Treona property did not bring him much profit, partly because he was not sufficiently mechanically inclined or at home long enough to give the small farm proper attention. In mid-1951, after checking accounts carefully, he became convinced that he should sell the property, which he did early the following year for $15,000.[6]

Meanwhile he had bought a farm of 117 acres about five miles west of Grantham, near Allen. In September, 1952, with the money obtained from the sale of the Treona property, he purchased for $21,000 a second farm of 210 acres about three miles south of Dillsburg. The first farm he appropriately termed the upper farm, the second the lower. He turned both into dairy farms, let them out to tenant farmers on a lease and profit-sharing basis, and proceeded to develop buildings and lands in a model fashion. On the lower farm he almost immediately began a major extension to the barn to provide for milking stables. For several months he met with dealers for barn equipment (stalls, milkers, manure cleaners), and ordered building supplies (cement, lumber, roofing). Construction was in full swing by examination time in January, 1953. On January 20, he wrote, "I gave my final exam to

Ethics class . . . . Excused myself part time and ran down to the farm."[7] At the same time that this construction was going on at the lower farm, he tore out the south end of the barn on the upper farm to provide room for thirty-two milking cows.

Improvements in buildings were matched by improvements in the land. For this he worked closely with the county agricultural agents. Soon after the purchase of the lower farm he went to York to sign up for benefit payments under the agricultural program. There he talked to the county commissioners, who, Hostetter proudly related in his diary, "after listening to me talk . . . said, 'You talk in such a way that I know you know something about farming.' "[8] Six days later he met the soil conservation agent from York County and the two went over the farm together and decided on the work for which aid would be given, including ditching, tiling and contouring.[9] By the time Hostetter completed his improvement on the lower farm, he had laid over 5,000 feet of tile to drain wet spots, had cleared several acres of land, and had built new fences around virtually the whole farm. Much the same improvements he made, with some government aid, on the upper farm.

These improvements cost him considerable money. Even with government assistance, he still had to take out loans totaling $25,000. To one as careful in financing as Hostetter, this was some cause for worry. Was he being a good steward of his money? he kept asking himself. The projects, he noted in one place, "are costing me much more than I had planned. Oh God, give me wisdom in stewardship planning so that this venture may be to the glory of God." "I hope we can find our way through with this large indebtedness," he wrote in another. "We prayed about our business and felt the Lord was guiding us in what we did."[11] By the spring of 1955 he had paid off the mortgage on both farms, in part by cashing some of the bonds that his wife had inherited.[12] However, continued improvements on buildings and equipment, and enlargement of stock (both often at the request of his farmers), seem to have meant more loans and no great profits.

Whatever the profit, or lack of it, Hostetter obviously took pride and found relaxation in his farms. On returning from a trip, one of the first things he would do was to jump in his car and make the rounds of the two farms. In fact, he was so delighted with them that he was occasionally tempted to buy a third. Thus we find him on September 28, 1957, at Cyrus Neisley's farm sale, where, according to the diary, he was kept from buying the farm only because it sold for $53,000. That was too much for the cautious financier, who confessed that "it would be nice to own that lovely farm, but the income could hardly make a satisfactory return for a landlord investment."[13]

In the mid-1950s the Hostetters invested in and became part of an ice-cream company. Their son Ray and Richard Minter (Ray's brother-in-law) initiated the venture (appropriately named the Rich Ray Industries), and located it near Pitman, New Jersey. Besides investing in the company, Hostetter arranged for loans, travelled to New Jersey to help set up the bookkeeping procedures, and served as president of the corporation. The costs for producing and delivering the ice cream, however, were high, and the company's ice cream could not compete effectively in price with that sold in the supermarkets. Thus in 1961 the family decided to withdraw from production and sold the plant.[14]

Over the years, especially in the 1950s and 1960s, the Hostetters invested in stocks and bonds. The few records available suggest that these were usually sound investments. Some of his stocks nearly doubled in value when two local banks merged in 1957.[15] In February of 1968, he estimated that he had nearly $25,000 in stocks, exclusive of his wife's holdings. These were spread over a number of companies, including General Motors (100 shares), Hershey Chocolate (50 shares), Standard Oil of New Jersey (50 shares), and North American Rockwell (28 shares).[16]

Hostetter's family relations for some of these years were not always as easy as his business endeavors. His frequent absences from home placed a strain on family life that many families of churchmen of Hostetter's period experienced. Not surprisingly, some difficulties developed with the sons. When Hostetter's diary begins again in 1949, these difficulties had come to a head, and his sons seemed bent on activities that were disturbing to their father. His diary entry on his fiftieth birthday reflects his feelings: "In my own home have been my greatest trials of faith. I assumed that as I put God first and worked diligently in His service, God would supply all my needs and call my children to serve Him. I now see I gave too little attention to rearing them."[17]

He began to make deliberate efforts to be more with his sons. In May, 1949, part of the family accompanied him and his wife to Greenville College in Illinois where he received an honorary degree; the trip, he thought, was "one of the best we ever had with the family."[18] In the summer of the same year, he took Lane, Ray, and Glenn for a holiday trip as far west as Salt Lake City and Yellowstone National Park, and among other activities went swimming in the Great Salt Lake and attended a rodeo at Colorado Springs (obviously doing what the sons enjoyed). This, he said in his diary, was a "rich experience," and he was obviously delighted when his sons presented him with a terry bath robe in appreciation of the trip.[19]

But the immediate results were not as fruitful as he had hoped. A few days after their return, the annual youth conference convened on campus, but his sons did not appear interested. "Oh God," he prayed, "forgive me for my failures! My God, what shall I do? Please save my sons at any price!"[20]

He continued under this heavy burden. As the winter revival meetings in early 1950 approached, his burden intensified. He became desperate for a spiritual response from his sons. On February 1, he spent the morning in "anguish and prayer." "Oh God," he exclaimed, "come to our help. . . . Why has God not done in me what I have earnestly, fervently asked? . . . Oh God, I cannot live. I do not care to live unless you work out your will in the lives of these boys."

The next day he began to fast. For twenty-nine days and covering the length of the revival, he took only small amounts of fruit juices, milk, and tea, even during the time that he travelled to Chicago for a conference with travel agents. "Oh Lord," he prayed on the fifth day of the revival, "this is not a hunger strike against thee, it is the outcry of a desperate soul who cannot live unless thou dost work." He ended his fast on March 3 when two of his sons went to the altar.[21]

Two weeks later, however, he was alarmed. He came home from Chicago to find that two sons had not been in church but had gone off instead to Harrisburg. "How shall I keep these boys from slumping back into irreligious living!" he prayed. "If my sons will not follow thee please take my life away, dear Lord."[22]

But that is the last entry of that nature to appear in the diary.

The sons began to find themselves spiritually, and to Hostetter's great joy, they took what he considered to be fine, Christian wives. In a matter of only months the tone of the diary concerning his sons began to change. Thus he wrote in February, 1952, that after an evening service Lane and June came home and "we talked about spiritual problems until 11:20. God bless them!"[23] Several months later, after preaching at Grantham on "Job Tested by Loss," he noted that many people gave him "comments of appreciation. I appreciated Ray and Lane's comments the most."[24] And in December, 1953, following a visit by Nelson and Ray and their families, he wrote: "How good God was to me to give to both Nelson and Ray fine girls as wives and mothers. They both are devoutedly helpful to their husbands and love their children. They are both very excellent housekeepers and both are earnest Christians."[25]

The diary suggests what one would suspect from these developments that from the early 1950s onward Hostetter's relations with the family were more relaxed and pleasant. This may be further illustrated by the occasions in which he played games with members of the family—from "Battleship" to "Easy" to "Sorry." In the spring of 1953 he went with Glenn to Carlisle to play miniature golf, which he found so "refreshing and restful" that he returned for another game eight days later with Glenn, Ray and Audrey, and several of their friends.[26] A deep sea fishing expedition in June, 1959, with Nelson's and Ray's families was one of the highlights of the year.[27]

He followed the careers of his sons with great interest. He and his wife went to Puerto Rico to attend Nelson's wedding to Esther Miller. When Nelson proposed to take over a funeral home in West Liberty, Ohio, he met with his son and carefully went over the financial arrangements with him.[28] He was grateful for Lane's decision to become a minister. After preaching for several years, Lane was ordained at the Lancaster Brethren in Christ Church in 1962. His father was there and had part in the service. "It was a great service," Hostetter wrote. "[My] tears flowed freely. To see one of my sons ordained to the ministry was an unforgettable experience."[29]

When Ray approached graduation from an M.A. program, Hostetter wrote to a number of local schools to inquire about a teaching position for his son.[30] When instead Ray obtained a teaching and coaching position at Tabor College in Kansas, Hostetter noted with interest that his son, with a salary of $3,000 a year, made more than his father who was president of a college, and he followed the sports sections of the daily paper to see how his son's teams had fared. Later when Ray was about to leave Tabor, Hostetter approached the president of Elizabethtown College about a position for him. Instead, his son joined the faculty at Messiah.[31]

The father lived long enough to see his sons engage in the kinds of ministries that had so much absorbed his own life. Nelson as Executive Coordinator of Mennonite Disaster Service (MCC); Lane as minister, evangelist, and in the publishing field; Ray as president of Messiah College; Glenn as teacher.

Glenn appears to have received the most attention from his father. This was probably owing in part to his being the youngest in the family, probably also in part because of health problems. Glenn accompanied his father on several lengthy trips, including one to Florida in early 1951.[32] When Glenn had two major operations in the Lancaster General Hospital within two months of each other in 1952, Hostetter visited his son virtually every day, sometimes two times a day.[33] And when Glenn with considerable apprehensions entered the University of Chicago for graduate studies, Hostetter arranged for an MCC meeting in Chicago at the same time, and then accompanied his son to help him get settled into the university. As he left, the diary reads, "We prayed together standing in the station and then [Glenn] carried my luggage to my car and kissed me goodbye. God bless him!"[34]

Glenn married Dorothy Shearer in March, 1956, and shortly afterward taught in a private school in Davenport, Iowa, and later, in 1963, in Beaver Dam, Wisconsin. Usually when Hostetter was in the Midwest, he visited with Glenn and Dorothy and their growing family of girls. In the spring of 1961, he found the parents taking instruction in the Episcopal Church. He appears not to have been surprised or disappointed. "He seems to have met a real spiritual crisis in his life," he wrote of Glenn. "He says now he could come back to [the] Brethren in Christ more easily than ever before."[35] In the next three years, the Hostetters spent two vacations with Glenn's family. Of the last, Hostetter's diary notes that "we had several wonderful evenings with the family as we played, read, talked and prayed together."[36]

A few months later, in December, 1964, Glenn died in an automobile accident. Hostetter received the news after prayer-meeting on December 23. He did not sleep that night and left the next morning to be with Dorothy and the children. In the diary, he spoke with gratitude of the many tributes paid to Glenn by his friends and colleagues.[37] After the funeral, the Hostetters placed $5,000 in trust in a local bank for Glenn's four daughters.

He now made even greater efforts to be with Glenn's family. Following a visit in February, 1969, he wrote that he did not know when his next trip to the central part of the country would occur (he was no longer chairman of MCC), "but the very next time that I get within one or two hundred miles of you, I will stop in to see you."[38]

The great attention he gave to his grandchildren, it is tempting to think, may have been an attempt to compensate for what he considered his lack of attention to his sons as they were growing up. That at best, however, can be only part of the explanation; he did have a genuine love for children—grandchildren or other-wise. Certainly he idolized his grandchildren. Kaye, the first one, at two years of age was "a lovely little girl who speaks quite well and is very poised and affectionate."[39] Rahn and Curtis, Ray's sons, he thought were "fine little fellows—good pals and very enjoyable children."[40] When he visited Glenn's family in July, 1959, he found the twins, Vickie and Ginnie, "developing and growing" and talking "like chatterboxes. They are quick of com-prehension, very affectionate and friendly."[41]

Hostetter made a practice of sending cards and pictures to his grandchildren when he travelled, particularly when he was over-seas. When he returned in 1961 from his world trip, he asked Debra, Lane's daughter, to show him all the cards he had sent her, and was obviously delighted that she could do so.[42] In February of the following year he wrote in his diary that he sent valentines to all eleven of his grandchildren.[43]

With his wife he shared a love of flowers. Anna was particu-larly fond of violets. In 1948 she and her husband attached a greenhouse to the back of their house. In late December, after spending part of a day sifting and mixing dirt and planting flowers, he confessed in his diary that "Anna's hobby interests me very much. I hope to find more time to work in the greenhouse with her."[44] In March, 1950, they attended the Philadelphia Flower Show, which he thought a "gorgeous and glorious display." "How many beautiful things," he added, "God has planted in this world for us to enjoy."[45]

His respect for his parents grew over the years. When he went to visit them he invariably came away impressed with the quality of their lives. "We had a lovely visit with them," he wrote of one occasion in February, 1952. "They are always cheerful and thoughtful and never complain. What lovely old people they are."[46] When his father died in 1954, Hostetter wrote of him: "Daddy left us a great heritage . . . . I never remember him speaking disrespectfully about anyone. He lived on a high level of ethical practice. He truly put Christ and the church first in his life."[47] The feeling seems to have been mutual. The senior Hostetter, especially when writing on church matters, sometimes saluted his son as "Dear Bro. Christ," or "Dear Brother," even on occasion as "Dear Brother Hostetter."[48]

His father's death was not a time to be spent wastefully in grief. The next day he did some work in his office (despite his wife's protest) and on the day following the funeral preached the state council sermon at Grantham. In so doing, he may have had in mind his father's own devotion to the church when some fifty years earlier he had gone off to do church work on the death of a young daughter.

A few months later, Hostetter's mother died. In between the two deaths occurred that of his mother-in-law (his father-in-law had died earlier). Thus within a few months his connections with the older generation of his family were severed. Of the slightly more than $4,000 he received as an inheritance from his parents, he gave $500 to each of his four sons. "This," his diary explains, "is the way my father would want me to do, I believe."[49]

XII

"To Return to the Pastorate"

s C. N. Hostetter, Jr., approached the end of his presidency, he felt some uncertainty about what employment he should take. He hesitated to accept the invitation of incoming President Arthur Climenhaga and the trustees to remain to teach; perhaps, he thought, it were best for all if he removed himself from the program of which he had so long been head. He rejected out of hand a suggestion from one board member that he remain at the college as a fund raiser.[1] Neither did he accept Bishop Charlie Byers' offer in early 1959 of the Martinsburg pastorate, because he had no "positive, immediate plans" for the future, and, besides, he wanted to reduce his load.[2]

He momentarily considered returning to his early days as salesman. In September, 1959, he wrote to the Kroger Company at Dayton, Ohio, asking for an employment application form and stating that his character, integrity, and ability to sell would qualify him for certain positions with the company. An official of the firm replied that he was not certain the company had a job big enough for Hostetter, but sent him an application form anyway. Hostetter responded a few days later that since he had received several other offers of positions (which, unfortunately, he does not name) he would not be filling out the application.[3] Such an inquiry is more a commentary on the human inclination to be protective of the future than of any serious thought on Hostetter's part that he might do anything else than serve the church. The inquiry undoubtedly also reflects his love for the salesmanship that he had practiced earlier in his life.

In the end he returned to teaching. "I would very much like to give myself to students," he wrote to Arthur Climenhaga in

December, 1959, in accepting a part-time assignment following a year's leave of absence.[4] After his world tour for the Mennonite Central Committee and the World Relief Commission, he returned to Messiah College in the fall of 1961 to serve as chairman of the Department of Religion and Philosophy, to teach part-time, and to act as Director of Christian Field Work, a program which placed ministerial students in Pennsylvania Brethren in Christ churches for training, and which he had been largely responsible in creating and developing while president.

His diary reflects a continuing enthusiasm for his teaching. Pastoral Theology remained a favorite course. Following a class period in which he had each student (most of them ministers) describe a personal experience in soul-winning and identify the greatest hindrance to soul-winning in his church, he remarked that they had had "a very warm and stimulating session."[5] At the end of the school year he "wept and prayed for these ministers again and again as I read their papers."[6]

He did not intend to grow rusty with age. A month after he began teaching again he taped one of his lectures for self-criticism. He ended up "embarrassed at my hesitations—'Urs'—and long involved and incomplete sentences."[7] He continued to demand quality work from his students: for the first semester of 1962 the grades he gave were lower than those of most of his fellow teachers, with over 50% of the students receiving C's, and less than 10% A's. His Biblical Literature class of the same semester disappointed him: the readings he gave them did not seem to have much effect; he was shocked at the students' grades.[8] On the other hand, he was not certain a year later that he agreed with the Curriculum Committee's increasingly tough stand on borderline cases between C's and D's: "Sometimes I think our academic office thinks we can't be a good college without sieving out a lot of students and sending them home."[9]

His teaching, with his other activities, did not give him the greater leisure he had anticipated upon retirement. On New Year's Day, 1963, after spending a rare quiet day at home reading the Wisdom of Solomon and Ecclesiasticus from the apocrypha he reflected in his diary: "I had hoped my times of retirement would give me the opportunity to read leisurely and do the many things that I had wanted to do. It seems I still have far too many things on my schedule so I'm planning to cut down activity so as to be able to get my schedule on a more leisurely pattern." It was a reflection that he made many times, but a hope he never fulfilled.

In the fall of 1963 he began to pastor the Palmyra Brethren in Christ church. This ended his teaching at Messiah College, except for a couple of courses which he consented to do during the year because no one else was available. He continued, however, to be interested and active in the life of the college. He maintained contact with the Klines in Harrisburg, and occasionally visited Mrs. Kline after her husband's death. He assisted in fundraising campaigns, and collected enough money ($20,000) among his Hostetter relatives to endow in honor of his father the small dining room in the new Eisenhower Campus Center (he himself gave $10,000 and his wife $5,000).[10] When the Philadelpha campus of the college was being launched, he arranged for his old friend Orie Miller to attend a dinner meeting for a discussion of the project.[11] One of his last services to the college was to lead the campaign to pay the remaining indebtedness of Upland College, which had merged with Messiah College in 1965.[12] By the terms of his will, he left $40,000 to the institution.

In turn, the college gave him appropriate honors. At the 1963 commencement, it announced his appointment as President Emeritus, to the "enthusiastic response" of the audience, Hostetter noted.[13] In 1968, he received the Distinguished Alumnus Award in recognition of the wide range of services he had given in the church and throughout the world.

Why should a former college president assume a pastorate at the age of sixty-four? For Hostetter, there were several reasons. For years, as he frequently said, he had been teaching about the pastoral ministry; now he wanted a chance to put into practice what he had been teaching. Moreover, the good memories of his early years of pastoring at Refton had remained with him. He once explained to a friend that he had always had "a great hunger to return to the pastorate again. I told Mrs. Hostetter, if she could make the adjustment I would like to become a pastor again. Wife agreed and we had a thrilling time seeing souls saved and the church grow."[14] And finally, it has been conjectured, his son Lane was having at the time a warm and fruitful ministry at the Lancaster church; the son's success inspired the father to share the same joys of the pastorate.

The Hostetters rented their new house on the college campus and moved to the Palmyra parsonage at the end of the summer. September 1 was his first Sunday as pastor. "Oh Lord," he prayed that day in his diary, "make us a blessing to this people! They need to be loved, led and fed and please do this thru thy servant by the direction and control of the Spirit." The following Sunday he preached on "The Work of the Pastor" and promised to visit everyone within ninety days.[15]

This suggests that Hostetter took his pastoral work seriously. He cancelled some of the revival meetings and speaking engagements he had earlier agreed to take; most of the remaining were on days other than Sunday. And he began immediately to visit in the homes of both the members of the congregation and non-members of the community. In late 1965 he reported to his bishop that consistently in each quarter of the year he made 150 to 200 pastoral calls.[161] By 1969 he had built up an "Active Prospect List" of more than 170 families whose parents were not members of the church and with whom he had made contact during 1969, sometimes with the help of his student pastor assistant.[17] He began to conduct Leadership Training Programs for the Sunday school, and developed a premarital counselling program, which included for each couple a series of four film strips requiring two hours for presentation.

And he wrote letters—literally hundreds of them. These went to persons who missed attending church or Sunday school, to each visitor (regardless of how many times he or she had attended), to the sick, to those who needed encouragement or advice. Some of his members thought that he overdid his letter writing. Hostetter, however, felt that this was what a good pastor should do (as he had often taught his students at the college), and he intended to write letters, regardless of the numbers, or of the time and effort they took.

Letters of thanks were among the many that he wrote. To Faith Hoffman in 1967 he sent words of appreciation for "the fine rendition of the Children's Choir last Sunday morning. It was a beautiful number and was done so very well that it made a real contribution to the morning worship service."[18] Elderly Anna Hershey he thanked for simply being in the service: "Here at

Palmyra we do especially appreciate our older members who help give solidity and strength to our congregational life . . . . We feel that our older members can do much in strengthening our efforts through prayer and consistent living for Christ and loving relationships toward the outsiders."[19]

As a former educator, he encouraged the Palmyra young people to continue their education, particularly at Messiah College. In 1966 the congregation provided grants-in-aid to young people attending one of the seminaries approved by the denomination, and declared itself ready to assist any needy student who wanted to attend Messiah College.[20] For several years he took young people from the congregation to attend college preview days at Messiah College. He was proud, he wrote to Charlie Byers in 1967, that eleven students from the Palmyra church were now attending school at Grantham.[21]

His lecture notes on pastoral work may serve as something of a guide to his practice at Palmyra. In counselling, he advised not to worry too much about approach: get interested in the person and the approach will take care of itself. Don't give advice too freely. Be honest, yet gentle and merciful.

Congregations, he taught, are built through visitation; usually twenty minutes was long enough. But preaching is also important. Good preaching is the result of reading and rereading the text, of studying from a wide variety of books, and, most importantly, of listening to God: "The minister who would speak effectively to his people must give God a chance to speak to him. If the minister would move his people in public, his own soul must be moved by the Spirit in secret." Stories (for which Hostetter had a well-earned reputation) should never be used to detract from the message of the sermon.

His notes on preaching are fullest when he discusses the reading of the Bible in public. He claimed that such reading was usually poorly done and thus too few paid attention. He advised practice by reading the scheduled passage aloud in the study, and in the pulpit using good tone, effective pauses, and proper speed. But avoid being an actor: "You are a voice. Keep yourself out of sight, but aim to make people hear the voice of God."[22]

The Palmyra congregation clearly considered themselves fortunate to have obtained Hostetter as pastor. At the end of his first term, members wrote such expressions as: "It would be a terrible loss not to continue our relationship with the Hostetters," "Your value to our youth has been stupendous *[sic]*," and "Lack of Pastor Hostetter's services would be a calamity. Grant all leaves necessary."[23] This last statement suggests that Hostetter was finding his pastoral work somewhat constricting in light of the demands for his services elsewhere. In any event, the congregational council in early 1966 decided to give him more latitude in absences on Sunday and to use a ministerial student from Messiah College more frequently."[24]

Anna Hostetter took a greater part in the life of the pastorate than she had for some years in activities at Grantham, perhaps because like her husband she was reminded of her own pleasant and younger days at Refton. She continued at Palmyra to share his interest in the Mennonite Central Committee, among other ways, by collecting soap and quilt patches for relief projects.

Toward the end of his pastorate, Hostetter led the Palmyra congregation in the opening stages of a building program that would eventually add a Christian Education wing to the main building. Before that was completed, however, his health deteriorated rapidly. He never fully recovered from the mild stroke that he probably suffered during his trip in Africa in 1967. In 1970 at Upland, California, he attended his last of many General Conferences. Before returning home he joined part of his family for a day in Disneyland, where among other amusements he took a grandchild for a ride on the rollercoaster. He was released from his pastoral duties by his congregation in January, 1971. He and his wife returned to their house on the college campus in Grantham, but repeated strokes led to their moving to Messiah Home (now Messiah Village). There he has lived in a comatose condition for nine years. He died at Messiah Village on June 29, 1980.

Postscript

The motifs of C. N. Hostetter, Jr.'s life invite observations on and questions about the man himself and the causes he served.

He was a person of great energy and discipline. This rather than great brilliance enabled him to move from one task to another and to do each one well. And yet his friendliness and composure belied the pressure of his schedule. Many driven people, in contrast, are tense and thus limited in their service to others.

Hostetter's instincts, nevertheless, told him that he attempted too much. That church and other religious leaders allowed, even encouraged, him to assume ever more responsibilities, at a cost to himself, his family, and others, says as much about the church's propensity to give many offices to the able few as it does about Hostetter himself.

In various ways he represents the last of a group of church leaders. He was among those church college administrators who almost literally saved string and went about with cup in hand collecting nickels and dimes from his constituency. He modelled in his personal life style the frugality that he considered necessary to make his collecting plausible (including wearing patched clothing and buying recapped rather than new tires for his old cars). Although the leading officer, he ran as a footsoldier with his troops. He lived long enough to see a style different from his own emerging, but he appears to have recognized the need for some change and thus to have been accepting of it.

Similarly, he was among the last college presidents to manage in great detail the environment of college life. He carried out his role, like everything else he did, with conviction and energy, partly because he believed the principles on which he worked to be sound, partly because of his great desire to keep college and church together.

But in his later years he helped to move both college and church from a considerable degree of legalism to a more moderate frame of mind and practice. He did so, however, only as he could affirm each step in his own thinking, and as he could move his people with him. The warmth and sincerity of his pastoral nature and his evident spiritual soundness guaranteed that he would have followers in making the move. Successful transitions in church life are undoubtedly based in large measure on leaders and attitudes such as these.

Hostetter was also one of the diminishing numbers of church leaders who knew and were connected with virtually all the wires in the church network, both within the denomination and in many places without. The growing complexity of church life means that leadership is correspondingly more broadly distributed. Despite the continuing tendency to overwork able leaders, we are not likely to see many of his kind again.

In his mediation between polarized groups, Hostetter also stood as an uncommon leader. He worked to bring together militant evangelicals and pacifist Mennonites, holiness groups and staid conservatives, the Church World Service of the National Council of Churches and the World Relief Commission of NAE. Few have cared or have been able to work at this too neglected task. That Hostetter did so sometimes in the face of entrenched power is a tribute to his sense of self-assurance and to his belief that men and women, regardless of their affiliations, may be reconciled to each other through the work of Christ and the ministry of the church.

Not least of the motifs in his life was his strong sense of compassion for and identification with those who suffered, whether that suffering was physical, spiritual, or mental. In the relief agencies he headed, in his counselling as president, in his role as pastor and bishop, he was on the side of those whom others find easy to ignore.

C. N. Hostetter, Jr., is a bright example of a talented and dedicated man giving his life to many causes, and thus becoming a blessing to untold numbers of people throughout the world. He was in his own life what his General Conference hymn called the church as a whole to be—a messenger of grace.

Bibliography

Only the major sources for the biography are listed below; minor ones appear in the notes. Unless otherwise indicated, all sources are to be found in the Archives of the Brethren in Christ Church and Messiah College, located at Messiah College, Grantham, Pennsylvania.

Papers

    C. N. Hostetter, Jr., Papers.

        Includes correspondence (college, denominational, MCC, NAE, etc.), the diaries, lecture and sermon notes, minutes of boards and committees

    Home Mission Board Correspondence, Brethren in Christ Church

College Sources

    Administrative Committee Minutes

    Alumni Association Minutes

    Board of Trustees Minutes

    Bulletin

    Clarion and *Orthos* (student publications)

    Faculty Minutes

District and Congregational Minutes

    Grantham District Council and Semi-Annual Council Minutes

    Palmyra Congregational Council Minutes

Mennonite Central Committee

    Minutes of Annual Meetings and of the Executive Committee Minutes, in Mennonite Archives, Goshen, Indiana

    MCC Correspondence, Archives Material, in Mennonite Archives

Denominational Sources
Evangelical Visitor
General Conference Minutes

Books

Engle, Albert, *Saved to Serve in Kentucky and Elsewhere* (Privately printed, 1977).

Erb, Paul, *Orie Miller: The Story of a Man and An Era* (Scottdale, PA.: Herald Press, 1969).

Poe, Evelyn, ed., *Tributes to Dr. C. N. Hostetter* (Nappanee, Indiana: Evangel Press, 1960).

Sider, E. Morris, *Fire in the Mountains* (Privately Printed, 1976).

_____, *Nine Portraits: Brethren in Christ Biographical Sketches* (Nappanee, Indiana: Evangel Press, 1978).

Wittlinger, C. O., *Quest for Piety and Obedience: The Story of the Brethren in Christ* (Nappanee, Indiana: Evangel Press, 1978).

Other

Beloved President (a collection of 470 letters written to Hostetter by friends and former students at the time of his retirement from the presidency in 1960).

Interviews (for listing of each interview see the Foreword).

Tape recordings of the business sessions of General Conference.

NOTES

Chapter 1

[1]Clipping in Hostetter Biography File, C. N. Hostetter, Jr., Papers, located in the Archives of the Brethren in Christ Church and Messiah College, Grantham, Pa. The papers will hereafter be referred to as the Hostetter Papers.

[2]Noah Heisey, interview, September 8, 1979. All interviews in this book are on tape and in the Archives of the Brethren in Christ Church and Messiah College.

[3]Christian N. Hostetter Diary, January 27-29, 1914. Hereafter referred to as Diary.

[4]Diary, February 13, 1914.

[5]Henry Hostetter, interview, March 3, 1979.

Chapter 2

[1]Alma Cassel in *To Our Beloved President Dr. C. N. Hostetter, Jr.,* (letters to C. N. Hostetter, Jr., on his retirement as president of Messiah College in 1960), p. 128. Hereafter referred to as *Beloved President.*

[2]See Diary, June 6 and December 5, 1915.

[3]Diary, June 4, 5, 9, 1916.

[4]Christian and Cora Sider, interview, April 22, 1979.

[5]Emma Kreider in *Beloved President,* p. 271.

[6]For these debates, see respectively Diary, March 17, 1916, April 27, 1916, January 19, 1917.

[7]Diary, December 15, 1950.

[8]Diary, April 18, 1916.

[9]See pages in the back of the diary for 1916.

[10]For some examples see Diary, April 4, May 24, October 9, November 18 and 24, December 3 and 4, 1915.

[11]For a series of these visits, see Diary entries for February, 1916.

[12]Paul Lenhert and Jacob Stern in *Beloved President,* pp. 8 and 413 respectively.

[13]Diary, February 13, 1917.

[14]Ernest J. Swalm, interview, March 21, 1978.

[15]Charles Eshelman in *Beloved President,* p. 27.

[16]Elizabeth Brechbill, *ibid.,* p. 98.

[17]George Paulus, *ibid.,* p. 361.

[18]Diary, October 16, 1915.

[19]Diary, February 28, 1917.

[20]See Diary entries from April 15 to June 10, 1916.

[21]*Orthos* (1922), p. 87.

[22]Diary, May 28, 1916.

[23]Jacob Long in *Beloved President,* p. 307.

[24]Roy Wenger, interview, December 8, 1978. Also diary, May 2, 1917.

[25]Diary, June 15, 1917.

[26]Diary, August 20-22, 1917, and November 30, 1918.

[27]Ruth Hunt Byers, interview, August 19, 1979.

[28]Diary, February 18, 1919.

[29]Swalm interview.

[30]Diary, June 2, 4, 12, 28, 1917.

[31]Swalm interview.

[32]Diary, June 9, 1953 and May 26, 1962.

[33]C. N. Hostetter, Sr. to C. N. Hostetter, Jr., February 22, 1922. In C. N. Hostetter, Sr. papers located in the Archives of the Brethren in Christ Church and Messiah College.

[34]John Martin, from an interview by the author with Cyrus Lutz, April 21, 1979.

[35]*Orthos* (1922), p. 62.

[36]*Evangelical Visitor,* September 4, 1922, pp. 11-12.

[37]George Paulus, in *Beloved President,* p. 361.

Chapter 3

[1]This account of Iron Springs is based on various sources, as follows: Interviews with Christian and Cora Sider (April 22, 1979), Anna Hostetter (December 12, 1978), and Jesse Steckley (October 23, 1978); letter from Iola Dixon to E. Morris Sider, January 22, 1979; *Evangelical Visitor,* June 8, 1953, p. 12; Diary, November 17, 1952; Albert Engle, *Saved to Serve in Kentucky and Elsewhere* (privately printed, 1977), pp. 25-27.

[2]Swalm interview.

[3]Diary, July 30, 1953. Most of the information on the Hostetters' courtship and wedding was given by Anna Lane Hostetter in two interviews with the author (December 12, and 13, 1979). Some of this information as well as other aspects of Hostetter's early life may be found in a paper written for my course in Historical Study and Writing by one of his granddaughters, Debra Hostetter, entitled, "C. N. Hostetter, Jr." (in Archives of the Brethren in Christ Church and Messiah College).

[4]Diary, January 1, 1923. For the revival, see letter of Iola Dixon to E. Morris Sider, January 22, 1979.

[5]Diary, January 8, 1923.

[6]Diary, July 30, 1949.

[7]Diary, January 29, 1923.

[8]Diary, February 28 and March 8, 1923.

[9]Diary, March 26, 1923.

[10]C. N. Hostetter, Jr. to John Hostetter, August 30, 1930, Hostetter Papers. In subsequent references C. N. Hostetter, Jr. will be referred to as C.N.H., Jr.

[11]C. N. H., Jr., to John H. Moseman, October 16, 1934, Hostetter Papers.

[12]Lane Hostetter, interview, February 3, 1979.

[13]C. N. H., Jr., to John Zercher, February 15, 1939. Hostetter Papers.

[14]See, for example, Hilda Baxter to Mr. and Mrs. Hostetter, October 27, 1930, Hostetter Papers.

[15]Cyrus Lutz, interview, April 21, 1979.

[16]*Clarion,* February, 1928.

[17]*Ibid.*

[18]Alice Grace Hostetter Zercher, interview, July 6, 1979.

[19]*Evangelical Visitor,* October 23, 1933, p. 4.

[20]*Ibid.,* October 23, 1933, p. 4; July 2, 1934, p. 11.

[21]Clara Hess, Mary Slaymaker, and Mr. and Mrs. Landis Ressler provided these and other insights into Hostetter's ministry in an interview on March 4, 1979.

[22]C. N. H., Jr., to Mary Baer, August 30, 1930, Hostetter Papers.

[23]M. G. Engle to C. N. H., Jr., April 11, 1934, Home Mission Correspondence in Archives of the Brethren in Christ Church and Messiah College.

[24]Lutz interview.

[25]For a biography of Zook, see E. Morris Sider, *Nine Portraits: Brethren in Christ Biographical Sketches* (Nappanee, IN: Evangel Press, 1978), pp. 123-155. For tent evangelism, see Carlton O. Wittlinger, *Quest for Piety and Obedience: The Story of the Brethren in Christ* (Nappanee, IN: Evangel Press, 1978) pp. 172-73, 192-93.

[26]Holy Spirit File and Church History File, Hostetter Papers.

[27]Swalm interview.

[28]*Evangelical Visitor,* August 20, 1923, p. 2.

[29]For this Howick revival, see the Diary, July 14-August 20, 1923.

[30]*Evangelical Visitor,* October 12, 1925, pp. 10-11.

[31]For these two tent campaigns see Earl and Elsie Sider, interview, July 24, 1978 and May 15, 1979.

[32]See, for example, Diary, April 24, 1955.

[33]Citation on the Fiftieth Anniversary of Ordination, Hostetter Papers.

[34]For this 1933 summer revival see Lutz interview.

[35]*Evangelical Visitor,* February 2, 1931, p. 31.

[36]*Ibid.,* November 20, 1933, p. 14.

[37]*Ibid.,* December 19, 1932, p. 409.

[38]Charlie Byers, interview, August 19, 1979.

[39]These articles, in order are: *Evangelical Visitor,* October 24, 1932, p. 339; November 7, 1932, p. 357; November 21, 1932, p. 373. See also: *Evangelical Visitor,* March 16, 1931, p. 86 for a presentation on the subject at Pennsylvania State Council.

[40]M. G. Engle to C. N. H., Jr., April 1, 1926, Home Mission Correspondence, 1926-1927.

[41]C. N. H., Jr., to M. G. Engle, April 19, 1926, Home Mission Correspondence, 1926-1927.

⁴²M. G. Engle to C. N. H., Jr., October 5, 1927, Home Mission Correspondence, 1927-1931.

⁴³M. G. Engle to C. N. H., Jr., May 9, 1944, Hostetter Papers.

⁴⁴For the revival and brief mention of Hostetter, see E. Morris Sider, *Fire in the Mountains* (privately printed, 1966).

⁴⁵Diary, August 10, 1923.

⁴⁶Diary, January 16, 1952.

⁴⁷Diary, April 24, 1954.

⁴⁸These incidents from family life were given me in interviews with Anna Hostetter, December 12 and 13, 1979.

Chapter 4

¹C. N. H., Jr., to Martha Mellinger, January 27 1936, Hostetter Papers.

²*Clarion,* January, 1934, p. 16; February, 1934, p. 16.

³Ruth Linkletter, in *Beloved President,* p. 304.

⁴See *Clarion,* February, 1930, p. 4, for student appreciation of his teaching.

⁵Earl Miller, interview, June 7, 1979. Also *Clarion,* March, 1927, p. 134.

⁶*Clarion,* May, 1927.

⁷*Evangelical Visitor,* May 23, 1927.

⁸*Clarion,* October, 1933.

⁹Alumni Association Business Meeting, June 3, 1924 and June 1, 1925.

¹⁰Emma Kreider, in *Beloved President,* p. 271. For the decisions taken by the Alumni Association see the minutes of their business meeting for June 3, 1929 and June 2, 1932.

¹¹Faculty Minutes, September 27, 1934.

¹²*Ibid.,* May 23, 1935.

¹³C. N. H., Jr., to B. E. Thuma, March 12, 1936, Hostetter Papers.

¹⁴*Clarion,* October, 1934, p. 9.

¹⁵Trustee Board Minutes, January 11, 1935.

¹⁶C. N. H., Jr., to Adam Byers, May 14, 1935, Hostetter Papers.

¹⁷See, for example, his letter to Joel Carlson, May 14, 1935, Hostetter Papers.

¹⁸C. N. H., Jr., to Jesse Brechbill, June 20, 1935, Hostetter Papers.

¹⁹See C. N. H., Jr., to D. H. Martin, January 7, 1935, Hostetter Papers, in which Hostetter insists on turning back all the offerings he receives, rather than the 50% suggested by the Board of Trustees.

²⁰C. N. H., Jr., to Miriam Steininger, September 4, 1934, Hostetter Papers.

²¹C. N. H., Jr., to Pennsylvania Power and Light Company, April 7, 1936, Hostetter Papers.

²²See, for example, C. N. H., Jr., to C. H. Moyer, February 18, 1936, Hostetter Papers.

[23]C. N. H., Jr., to Musser Brothers, October 23, 1936, Hostetter Papers.

[24]C. N. H., Jr., to V.C.W., March 20, 1936.

[25]C. N. H., Jr., to H. L., April 25, 1940, Hostetter Papers.

[26]See the correspondence between Hostetter and Robert Lee Stuart during summer and early fall of 1938, Hostetter Papers.

[27]Harold K. Sheets, to C. N. H., Jr., April 22, 1936, Hostetter Papers.

[28]See, for example, C. N. H., Jr., to Lee Schriber, May 11, 1936, Hostetter Papers.

[29]For example, see C. N. H., Jr., to Jacob Bowers, December 20, 1934, Hostetter Papers.

[30]For another example, see C. N. H., Jr., to Esther Hoover (late 1938), Hostetter Papers.

[31]Trustee Board Minutes, January 18, 1951.

[32]C. N. H., Jr., to D. H. Hostetter, May 28, 1940, Hostetter Papers.

[33]C. N. H., Jr., to Hartman Landis, June 29, 1936, and August 2, 1938, Hostetter Papers.

[34]C. N. H., Jr., to Henry Trump, August 23, 1937, Hostetter Papers.

[35]C. N. H., Jr., to Bishop and Mrs. H. L. Trump, January 11, 1936, Hostetter Papers.

[36]C. O. Musser Estate File, Hostetter Papers.

[37]C. N. H., Jr., to Mr. and Mrs. C. O. Musser, December 16, 1947, and C. O. Musser to C. N. H., Jr., December 23, 1947, in C. O. Musser Letters, Hostetter Papers.

[38]See the exchange on this issue in the C. O. Musser Letters, in Hostetter Papers.

[39]*Bulletin,* August, 1935.

[40]Trustee Board Minutes, September 29, 1939.

[41]C. N. H., Jr., to Martin S. Musser, September 10, 1938, Hostetter Papers.

[42]For a report in 1943, see Trustee Board Minutes, October 9, 1943.

[43]Trustee Board Minutes, May 30, 1944.

[44]Trustee Board Minutes, February 22, 1945.

[45]*Bulletin,* August, 1945.

[46]Trustee Board Minutes, October 20, 1949.

[47]Diary, January 3 and 4, 1949.

[48]Diary, May 14, 1949.

[49]Diary, March 8, 1949.

[50]Diary, November 6, 1949.

[51]*Bulletin,* November, 1952.

[52]Trustee Board Minutes, April 23, 1953. See also Diary, April 23, 1953.

[53]Trustee Board Minutes, October 29, 1953.

[54]Diary, September 25, 1953.

[55]Diary, October 20, 1955.

[56]Diary, August 18, and 23, 1955.

249

[57]Diary, September 22, 1955.

[58]Diary, August 20 and 23, 1955.

[59]Diary, November 18, 1954.

[60]Diary, July 11-22, 1955.

[61]Diary, October 10, 1956.

[62]Diary, November 9, 1956.

[63]Diary, January 24, 1956. Also Isaiah Harley, interview, August 22, 1979.

[64]Diary, January 25, 1956.

[65]Diary, May 20-21, 1957.

[66]Diary, December 23, 1958.

[67]For examples, see Diary, March 16, 21, 30, 1960.

[68]Diary, November 19, 1956.

[69]Diary, March 30, 1957.

[70]Diary, March 2, 1959.

[71]Diary, July 23, 1959.

[72]Diary, July 28, 1959.

[73]Diary, February 17, 1960.

[74]Trustee Board Minutes, September 4 and October 31, 1958.

[75]Marts and Lundy to C. N. H., Jr., October 9, 1958. File on Marts and Lundy, Hostetter Papers.

[76]Diary, December 22, 1958 and March 14, 1959.

[77]Diary, November 14, 1958.

[78]Diary, March 29, 1960.

[79]Diary, May 12 and June 29, 1960.

[80]Diary, May 27, 1957.

[81]C. N. H., Jr., to Jack Snell, January 3, 1953, File on Annuity: Letters for New Homes, Hostetter Papers. See also Roy Wenger, interview, September 28, 1959 and Ray Hostetter, interview, February 16, 1979, for observations about his fund raising abilities.

[82]John Zercher to C. N. H., Jr., April 9, 1957, Hostetter Papers.

[83]Cyrus Lutz, in *Beloved President,* p. 315.

[84]E. J. Swalm in Evelyn Poe, ed., *Tributes to Dr. C. N. Hostetter, Jr.* (Nappanee, Ind.: Evangel Press, 1960), p. 38.

[85]Diary, March 31, 1950.

[86]Diary, March 26-April 9, 1955.

[87]Diary, December 14, 1955.

[88]C. N. H., Jr., to Musser Martin, February 29, 1952, Hostetter Papers.

[89]See, for example, C. N. H., Jr., to LeRoy Mann, October 3, 1957, Hostetter Papers.

[90]Diary, August 13, 1960.

Chapter 5

[1]Diary, October 30, 1951.

[2]See, for example, Diary, December 16, 1949.

[3]For a few examples, see Diary September 16 and 22, 1949, and July 8, 1957.

[4]See, for example, Diary, March 21, 1949.

[5]Diary, August 20, 1953.

[6]Diary, May 10, 1955.

[7]For an example of how he went to look for equipment and furnishings for the women's dormitory, see Diary, July 12, 1949.

[8]C. N. H., Jr., to Leo Kolb, November 9, 1937, Hostetter Papers.

[9]Gerald Wingert in *Beloved President,* p. 452.

[10]Trustee Board Minutes, October 2, 1949.

[11]See Diary for July, 1951

[12]Diary, June 24, 1959.

[13]Diary, October 9, 1956.

[14]Diary, March 13, 1956.

[15]See, for example, Homer Kraybill in *Beloved President,* p. 268.

[16]See Diary, March 15, 1952 for his using the station master's office in Dearborn, Michigan.

[17]See *Bulletin,* May, 1956 for appointments.

[18]The letter is in a file marked C. N. Hostetter, Jr., personal correspondence, 1950-51, Hostetter Papers.

[19]Trustee Board Minutes, October 24, 1941.

[20]Trustee Board Minutes, October 10, 1946.

[21]Trustee Board Minutes, April 19, 1956, May 30, 1958, April 22, 1960.

[22]Samuel Winger, interview, September 18, 1979.

[23]Helen Bucher to C. N. H., Jr., March 23, 1941, Hostetter Papers.

[24]Diary, January 21, 1955.

[25]Diary, May 6, 1958.

[26]See folder on Ministers' Seminar, 1960, Hostetter Papers.

[27]Trustee Board Minutes, November 7, 1949 and April 27, 1950.

[28]C. N. H., Jr., to Investment Committee, February 19, 1951, Committee and Group Letters file, Hostetter Papers.

[29]C. N. H., Jr., to Board of Trustees, June 9, 1953, Board Members letters, 1952-53, Hostetter Papers.

[30]C. N. H., Jr., to Bureau of Publications, Department of Property and Supplies, Commonwealth of Pennsylvania, December 22, 1958, Hostetter Papers.

[31]See, for example, Diary, July 20, 1951.

[32]Diary, September 12, 1951. See also Grantham Water Company to Public Utilities

Commission, September 13, 1951, Grantham Water Company File, Hostetter Papers.

[33]Trustee Board Minutes, October 11, 1951, and C. N. H., Jr., to Roy Wenger and Kenneth Hoover, October 24, 1951, Committee and Group Letters, 1951-52, Hostetter Papers.

[34]Diary, February 5, 1952.

[35]See, for example, *Bulletin,* November, 1941.

[36]Response from Henry Landis, May 24, 1937, Hostetter Papers.

[37]*Evangelical Visitor,* October 25, 1937, p. 11. See also E. J. Swalm to C. N. H., Jr., (1937), Hostetter Papers.

[38]H. D. H. to C. N. H., Jr., September 1, 1938, Hostetter Papers.

[39]Charlie B. Byers to C. N. H., Jr., May 5, 1940, Hostetter Papers.

[40]Earl Sider to C. N. H., Jr, March 13, 1939, Hostetter Papers.

[41]C. R. Heisey to C. N. H., Jr., June 15, 1935, Hostetter Papers.

[42]Administration Committee Minutes, April 30, 1947.

[43]Diary, May 16, 1951.

[44]C. N. H., Jr., to Earl Miller, April 11, 1950, Hostetter Papers.

[45]Diary, November 3, 1949.

[46]C. N. H., Jr., to members of the Ladies Quartet, January 20, 1948, Quartet Letters, Hostetter Papers.

[47]C. N. H., Jr., to Frances A. Smith, November 11, 1949, Administrative Staff Correspondence, Hostetter Papers.

[48]Avery Musser to C. N. Hostetter, Jr., April 26, 1937, Hostetter Papers.

[49]C. N. H., Jr., to Abram Lehman, April 18, 1937, Hostetter Papers.

[50]C. N. H., Jr., to Earl Miller, October 11, 1954, Faculty member's correspondence, Hostetter Papers.

[51]C. N. H., Jr., to presidents of the graduating classes and their advisers, April 7, 1937, Hostetter Papers.

[52]C. H. to C. N. H., Jr., August 27, 1957, Hostetter Papers.

[53]C. N. H., Jr., to Jacob Kuhns and D. Ray Heisey, September 5, 1957, Committee and Group Letters, Hostetter Papers.

[54]C. N. H., Jr., to Jesse Lady, August 29, 1935, Hostetter Papers.

[55]Jesse Lady to C. N. H., Jr, August 12, 1935, Hostetter Papers.

[56]Lady to Hostetter, August 23, 1935, Hostetter Papers.

[57]See, for example, C. N. H., Jr., to J. H. Martin, October, 1935, Hostetter Papers.

[58]C. N. H., Jr., to J. B. Cressman, February 26, 1940, Hostetter Papers.

[59]J. B. Cressman to C. N. H., Jr., February 29, 1940, Hostetter Papers.

[60]C. N. H., Jr., to Cressman, March 1, 1940, Hostetter Papers.

[61]C. N. H., Jr., to Cressman, March 14, 1940, Hostetter Papers.

[62]See especially Howard Book to C. N. H., Jr., January 20, 1940, and C. N. H., Jr., to Howard Book, May 20, 1940, Hostetter Papers.

[63]C. N. H., Jr., to Charles Eshelman, November 17, 1954, Hostetter Papers.

[64]Faculty Minutes, February 27, 1951.

[65]C. N. H., Jr., to Carl J. Ulery, September 8, 1959, Board of Trustees Correspondence, Hostetter Papers.

[66]C. N. H., Jr., to John Hoke, April 16, 1936, Hostetter Papers.

[67]Charlie Byers, interview, August 19, 1979.

[68]L. M. to C. N. H., Jr., December 28, 1938, Hostetter Papers.

[69]C. N. H., Jr., to L. M., January 3, 1939, Hostetter Papers.

[70]Charlie Byers in *Beloved President*, p. 2.

[71]C. N. H., Jr., to Samuel Wolgemuth, November 11, 1953, Grantham District File, Hostetter Papers.

[72]Diary, November 14, 1956.

Chapter 6

[1]Diary, May 28-31, 1949, for the family trip and the graduation exercises.

[2]*Bulletin,* February, 1935.

[3]*Evangelical Visitor,* Missionary Supplement, November 3, 1947, p. 1.

[4]*Clarion,* October, 1945, p. 1.

[5]*Evangelical Visitor,* May 16, 1960.

[6]"The Good Way." Dedication sermon for the new buildings at Upland College. *Evangelical Visitor,* March 21, 1947, pp. 4, 12, 14.

[7]C. N. H., Jr., to Edward Farner, April 30, 1957, Hostetter Papers.

[8]C. N. H., Jr., to John Z. Martin, January 28, 1959, Hostetter Papers.

[9]Isaiah Harley, interview, and Diary, February 19, 1963.

[10]C. N. H., Jr., to Frank Hennigh, January 21, 1939, Hostetter Papers.

[11]C. N. H., Jr., to Rhoda Haas, May 19, 1938, Hostetter Papers.

[12]C. N. H., Jr., to Emerson Frey, June 25, 1941, Hostetter Papers.

[13]C. N. H., Jr., to Paul Martin, Jr., August 14, 1958, Hostetter Papers.

[14]See, for example, C. N. H., Jr., to Christian Oberholser, Jr., February 17, 1959, Hostetter Papers.

[15]*Evangelical Visitor,* September 5, 1960, p. 3.

[16]C. N. H., Jr., to Enos Hess, April 2, 1938, and Hess to Hostetter, July 22, 1938, Hostetter Papers.

[17]C. N. H., Jr., to Mary Hoffman, April 2, 1938, Hostetter Papers.

[18]C. N. H., Jr., to Asa Climenhaga, July 9, 1936, Hostetter Papers.

[19]Faculty Minutes, October 17, 1940.

[20]Administrative Committee Minutes, October 21, 1943.

[21]Diary, January 11, 1949.

[22]Diary, June 25-28, 1952.

[23]C. N. H., Jr., to Claude Rees, August 25, 1937; Hostetter to Stephen W. Paine, September 8, 1937, Hostetter Papers.

[24]C. N. H., Jr., to B. E. Thuma, January 14, 1936, Hostetter Papers.

[25]See file on Pennsylvania Association of Junior Colleges, Hostetter Papers.

[26]Trustee Board Minutes, January 9, and April 10, 1947.

[27]*Ibid.,* April 10 and October 2, 1947.

[28]Memorandum to President Hostetter, April 19, 1948, File on Bible College Accreditment, Hostetter Papers.

[29]For a report, see *General Conference Minutes,* 1950, p. 125.

[30]Trustee Minutes, October 10, 1947.

[31]C. N. H., Jr., to African missionaries, November 3, 1948, File on Committee and Group Letters, Hostetter Papers.

[32]Trustee Minutes, November 7, 1949.

[33]C. N. H., Jr., to Ruth Dowling, February 22, 1951, Hostetter Papers.

[34]Faculty Minutes, December 2, 1952.

[35]For these developments, see Faculty Minutes, November 20, 1951; Diary, January 6, 1953; Trustee Minutes, June 2, 1953.

[36]See *Bulletin,* July, 1954 for a good explanation for this step gained.

[37]C. N. H., Jr., to S. A. Witmer, May 23, 1958, File on Accrediting Association of Bible Institutes and Bible Colleges, Hostetter Papers.

[38]Diary for January 19, and 22, 1954.

[39]Trustee Minutes, April 10, 1958.

[40]Diary, March 10-11, 1958.

[41]Salary Agreement File in Correspondence for 1934-36. See also C. N. H., Jr., to Ben Thuma, January 14, 1936, Hostetter Papers.

[42]C. N. H., Jr., to J. B. Cressman, March 1, 1941, Hostetter Papers.

[43]Trustee Minutes, April 10, 1958.

[44]Trustee Minutes, October 14, 1957.

[45]C. N. H., Jr., to Charles Eshelman and C. O. Wittlinger, November 8, 1954, Hostetter Papers.

[46]For these and other explanations, see the statement of Charles Eshelman to the trustees, Trustee Minutes, October 14, 1957.

[47]Sara Lehman to C. N. H., Jr., March 12, 1958, High School Continuation File, Hostetter Papers, for this letter and reports.

[48]See Board of Trustees Minutes, April 10, 1958 for the committee's report.

[49]*General Conference Minutes,* 1958, pp. 125-26.

[50]For the report to General Conference, see *General Conference Minutes,* 1959, pp. 47-48. For the minutes of the committee's work see Academy Restudy Committee, File on High School Study Committee, Hostetter Papers. Note also diary, December 22, 1958.

[51]Diary, July 14, 1959.

[52]Diary, March 15, 1960.

[53] Diary, April 4, 1960.

[54] Diary, May 12, 1960.

[55] C. N. H., Jr., to Landis Miller, March 26, 1936, Hostetter Papers.

[56] Faculty Minutes, February 18, 1938.

[57] Board of Trustees Minutes, May 14, 1942.

[58] Administration Committee Minutes, May 4, 1943.

[59] Paul and Lela Hostetler, interview, July 19, 1979.

[60] Administration Committee Minutes, March 1, 1948.

[61] Administration Committee Minutes, March 1, 1948.

[62] Diary, February 2, 1950.

[63] Hostetler interview.

[64] C. N. H., Jr., to Hannah Eyer, October 27, 1937, Hostetter Papers.

[65] C. N. H., Jr., to Will Houghton, November 14, 1938, Hostetter Papers.

[66] Diary, May 16, 1949.

[67] Jacob Kuhns, interview, November 9, 1981.

[68] Diary, May 14, 1949.

[69] Faculty Minutes, January 24, 1950 and February 24, 1953.

[70] See Faculty Minutes, February 28, 1955 for permission to do so.

[71] Diary, May 30, 1958.

[72] C. N. H., Jr., to Norman Brubaker, October 21, 1936, Hostetter Papers.

[73] Administration Committee Minutes, October 24 and November 7, 1950.

[74] Faculty Minutes, April 9, 1941.

[75] Faculty Minutes (Special Meeting), February 26, 1943.

[76] Administrative Committee Minutes, March 15, 1946; Faculty Minutes, March 19, 1946.

[77] Administrative Committee Minutes, May 17, 1954.

[78] Administrative Committee Minutes, November 19, 1956.

[79] Diary, January 14, 1958.

[80] Diary, May 10, 1951.

Chapter 7

[1] For illustrations, see C. N. H., Jr., to Robert Stewart, July 4, 1936, Hostetter Papers, and Gerald and Lois Weaver, interview, August 26, 1979.

[2] For examples of these, see diary, January 29 and November 8, 1954, and Ruth Byers interview.

[3] C. N. H., Jr., to Mildred Stump, August 18, 1938, Hostetter Papers.

[4] C. N. H., Jr., to Mr. and Mrs. Willie Jantz, December 12, 1939, Hostetter Papers.

[5]For several examples, see Miriam Kniesly Brubaker in *Beloved President,* p. 108; Richard Gordon in *Beloved President,* p. 179; Esther Engle Eshelman in *Beloved President,* p. 152; Esther Ebersole in *Beloved President,* p. 55 and interview, June 13, 1979.

[6]Ralph Palmer in *Beloved President,* p. 360.

[7]Earl Miller interview.

[8]John R. Sider in *Beloved President,* p. 437.

[9]C. N. H., Jr., to Harold Engle, November 11, 1937, Hostetter Papers.

[10]Carlton O. Wittlinger to C. N. H., Jr., December 8, 1937, Hostetter Papers.

[11]Feyline Ballou to C. N. H., Jr., February 13, 1938, Hostetter Papers.

[12]James Lesher in *Beloved President,* p. 302.

[13]*Clarion,* March, 1936, p. 4, and diary, December 21, 1951.

[14]Faye Byers in *Beloved President,* p. 121. For examples of similar statements from the same source, see Anita Brechbill, p. 99; Esther Brubaker, p. 107; Barbara Hankey, p. 190; Stanley Hoke, p. 233.

[15]Diary, January 15, 1953.

[16]Esther Ebersole interview.

[17]Diary, March 12, 1951.

[18]Diary, May 25, 1955.

[19]Erwin Thomas, interview, July 5, 1979.

[20]Aaron Stern, interview, July 6, 1979.

[21]There are several versions of this story. See Dorothy and Eugene Wenger, *Beloved President,* p. 436, and Eber Dourte, interview, March 8, 1979.

[22]Henry N. Miller in *Beloved President,* p. 339.

[23]Diary, March 1 and 8, 1955.

[24]C. N. H., Jr., to Isaiah Harley, March 17, 1955, Administrative Staff Correspondence, Hostetter Papers.

[25]Diary, October 6, 1954.

[26]Diary, January 13, 1950.

[27]Naomi Heise Marr in *Beloved President,* p. 323.

[28]Ann Ginder in *Beloved President,* p. 174.

[29]Keith Ulery, interview, August, 1980.

[30]C. N. Hostetter, Jr., to H. H., October 27, 1952. C. N. H., Jr., Personal file, Hostetter Papers.

[31]C. N. H., Jr., to L. R., March 1, 1957, Hostetter Papers.

[32]C. N. H., Jr., to B. F., November 18, 1958, Hostetter Papers.

[33]C. N. H., Jr., to Mr. and Mrs. C. G., February 22, 1960, Hostetter Papers.

[34]William Hoke in *Beloved President,* p. 234.

[35]Ethel Musser in *Beloved President,* p. 212.

[36]C. N. H., Jr., to George Lenhert, November 17, 1954, Administrative Staff Correspondence. For other examples of such commendation to the staff, see C. N. H., Jr., to

Frances A. Smith, December 19, 1947. Administrative Staff Correspondence; and C. N. H., Jr., to Anna Climenhaga, April 2, 1938, Hostetter Papers.

[37]Diary, December 18, 1957.

[38]C. N. H., Jr., to Administrative Committeee, October 10, 1953, File on Committee and Group Letters, Hostetter Papers.

[39]For a study of the Sakimuras, see Howard Kauffman, "Conflicting Culture for the Sakimuras," a research paper written for the class in Historical Study and Writing (1977) at Messiah College. See also *Evangelical Visitor,* October 24, 1955, p. 15.

[40]C. N. H., Jr., to Arthur Climenhaga, December 17, 1959, Hostetter Papers.

[41]Diary, March 24, 1950.

[42]Diary, January 20, 1954.

[43]Diary, October 7, 1952.

[44]John and Alice Grace Zercher, interview, July 6, 1979.

[45]Eber Dourte, interview, March 8, 1979.

[46]For examples, see the following in *Beloved President;* Ruth (Mrs. Harold) Zercher, p. 465; Blanche Landis Kipe, p. 258; Glenn Ginder, p. 173.

[47]C. N. H., Jr., to Carlton O. Wittlinger, March 11, 1950, File on Administrative Staff Correspondence, Hostetter Papers.

[48]Edgar Stoesz, interview, March 8, 1979.

[49]Diary, June 30, 1960. The first occupant of the chair (Owen Alderfer) was installed in 1980.

Chapter 8

[1]Semi-annual District Minutes, September 14, 1934.

[2]*Ibid.,* March 13, 1936.

[3]*Ibid.,* March 16, 1937.

[4]District Council Minutes, January 5, 1956.

[5]Semi-annual District Council Minutes, February 8 and 11, 1947.

[6]Virgie Kraybill, interview, November 9, 1978.

[7]Diary, March 13, 1949.

[8]Diary, April 3, 1955.

[9]Diary, September 23, 1952.

[10]Diary, February 2, 1954.

[11]Diary, July 25, 1949.

[12]Diary, September 2, 1951.

[13]Diary, July 4, 1962.

[14]See Semi-annual District Council Minutes, February 2 and September 29, 1951. Also diary, January 1, February 2, September 29-30, and Isaiah Harley interview.

[15]Semi-annual District Council Minutes, February 5, 1953.

[16]For the revival, see diary, October 30-November 7, 1955.

[17]General Conference, 1954, File, Hostetter Papers.

[18]Diary, December 27, 1954.

[19]*Evangelical Visitor,* April 27, 1957, p. 3.

[20]Diary, June 12 and 15, 1962.

[21]For some examples, see C. N. H., Jr., to M. G. Engle, November 1, 1943, Home Missions Correspondence; Hostetter to Western Clergy Bureau, June 14, 1937, Home Missions Correspondence; Hostetter to Martha Sentz, July 9, 1938, Home Missions Correspondence, Hostetter Papers.

[22]Circular letter from Hostetter, November 1, 1945, Home Missions Correspondence, Hostetter Papers.

[23]S. G. to C. N. H., Jr., December 18, 1947, Home Mission File, Hostetter Papers.

[24]C. N. H., Jr., to Albert Engle, July 16, 1952, Home Mission Board Members Correspondence, Hostetter Papers.

[25]*Evangelical Visitor,* January 27, 1958, p. 6.

[26]See Home Mission Correspondence for 1936-1937, Hostetter Papers.

[27]See *ibid.,* for 1944-46, Hostetter Papers.

[28]See *ibid.,* for 1934, Hostetter Papers.

[29]For a fuller account of Sarah Bert, see E. Morris Sider, *Nine Portraits: Brethren in Christ Biographical Sketches* (Nappanee, Indiana: Evangel Press, 1978).

[30]Report of Home Mission Board, October 1933, Home Missions Correspondence, Hostetter Papers.

[31]For a review of the case up to 1942 from the point of view of the Home Mission Board, see M. G. Engle to C. N. H., Jr., October 1, 1942, Home Mission Correspondence. For the Arcadia member's point of view, see A. B. S. to C. N. H., Jr., May 13, 1944, Home Missions Correspondence, Hostetter Papers.

[32]C. N. H., Jr., to M. G. Engle, December 9, 1925. See Engle's reply of January 28, 1926, both in Home Missions Correspondence, Hostetter Papers.

[33]C. N. H., Jr., to M. G. Engle, February 10, 1926, Home Missions Correspondence, 1926-1927, Hostetter Papers.

[34]C. N. H., Jr., to Wilber Snider, February 24, 1928, Home Missions Correspondence, 1927-1931, Hostetter Papers.

[35]C. N. H., Jr., to M. G. Engle, September 23, 1926, Home Missions Correspondence, 1926-1927, Hostetter Papers.

[36]C. N. H., Jr., to M. G. Engle, November 3, 1939, Home Missions Correspondence, 1938-1944, Hostetter Papers.

[37]C. N. H., Jr., to H. Wagaman, November 7, 1932, Home Missions Correspondence, 1931-1934, Hostetter Papers.

[38]C. N. H., Jr., to Carl Baker, November 22, 1935, Home Missions Correspondence, 1935-1936, Hostetter Papers.

[39]Examples may be found in C. N. H., Jr., to Floyd Wingert, November 14, 1933, Home Missions Correspondence, 1931-1934; and in Hostetter to Albert Engle, July 12, 1937, Home Missions Correspondence, 1936-1938, Hostetter Papers.

[40]C. N. H., Jr., to Wilber Snider, December 17, 1937, Home Missions Correspndence, 1936-1938, Hostetter Papers.

[41]For Engle's letter, see M. G. Engle to Abner Martin and C. N. H., Jr., September 5, 1933, Home Missions Correspondence, 1931-1934, Hostetter Papers.

[42]Henry Ginder to Dale Ulery, December 22, 1952, Home Missions Correspondence, Hostetter Papers.

[43]See, for example, Paul McBeth to C. N. H., Jr., February 22, 1932, Home Missions Correspondence, 1931-1934; Denny Jennings to Hostetter, September 29, 1935; Denny and Marie Jennings File, Hostetter Papers; and Ross Morningstar to Hostetter, January 9, 1951, Home Missions Correspondence, Hostetter Papers.

[44]See, for example, C. N. H., Jr., to M. G. Engle and Abner Martin, September 7, 1931, Home Missions Correspondence, 1931-1934, Hostetter Papers.

[45]C. N. H., Jr., to Irwin Heisey, August 16, 1935, Hostetter Correspondence Box for 1934; Hostetter to J. B. Funk, February 18 and March 18, 1936, Home Missions Correspondence, 1935-1936, Hostetter Papers.

[46]Evangelical Visitor, November 3, 1947, p. 1 of Supplement.

[47]C. N. H., Jr., to Paul McBeth, March 3, 1931, Home Missions Correspondence, 1931-1934, Hostetter Papers.

[48]Albert Engle to C. N. H., Jr., November 16, 1927, Home Missions Correspondence, 1927-31, Hostetter Papers.

[49]C. N. H., Jr., to Mr. and Mrs. Ralph Winger, February 26, 1937, Home Missions Correspondence, 1936-1938, Hostetter Papers.

[50]Diary, November 12, 1957.

[51]Diary, April 17, 1955.

[52]C. N. H., Jr. to Albert Engle, September 6, 1938, Home Missions Correspondence, 1938-1944. For the other correspondence see Hostetter to Engle, October 8, 1937, Home Missions Correspondence, 1938-1944; Hostetter to Engle, September 8, 1938, Home Missions Correspondence, 1938-1944; Engle to Hostetter, September 23, 1938, Home Missions Correspondence, 1938-1944, Hostetter Papers.

[53]C. N. H., Jr., to Albert Engle, March 22, 1944, Home Missions Correspondence, 1938-1944, Hostetter Papers.

[54]Diary, July 16, 1949.

[55]Diary, June 8, 1949, and January 3, 1950.

[56]Diary, June 23, 1949.

[57]I owe this insight about the termination of his service with the Home Mission Board to John Hostetter.

[58]C. N. H., Jr., to Marie Switzer, February 2, 1966, Hostetter Correspondence. See also Hostetter to Rachel McBeth, March 27, 1957, Hostetter Correspondence, Hostetter Papers, for a description of the committee's work.

[59]Diary, January 22, 1962.

[60]Diary, November 29, 1961.

[61]General Conference Minutes, 1950, p. 31.

[62]General Conference Minutes, 1951, pp. 9-12.

[63] Carlton O. Wittlinger, *Quest for Piety and Obedience: The Story of the Brethren in Christ* (Nappanee, Indiana: Evangel Press, 1978), pp. 481-92.

[64] Diary, March 13 and 14, 1951.

[65] C. N. H., Jr., to Arthur Climenhaga, February 13, 1953, Faculty Members Correspondence, 1953, Hostetter Papers.

[66] C. N. H., Jr., to Henry Ginder, October 22, 1945, Home Missions Correspondence, 1944-1946, Hostetter Papers.

[67] C. N. H., Jr., to A. G. Brubaker, December 27, 1951, Hostetter Papers.

[68] Diary, November 11, 1956.

[69] C. N. H., Jr., to J. Howard Kauffman, July 8, 1967, Hostetter Papers.

[70] Clyde and Dorothy Jean Sollenberger, interview, August 7, 1979.

[71] Home Mission Board Members Correspondence, Hostetter Papers.

[72] Luke Keefer, interview, July 8, 1979. See also Hostetter's letter to Mrs. J. A. E., April 30, 1959, Hostetter Papers.

[73] See tape cassette recording of General Conference of 1963 (index available in the Archives of the Brethren in Christ Church and Messiah College).

[74] Diary, June 14, 1963.

[75] See File on Wedding Licenses, Hostetter Papers.

[76] C. N. H., Jr., to R. D., April 19, 1963, Hostetter Papers.

[77] Diary, May 20, 1961.

[78] Diary, June 8, 1951. For the sermon, see *Evangelical Visitor,* June 12, 1961, pp. 3-8.

[79] E. J. Swalm interview.

[80] For other similar evaluations see Paul Hostetler interview, July 17, 1979, Roy Wenger interview, and John Hostetter, interview, October 7, 1978.

[81] *Evangelical Visitor,* June 4, 1945, p. 7.

[82] For examples of these services, see diary entries for November 27-December 2, 1949 (Maytown), December, 1949 (Souderton), and January, 1951 (Lancaster).

[83] Diary, January 21, 1953.

[84] Diary, August 6, 1956.

[85] Diary, January 31, 1962.

[86] Diary, March 18, 1962.

[87] Diary, March 22, 1963.

[88] Diary, January 30, 1957.

[89] Diary, December 11, 1950.

[90] Diary, August 29, 1951.

[91] Diary, October 3-5, 1953.

[92] Diary, July 30-31, 1960.

[93] Diary, August 26-27, 1949.

[94] C. N. H., Jr., to Abner Martin, December 14, 1927, Home Missions, Classified Report, Home Missions Correspondence, Hostetter Papers.

260

95Keefer interview.

96"Implications of Holiness for the Church Today," Elkhart Seminar, Holiness File, Hostetter Papers.

97Diary, August 24, 1961.

98John Rosenberry, interview, August, 1979.

99Diary, August 7, 1961.

100See, for example, Hostetter taking a handkerchief to Earl Bossert, accompanied by Will Charlton, diary, August 26, 1960.

101Diary, June 11, 1956.

Chapter 9

1C. N. H., Jr., *Rethinking our Peace Position* (Nappanee, Ind.: E. V. Publishing House, 1951).

2For a report, see *Clarion,* November, 1941, p. 7.

3Orie Miller to C. N. H., Jr., September 30, 1941, Conscientious Objector File, Hostetter Papers.

4See, for example, his report to Henry Fast, December 17, 1941, Correspondence 1938-1941, Hostetter Papers. Also *Clarion,* March, 1942, pp. 7, 4, and *Evangelical Visitor,* March 16, 1942, p. 14.

5Henry Fast to C. N. H., Jr., December 30, 1941, Correspondence Box, 1938-1941, Hostetter Papers.

6Harry Martens, interview, January 15, 1979.

7Wilmer Heisey, interview, July 31, 1979.

8*General Conference Minutes,* 1942, p. 26.

9*Ibid.,* 1943, p. 58. For a fuller discussion, see Carlton O. Wittlinger, *Quest for Piety and Obedience,* pp. 389-91.

10John Zercher interview. See also my chapter of biography in E. Morris Sider and Paul Hostetler, eds., *Lantern in the Dawn: Selections from the Writings of John Zercher* (Nappanee, Ind.: Evangel Press, 1980). For a similar illustration see C. N. H., Jr., to Joseph Brechbill, May 21, 1953, Grantham District folder, Hostetter Papers, and Semi-annual District Council Minutes, October 2, 1953.

11See, for example, Semi-annual District Council Minutes, September 26, 1942; February 5, 1944; January 29 and February 5, 1945.

12C. N. H., Jr., to E. J. Swalm, John Hoffman, Eber Dourte, April 2, 15, 21, 1948 in Universal Military Training and Selective Service file, Hostetter Papers. And C. N. H., Jr., to members of the Peace, Relief and Service Committee, July 2, 1948, Peace Relief and Service File, Hostetter Papers.

13Diary, December 27 and 28, 1950.

14Edgar Metzler, interview, January 11, 1979.

15Diary, January 29, 1951.

16C. N. H., Jr., to Ernest E. Miller, November 5, 1947, File on Foreign Student

Exchange, Hostetter Papers. For some of these visits to Washington, D. C., see Diary, October 2, November 30, and December 1, 1950, and C. N. H., Jr., to James A. Donavan, Jr., Department of State, December 23, 1950, File on Exchange Visitor Program, Hostetter Papers.

[17]Hannah Godsch-Kahners in *Beloved President,* p. 264.

[18]Diary, April 24, 1952.

[19]For his instructions, see MCC Correspondence/Archives Material/1950 Hostetter, C. N. in the Mennonite Archives, Goshen, Indiana. For the details of his trip, see the diary, June 15-August 31, 1950.

[20]Travel Tips File, Hostetter Papers.

[21]Summer Tour Evaluations (1950), File Folder, Hostetter Papers.

[22]*Bulletin,* November, 1947, and diary, April 22, 1950.

[23]Mennonite World Conference, 1948-1952, File Folder, Hostetter Papers.

[24]Diary, September 12, 1949.

[25]Diary, November 2, 1951. For the invitation, see Harold Bender to C. N. Hostetter, Jr./ Hist MSS/1.278/Box 64/H. S. Bender Collection, Pres. C. N. Hostetter Correspondence, Mennonite Archives.

[26]Diary, May 3-5, 1951.

[27]C. N. H., Jr., to Orie Miller, October 29, 1945, Mennonite Central Committee, C. P. S. and Other Correspondence, 1940-1945, Mennonite Archives.

[28]Henry Fast to E. Morris Sider, March 6, 1979, Hostetter Papers.

[29]Diary, March 22, 1952.

[30]Diary, January 2, 1953.

[31]*Evangelical Visitor,* February 2, 1953, p. 15.

[32]Edgar Stoesz interview.

[33]William Snyder, interview, February 1, 1979.

[34]William Snyder to C. N. H., Jr., July 19, 1963, MCC Correspondence, Hostetter, 1963 File, Mennonite Archives.

[35]Winfield Fretz to C. N. H., Jr., February 13, 1968, loose letter in back of *Beloved President.*

[36]C. N. H., Jr., to Orie Miller, November 15, 1954, MCC Correspondence, Archives Material, 1954, Hostetter, Mennonite Archives.

[37]Diary, December 18, 1954.

[38]Diary, October 1, 1955.

[39]Harold Bender to C. N. H., Jr., October 18, 1955, and Hostetter to Bender, October 20, 1955, Seminaries Correspondence Folder, Hostetter Papers.

[40]Diary, February 2, 1955.

[41]C. N. Hostetter, Jr., to Albert M. Gaeddert, MCC Correspondence, Archives Material/ 1955/Hostetter, Mennonite Archives.

[42]Diary, September 21, 1956.

[43]George McGovern to William Snyder, May 10, 1961, Food for Peace Council Folder, Hostetter Papers.

[44]Diary, June 27, 28, 1961.

[45]Diary, September 30, 1963. See also general information in Food for Peace Folder, Hostetter Papers.

[46]For these developments, see Peace Corps File, Hostetter Papers; Minutes of an MCC meeting on May 12, 1961; MCC Executive Committee Minutes, November 4 and December 15-16, 1961; *Evangelical Visitor,* September 3, 1962, pp. 3, 4, 10, 11.

[47]Paul Erb, *Orie O. Miller: The Story of a Man and an Era* (Scottdale: Herald Press, 1969), pp. 128-29.

[48]Vietnam Testimony Before Senator Kennedy's Committee file folder, Hostetter Papers. Also *Evangelical Visitor,* August 30, 1965, p. 16.

[49]See White House Conference file folder, and White House Message: July 12, 1966, file folder, Hostetter Papers. Also *Evangelical Visitor,* November 20, 1967, p. 15.

[50]See MCC Executive Committee Minutes, September 14, 1957.

[51]MCC-Voluntary Service file folder, 1959-1960, Hostetter Papers.

[52]See Exhibit 2, MCC Executive Committee Minutes, May 17, 1958.

[53]For Hostetter's comments on these developments, see Diary, July 17, 1958; May 1, 1959; January 21, 1960.

[54]Willis Detwiler, interview, March 8, 1979.

[55]C. N. H., Jr., to Ronald Lofthouse, December 28, 1966, Bishops' Nominating Committee (1967) file, Hostetter Papers.

[56]MCC Executive Committee Minutes, December 13-15, p. 12.

[57]"The Urgency of World Relief," in Relief NAE file folder, Hostetter Papers.

[58]MCC (Canada) file folder, Hostetter Papers.

[59]*Gospel Herald,* April 16, 1963, pp. 317-18.

[60]C. N. H., Jr., to William Snyder, March 10, 1958, MCC Correspondence/Hostetter, C. N./1958, Mennonite Archives.

[61]C. N. H., Jr., to Jacob Klassen, July 16, 1962, MCC Correspondence/Hostetter, C. N./1962, Mennonite Archives.

[62]C. N. H., Jr., to Peter G. Wiwcharuck, August 20, 1966, Peter Wiwcharuck file, Hostetter Papers.

[63]For some occasions when Hostetter was at Brook Lane for business and consultation, see diary, January 19, 1960, and May 27, 1961.

[64]Howard Musselman, interview, April, 1979.

[65]*Evangelical Visitor,* April 12, 1954, p. 13.

[66]J. M. Klassen to C. N. H., Jr., January 13, 1965, MCC Addresses file, Hostetter Papers.

[67]J. M. Klassen to C. N. H., Jr., February 9, 1965, Manitoba file, Hostetter Papers.

[68]For the setting up of MCC (Canada) and Hostetter's role in it, see Jacob M. Klassen, interview, February, 1979.

[69]For support for these views, see William Snyder and Edgar Stoesz interviews.

[70]Diary, October 5, 1961.

[71]Notes on Interview with Dr. Carl McIntire on September 9, 1964, Carl McIntire

Interview folder, Hostetter Papers.

[72]Metzler interview.

[73]For the complete text of the address, see *Evangelical Visitor,* October 21, 1957, pp. 4-5.

[74]For this trip, see diary, July 22-August 28, 1957.

[75]MCC Executive Committee Minutes, May 6-7, 1960. Also Robert Miller's instructions in MCC correspondence, Hostetter, 1960 file, Hostetter Papers.

[76]Diary, September 29, 1960.

[77]Diary, October 13, 1960.

[78]Jacob M. Klassen interview.

[79]Diary, October 30, 1960.

[80]Diary, November 16, 1960.

[81]Diary, November 28, 1960.

[82]Diary, December 4, 1960.

[83]Diary, December 20, 1960.

[84]For the details of the trip see diary, September 20, 1960-April 7, 1961. For Hostetter's detailed reports to MCC, see C. N. Hostetter, Jr. Reports, World Tour—1960-1961 file, Hostetter Papers.

[85]For example, see his General Conference sermon of 1961 in which he praises the strength of the national churches, on tape in the Archives of the Brethren in Christ Church and Messiah College. For his even stronger conviction for the need of relief and missions to work together, see MCC Minutes of a Conjoint Meeting of the Executive Committee and the Continuation Committee of the Mennonite Mission Board Secretaries, May 11-12, 1961.

[86]William Snyder to C. N. H., Jr., March 3, 1961, MCC Correspondence, Hostetter, 1961, Mennonite Archives.

[87]For these tours and addresses in many other churches outside the itinerary, see diary entries for April to June.

[88]MCC Executive Committee Minutes, May 13, 1961.

[89]For Hostetter's comments on this address, see diary, August 5, 1962.

[90]For this trip, see diary, November 6-16, 1962, and the report of Hostetter and Stoesz to MCC in Haiti Visit, 1962 file, Hostetter Papers.

[91]For this summer tour, see diary, June 20-August 20, 1963. Also Report of C. N. Hostetter, Jr., on Algeria, Greece, Jordan Visit in Report on Algeria, Greece, Jordan Trip, 1963 file, Hostetter Papers.

[92]See Report on Relief Situation in Haiti, 1966, file, Hostetter Papers.

[93]See diary for July 30-August 28, 1967. Also his reports to MCC in Reports—1967 Trip to Africa file, Hostetter Papers. Unfortunately, his report on Zambia and Rhodesia are missing from the file.

[94]Peter Dyck, interview, February 1, 1979.

[95]Stoesz interview.

[96]William Snyder to C. N. H., Jr., March 3, 1961, MCC Correspondence/Hostetter/1961, Mennonite Archives.

[97]Ivan Eikenberry to C. N. H., Jr., September 15, 1967, Report—1967 Trip to Africa folder, Hostetter Papers.

[98]C. N. H., Jr., to Peace, Relief and Service Committee, March 27, 1953, Peace, Relief and Service Committee file, Hostetter Papers.

[99]C. N. H., Jr., to Brethren in Christ pastors, October 10, 1962, Harold Martin Project file, Hostetter Papers.

[100]C. N. H., Jr., to E. J. Swalm, Kenneth B. Hoover, Clair H. Hoffman, August 3, 1964, Peace, Relief and Service Committee Correspondence and Business file, Hostetter Papers. He repeats this theme of failing contributions in a letter to the Atlantic Conference churches, July 30, 1964, and in a letter to E. J. Swalm and Clair H. Hoffman, July 15, 1964 in the same file.

[101]C. N. H., Jr., to E. J. Swalm, April 11, 1967, Correspondence, 1967 file, Hostetter Papers.

[102]John Zercher interview.

[103]For comments on the Institute, see diary, June 27, 1960, and June 29, 1962.

[104]Minutes of the Exploratory meeting, December 21, 1954 in the files at the Associated Mennonite Biblical Seminaries, Elkhart, Indiana. Also see diary, December 21, 1954.

[105]Erland Waltner to C. N. H., Jr., July 30, 1955, Associated Mennonite Seminaries Correspondence file, Hostetter Papers.

[106]C. N. H., Jr., to Erland Waltner, August 3, 1955, Associated Mennonite Seminaries, Correspondence file, Hostetter Papers.

[107]Erland Waltner to C. N. H., Jr., December 24, 1955, Associated Mennonite Seminaries, Correspondence file, Hostetter Papers.

[108]Associated Mennonite Seminaries, Reports, minutes, etc., file, Hostetter Papers. Also diary, June 8, 1956.

[109]Arthur Rosenberger to C. N. H., Jr., June 16, 1956, Associated Mennonite Seminaries, Correspondence file, Hostetter Papers.

[110]S. F. Pannebecker to C. N. H., Jr., September 11, 1956, Hostetter, C. N., MCC and Mennonite Affiliated Colleges file, Hostetter Papers.

[111]Diary, February 28, 1957. Erland Waltner to C. N. H., Jr., March 9, 1957, Associated Mennonite Seminaries, Correspondence file, Hostetter Papers.

[112]C. N. H., Jr., to Members of the Board for Schools and Colleges, June 4, 1957, Associated Mennonite Seminaries, Correspondence file, Hostetter Papers.

[113]General Conference Minutes, 1959, pp. 108-110.

[114]C. N. H., Jr., to Nelson Kaufman, September 1, 1959, Minutes, Joint Coordinating Committee, Correspondence, 1956-1965, Hostetter Papers.

[115]For the text of the dedication speech, see Mennonite Life, April, 1959.

[116]Diary, July 25, 1960.

[117]C. N. H., Jr., to Erland Waltner, August 31, 1965, Joint Coordinating Committee Correspondence, 1956-1965, Hostetter Papers.

Chapter 10

[1]Evangelical Visitor, October 11, 1937, p. 9.

[2]*Clarion,* May, 1939, p. 13.

[3]*Ibid.,* March, 1942.

[4]See C. N. H., Jr., to Henry Morrison, April 4, 1940, Correspondence, 1938-41, Hostetter Papers.

[5]Diary, April 14 and 15, 1950.

[6]Diary, May 1, 1953.

[7]Diary, April 19-22, 1949.

[8]Diary, April 21, 1950.

[9]Diary, April 27, 1954.

[10]Diary, October 12, 1954.

[11]*Evangelical Visitor,* June 16, 1958, p. 2.

[12]Diary, April 11, 1951.

[13]C. N. H., Jr., to Asa Climenhaga, December 10, 1951, Hostetter Correspondence.

[14]Diary, April 28, 1954.

[15]C. N. H., Jr., to Carl F. H. Henry, December 14, 1954, NAE: Correspondence, 1949-1955 file, Hostetter Papers.

[16]C. N. H., Jr., to James DeForest Murch, n.d., National Association of Evangelicals file, Hostetter Papers.

[17]For Hostetter's comments, see diary, April 19, 1955. For two other accounts of this event, see George Ford, interview, February, 1979, and E. J. Swalm interview.

[18]C. N. H., Jr., to Carl F. H. Henry, May 2, 1955, National Association of Evangelicals Correspondence, Hostetter Papers.

[19]Carl F. H. Henry to C. N. H., Jr., May 6, 1955, National Association of Evangelicals Correspondence, Hostetter Papers.

[20]J. Harold Sherk to C. N. H., Jr., October 28, 1955, MCC Correspondence, Archives Material 1955, Mennonite Archives. See Hostetter's reply of November 3, 1955—MCC Correspondence, Archives Material 1955, Mennonite Archives, in which he reports that he has written to Henry but isn't very optimistic about the results.

[21]Carl F. H. Henry to C. N. H., Jr., November 14, 1955. National Association of Evangelicals Correspondence, 1949-55, Hostetter Papers.

[22]For arrangements and the talks in October, 1959, see MCC Executive Committee Minutes, November 7, 1959, Exhibit X.

[23]John Howard Yoder to Guy Hershberger, May 2, 1960, Social Action Committee—NAE file, Hostetter Papers.

[24]Minutes of the Mennonite Representatives, Grand Rapids, Michigan, April 12, 1961, NAE Mennonite Group file, Hostetter Papers.

[25]*United Evangelical Action,* April, 1963, pp. 18-19.

[26]Diary, June 30, 1961.

[27]Diary, April 11, 1962.

[28]C. N. H., Jr., to John Howard Yoder, January 19, 1960, NAE Mennonite Group file, Hostetter Correspondence.

[29]C. N. H., Jr., to Leo Driedger, August 9, 1960, Hostetter Papers, and Guy Hersh-

berger to J. A. Toews, July 20, 1960, Hostetter Papers. Hershberger in his letter to Toews says that Hostetter has written to him to suggest that perhaps we should not try too hard to continue the discussion within NAE. Perhaps more progress should be made outside the structure by working with men such as Everett Cattell and Mahlon Macy. Unfortunately, Hostetter's letter to Hershberger is not in his collected papers.

[30]Diary, January 12, 1963.

[31]For the conference, see Diary, March 6-8, 1963.

[32]MCC—Billy Graham Meeting—Report file, Hostetter Papers. MCC Peace Section, Executive Committee Minutes 9/23/61 and 5/12/62.

[33]From a pamphlet "Seeking Foundation Support," in Foundation Support file, Hostetter Papers.

[34]See Annual Report for 1957 in WRC file, Miscellaneous Materials, Hostetter Papers. Also diary, June 6, 1957.

[35]See Executive Committee Minutes, February 13, 1957, World Relief Commission file, Hostetter Papers.

[36]I owe this insight to Jacob Klassen interview.

[37]William Snyder interview.

[38]Wendell Rockey to E. Morris Sider, February 24, 1979, Hostetter Papers.

[39]Executive Committee Minutes, June 23, 1960, WRC file, Hostetter Papers.

[40]Executive Committee Minutes, October 5, 1964, WRC 1965 Correspondence, Hostetter Papers.

[41]William Snyder to C. N. H., Jr., April 22, 1965, in Executive Committee Minutes, WRC file, Hostetter Papers.

[42]Clyde Taylor to Wendell Rockey, September 17, 1965, WRC 1965 Correspondence, Hostetter Papers.

[43]C. N. H., Jr., to Herbert Mckeel, January 17, 1962, Hostetter Papers. For arrangements to send Miller, see Notes from a Staff Meeting at Akron, October 16, 1966, MCC, Executive Secretary, Pro Tem Items file, Hostetter Papers.

[44]See William Snyder to Robert Miller, December 7, 1961 in Samuel Miller file, Hostetter Papers. Also diary, March 16, 1962.

[45]See the exchange between Ockenga and Hostetter in Park Street—Ockenga file, Hostetter Papers.

[46]See Wilbert Shenk to C. N. H., Jr., August 18, 1964, Robert Davis file, Hostetter Papers.

[47]Robert Miller to Wendell Rockey, December 22, 1965, MCC, C. N. Hostetter, Jr., Viet Nam file, Hostetter Papers.

[48]Clay Mitchell to C. N. H., Jr., August 23, 1966, Mailing Lists and Clay Mitchell file, Hostetter Papers.

[49]Elmer Kilbourne to Wendell Rockey, October 20, 1966. Elmer Kilbourne file, Hostetter Papers.

[50]C. N. H., Jr., to Elmer Kilbourne, February 4, 1969, Correspondence 1968, Hostetter Papers.

[51]Small notebook containing mainly sermon outlines, with record beginning September 1, 1934, Hostetter Papers.

[52]See, for example, diary, January 29, 1949.

[53]Diary, January 29, 1949.

[54]Diary, August 31, 1962. For a fuller account of the division and merger efforts, see Carlton O. Wittlinger, *Quest for Piety and Obedience,* pp. 134-40.

[55]United Zion file, Hostetter Papers.

[56]Luke Showalter, interview, August 7, 1979.

[57]Charles Ronald Burgard in *Beloved President,* p. 118.

[58]See diary for August 11-16, 1953.

[59]Diary, September 20, 1953.

[60]Diary, January 31, 1954.

[61]C. N. Hostetter, Jr., to B. Ewing, March 3, 1955, Pennsylvania Temperance League folder, Hostetter Papers.

[62]For these dates, see Doris S. Rupp to E. Morris Sider, March 29, 1979, Hostetter Papers. Doris Rupp is Assistant Executive Director, South Central Pennsylvania Lung Association.

[63]Diary, September 25, 1958.

[64]Diary, October 29, 1951.

Chapter 11

[1]For his interest in the Republican convention, see diary entries for July, 1952.

[2]Diary, January 20, 1953.

[3]Diary, November 6-7, 1956.

[4]Diary, June 8, 1949.

[5]For these activities, see diary for March 19 and April 18, 1949; May 5, 1951; July 15, 1949.

[6]Diary, February 8, 1952.

[7]Diary, January 20, 1953.

[8]Diary, December 23, 1952.

[9]Diary, December 29, 1952.

[10]See, for example, diary, July 26, 1955.

[11]Diary, May 5, 1954.

[12]Diary, March 31, 1955.

[13]Diary, September 28, 1957.

[14]For significant diary entries, see August 4, 1955; April 29, 1955; February 19, 1957; March 12, 1959.

[15]Diary, April 23, 1957.

[16]Miscellaneous Papers, Hostetter Books, Hostetter Papers.

[17]Diary, January 22, 1949.

[18]See diary entries for May 28 to 31, 1949.

[19]Diary for August 10-23, 1949.

[20]Diary, August 27, 1949.

[21]See diary entries between February 1 and March 3, 1950.

[22]Diary, March 19, 1950.

[23]Diary, February 24, 1952.

[24]Diary, August 17, 1952.

[25]Diary, December 3, 1953.

[26]Diary, May 14, 1953, and May 22, 1953.

[27]Diary, June 17, 1959.

[28]Diary, April 17, 1953.

[29]Diary, April 8, 1962.

[30]See C. N. H., Jr., Personal Correspondence, 1950-51, Hostetter Papers.

[31]C. N. H., Jr., to Ray Hostetter, April 11, 1952, C. N. Hostetter, Jr., Personal file, Hostetter Papers.

[32]See the diary for interesting details, including attending an exhibition baseball game and watching water skiiers at Cypress Gardens.

[33]See diary for August and September, 1952.

[34]Diary, September 30-October 1, 1955.

[35]Diary, May 24, 1961.

[36]Diary, August 4-19, 1964.

[37]For the death and Hostetter's thoughts, see the diary for December 23-25, 1964.

[38]C. N. H., Jr., to Mrs. Glenn Hostetter, February 4, 1969, Correspondence, 1969, Hostetter Papers.

[39]Diary, December 2, 1953.

[40]Diary, March 11, 1956.

[41]Diary, July 3, 1959.

[42]Diary, April 23, 1961. Debra Hostetter of Mechanicsburg, PA is in possession of a collection of these cards.

[43]Diary, February 12, 1962.

[44]Diary, December 27, 1949.

[45]Diary, March 22, 1950.

[46]Diary, February 18, 1952.

[47]Diary, April 5, 1954.

[48]For an example, see C. N. Hostetter to C. N. H., Jr., April 26, 1940, Hostetter Papers.

[49]Diary, September 23, 1955.

Chapter 12

[1]C. N. H., Jr., to Employment Committee, October 20, 1959, Committee and Group Letters, 1959-1960, Hostetter Papers.

²C. N. H., Jr., to Charlie Byers, January 13, 1959, General Correspondence, 1958-59, Hostetter Papers.

³C. N. H., Jr., to C. W. Hershey, September 21, 1959. Also Hershey to Hostetter, September 17, 1959, C. N. Hostetter, Jr. Personal, 1959-60, Hostetter Papers.

⁴C. N. H., Jr., to Arthur Climenhaga, December 17, 1959, Correspondence, 1959-60, Hostetter Papers.

⁵Diary, December 5, 1961.

⁶Diary, January 29, 1962.

⁷Diary, October 24, 1961.

⁸Diary, February 12, 1962.

⁹Diary, January 14, 1963.

¹⁰C. N. Hostetter, Sr., Memorial File, Hostetter Papers.

¹¹C. N. H., Jr., to Orie Miller, February 14, 1968, Correspondence, 1968-70 file, Hostetter Papers.

¹²For Hostetter's activities in this successful campaign, see Upland College Debt file, Hostetter Papers.

¹³Diary, June 1, 1963.

¹⁴C. N. H., Jr., to Elizabeth Evans, May 20, 1969, Correspondence, 1969, Hostetter Papers.

¹⁵Diary, September 8, 1963.

¹⁶C. N. H., Jr., to Henry Ginder, December 22, 1965, File on Palmyra Church Board Minutes, Hostetter Papers.

¹⁷Palmyra Congregational Council Minutes for January, 1969.

¹⁸C. N. H., Jr., to Faith Hoffman in Correspondence 1967 file, Hostetter Papers.

¹⁹C. N. H., Jr., to Anna Hershey, November 10, 1969, Sunday School Letters file, Hostetter Papers.

²⁰Palmyra Congregational Council Minutes, January 19, 1966.

²¹C. N. H., Jr., to Charlie Byers, December 12, 1967, Correspondence, 1967, Hostetter Papers.

²²For these notes on pastoral work, see his lecture materials in his collected papers (Hostetter Papers).

²³Miscellaneous Papers, Hostetter Books File, Hostetter Papers.

²⁴Palmyra Congregational Council Minutes, January 19, 1966.

Index

(This is a selective index in that no attempt has been made to include all details, and most names have been omitted.)